T0095354

Through The Barracks Window

A Time of Waves

Stacey L. Bolin

Order this book online at www.trafford.com
or email orders@trafford.com

Most Trafford titles are also available at major online book retailers.

© Copyright 2011 Stacey L. Bolin.
All rights reserved. No part of this publication may be reproduced, stored in a retrieval
system, or transmitted, in any form or by any means, electronic, mechanical, photocopying,
recording, or otherwise, without the written prior permission of the author.

Author Credits: Bering Hill Barracks Photo, Adak, AK -
Photo inside book by Ronald D. Bolin /
Cover and Biography Photo by Allison "Nikki" Greever Pasadena, Maryland

Printed in the United States of America.

ISBN: 978-1-4269-6637-8 (sc)
ISBN: 978-1-4269-6638-5 (e)

Trafford rev. 06/22/2011

 www.trafford.com

North America & international
toll-free: 1 888 232 4444 (USA & Canada)
phone: 250 383 6864 ♦ fax: 812 355 4082

To my husband - Ron Bolin, You are my best friend, my lover, my soul mate. I've loved you long before I ever met you, and will love you past the point of dying. You are my forever and that is still not long enough. Without you, my story could not be told. ~ "Elephant Shoes"

To my boys – Ryan and Reese, I Love you both with all of my heart and soul, you are my miracles. Never be afraid to dream your wildest dreams, but always remember, while some of your dreams could happen over night, others may take a life time. Be happy with who you are, with what you have, and let the other pieces of life fall into place when the time is right.

All my heart and soul to the three of you.

Stacey aka. Mom

What you need to know about the past is that no matter what has happened, it has all worked together to bring you to this very moment. And this is the moment you can choose to make everything new. Right now. So stop looking at that broken watch in the desolated and withering walls of your mind. Look ahead and redesign yourself! Author unknown

Never under estimate the power of a woman, as only she knows the magic within herself. Author ~ Stacey L. Bolin 1986

PROLOGUE

"I can't do this! Please let me up! Please!" She screamed with horror. She feared the procedures that her body was about to undergo. "Please Stop!"

Brilliant flashes of light blinded her as she tried helplessly to fixate on the turmoil that filled the room. Endless touches of unknown hands, positioned her to sit onto the hardness of a cold steel table. As if she were part of a sick sadistic form of bondage, her arms were bound with a sheet. Slowly she was helped to lean back onto the sheet and table to become her own restraint.

Her breathing-labored as the utterances and commotion intensified as the silhouettes in the glow of the lights grew closer.

"Are we ready to begin?" a distinguished voice, questioned. "You should feel extremely privileged Petty Officer...this surgical unit is the one we use for the President of the Unites States."

Maybe another day and place, this would have made her happy, but this comment did not comfort her at all.

"Please! Put me to sleep! Give me something!"

Though muffled by a cloth surgical mask, she somehow understood the deep voice that answered her cries. "Relax ma'am, I am going to give you a local, just a little something to take the edge off. As far as we know, this medication won't hurt the baby. I'm sorry that we can't put you under, it's too dangerous."

Finally someone was listening, they knew she was frightened with what was about to take place. Following an increased coolness into her left arm, she could feel the tenseness, throughout her body, slowly subsiding. Whatever the drug was, it worked quickly. Images became rather blurry, but she never revealed its effect. She knew she needed more.

"It isn't working! Please stop!" knowing perfectly well that it was working, just not enough to put her to sleep and relieve her fears and concerns.

Again, another short burst of coolness danced into her wanting veins. Still never revealing its effect, she pleaded for more.

"We must begin the procedure," ordered the surgeon.

She lay there unable to avoid the prick of the needle as it entered the tissue framed by her right collar bone. As the needle was pushed deeper, warm bursts followed by sharp stings radiated across her shoulders and up into her neck. The constant pain was nothing she had ever felt before, until the event that shortly followed the procedure.

"Nurse, how is the monitor on the Petty Officer's baby looking? Any distress or change in the heart rhythm?"

"All is reading normal at this time Sir."

As the deep voice spoke into her left ear to keep her attention, a startling, intense, and overwhelming pain ripped through her body. She shrieked in intense horror, "WHAT ARE YOU DOING TO ME! STOP... STOP...STOP!"

CHAPTER ONE

IF I ONLY KNEW THEN

The sounds of the room were still as I gazed out of the ninth story window from a darkened waiting room. Motionless I stood as pieces of the past appeared within my subconscious, moments set in time that seemed so very far away. My memories left me feeling as if I had been watching a slide show, yet not all the images were filled with happiness.

"How did I get here?" I said in a soft and somber whisper into the emptiness of the room.

The sun felt warm upon my face as its rays filtered through the pane glass of the window. All I had with me, was a bag of two-day-old donuts and my thoughts. It had been eleven years since I made that fateful choice to join the military. My dreams, as I signed a contract with the Navy in the summer of 1990, were dreams of adventure, travel, education and finding a love of a lifetime.

After a while I began to believe I didn't know how to feel except numb. It had been a long hard road to get to this day and I feared what the outcome would be. Trying to keep a positive outlook, I prayed that I would be able to go home to get on with the remainder of my life. But were these prayers for what I truly wanted?

What would their decisions be? There was no way to know. Could I finally make them see what I had been through? While in the Navy, the chain of events that I had undergone, were no-fault of mine. How could I help them feel my pain? To see a life on paper would not express the woman who would stand before them today. Would they see? Would they feel? I was so glad to be alive, but what about the future? What would the future hold for me? Could this day have been prevented? Yes!

So intertwined in my thoughts, I never acknowledged the life that was filtering into the offices and the areas surrounding the waiting room.

"Good Morning Petty Officer Bentley, how are you? Can I get you anything?" Lt. Parker commented, in her usual cheerful voice.

There was something in her voice that made you feel she truly understood the hardships a person had experienced in his or her life. Even with the work load she had, she always made time to listen, without fail, to the fears and concerns of all the military members facing their day in the court room. A funny thing about all this, most of the military members were being represented by many other counselors that had the personality of a wet mop. They had an overwhelming arrogance and lack of compassion that rendered them unable to be sincere.

Startled, I replied trying to bring tone into my voice, "No thank you ma'am. I just need a little time to collect my thoughts. Thank you for asking." And with that, I turned to look back out the window.

A small tear began to roll down my face, as I allowed myself to go deep into my thoughts to look back on the journey that brought me here.

CHAPTER TWO

D-DAY

My military saga began January 15, 1991 in Concord, New Hampshire. Realizing that my life was about to change forever I arrived at the recruiting station. With a deep breath to ease my fear I accepted my travel arrangements along with a one way ticket on a Greyhound bus to Boston, Massachusetts, to begin my registration for old Uncle Sam and his fine military service. *Little did I know.*

Before I knew it I found myself on a three-hour stop and go trip, my thoughts filled with getting out of this crazy decision with every stop we made. We finally arrived in a dirty old bus depot in a bad part of town just outside of the Boston city limits. I got off the bus and looked for someone to point me in the right direction to the Holiday Inn.

"What a bad place for a hotel" I thought to myself. *"This is the Navy's finest?"*

I went inside and asked a lady that was sitting in a caged ticket booth for information about the Holiday Inn where I was to report.

"Sorry friend, you are at the wrong bus station on the other side of town," she said as her voice was accompanied with laughter and the snapping of the gum she was chewing. "The only way to get there from here is to take one of our best, luxury taxis for the low, low price of 53 non-refundable dollars." Her laughing was even louder after her smart ass remark.

"You're a royal bitch," is what I felt like screaming, *"A goddam bitch!"*

It took all the strength I could muster up to keep from kicking my luggage across the dirty bus station floor.

Frustrated, I forced somewhat of a smile on my face and walked around the bus station to see if others had experienced the same situation. I spoke with two other gentlemen that were also on the wrong bus, but were headed in the same direction. Their recruiting officer had also assigned their travel orders as well. It was then and there I knew that this was just the beginning of many long and complicated journeys that awaited me.

The three of us got a cab and split the difference so that we could arrive on time, get settled, and save what little money we had. Our cab was not one of luxury. It was flu bug phlegm yellow accented with beautiful, *and I mean that most sarcastically,* black, neon green, and purple spray painted graffiti of various slang. The back seat on which we sat was frayed and torn red vinyl with rusted springs. *Thank God we had our luggage to sit on.*

It had an engine and four tires that were bald and no hub caps. The one thing this taxi did have, the best Bose music system that could be heard for a ten-mile radius. The bass was so loud, I feared that the vibration would cause the fuel tank to spark and catch fire. We rode 32 miles in our wonder on wheels and were relieved to reach our destination. *I hoped I never had to do that again.*

When I arrived at the hotel, I found myself standing in a long line with others like myself, clueless and confused. *That seemed to be the popular look for the day.* When it was my turn to approach the check-in desk, I gave my name, social security number, and branch of service. The desk clerk looked at me in the same manner as the ticket lady at the bus station.

"Christ sakes, not again!" I said under my breath, but was heard by the clerk.

I was asked to wait just a moment while he spoke to another clerk working with him. In my mind I was praying he was just asking a question because he was a new employee. *Unfortunately, that wasn't the case.*

"I'm sorry Miss Lake, but your name does not appear on our check-in roster, are you sure you're to be in Boston? This has happened before to others and they were to be in Maine."

"Excuse me?" I said in the most sarcastic voice I could conjure up, hoping it would change the outcome of this problem.

I showed him my travel arrangements, the hotel name and address and the airport that I was leaving from, that indicated that I was to be in Boston.

"I'm truly sorry, Miss Lake, but like I said, your name does not appear on our check in rosters."

This was the only explanation that I could get out of him? Not one bit of advice on what to do next?

hear me. I rushed into the ladies room, kicked open the stall door and in a blink of an eye, while my pants were going down and I was bending forward to prepare to sit down, my bladder gave way. It flooded part of the floor, covered the toilet seat, which I sat in and what was left trickled into the bowl. I felt as though I had just lost twenty pounds, and judging by the amount of toilet paper I used to wipe everything up that I would say I was just about right.

Humiliated and embarrassed I took a good long look in the mirror, with a tremendous sigh I then dropped my head to cry. Feeling exhausted and overwhelmed by the events of the past twenty-four hours I melted into an emotional realization that I was really leaving my home. Twenty one years I had been doing everything I could to get out of town. I felt empty where I was living and there was nothing else I could do. Deep inside I knew the real reason was that I was running away from the bad and abusive relationships, money troubles, and jobs that would never get me anywhere in life. I needed so much more in my life that New Hampshire could never offer or fulfill for me.

"You can do it, Fallon" I said as I picked up my head and wiped my running nose. "This is finally your time to shine, make the best of it and give it your all, someone out there is waiting for you to find them."

I got myself cleaned up, went back upstairs to get my things and then sat quietly in the hotel restaurant to eat my breakfast. My time between breakfast and going to the Military Enlisted Processing Station, aka M.E.P.S, was a complete blur.

Before I knew it time had quickly passed and I found myself standing in a huge meeting room, with other recruits, in the M.E.P.S. with my right hand in the air. With fifty seven other male and female adolescents, we repeated the following words a chief was reciting at the front of the room.

"I, Fallon Lake, do solemnly swear that I will support and defend the Constitution of the United States against all enemies, foreign and domestic; that I will bear true faith and an allegiance to the same; and that I will obey the orders of the President of the United States and the orders of the officers appointed over me, according to regulations and the Uniform Code of Military Justice. So help me God!"

A million thoughts then raced through my head, most of them in disbelief that I had just taken the military oath into the armed forces of the United States Navy.

I did learn one very interesting fact later in my military career that could have changed my destiny had I known about this on the day of my enlistment.

What recruits are not told about this oath that is taken in the M.E.P.S., it is not the official oath that binds your contact with the military. It is done so that it will ensure your recruiter that you will arrive at the recruit training facility for they fear recruits will go AWOL, which stands for unauthorized absence without leave, and that in turn means your recruiter will not get his bonus for signing you up.

I would not be allowed to go into my work field, as a builder in the Seabee's until I completed and graduated from my eight weeks of recruit training in Orlando, Florida or otherwise known as boot camp. My entire day consisted of a grueling process which is known in the military as hurry up and wait. Over the course of eight hours we sat around waiting to be taken to the airport, with the exception of an hour signing papers and taking the oath. I found myself sitting in a small room with the other fifty seven new recruits all dealing with the anxiety of a never ending wait. With the exception of the young man that was enjoying a good nose picking, as I already knew what he was thinking, I peered around the room trying to decipher the facial expression of those around me.

What were they thinking? Were they scared of what boot camp would be like? Were they regretting their decision to join the military? Did they leave a boy or girlfriend back home to wait? I wondered, as this was what I was thinking about myself.

As I sat speechless and trying to make the most of what seemed to be a bad situation that just kept getting worse with each passing hour. I couldn't help but think this was not what my recruiter said Navy life would be like. *This would be a sentence that I would be saying and hearing by others around me for the next several years. Our recruiters lied to us.*

At about quarter to four that afternoon a man in a Navy uniform finally came into the room.

"Pack up your crap! We're heading for the airport!" He said in a sharp tone of voice.

We were taken to the airport in a large white van with government tags and extremely darkened windows. The only thing that was missing was the handcuffs, shackles, a neon jumpsuit with big numbers on the back, and a trash stabber for working the sides of the highway. In the front seats you could hear the military personnel, assigned to carting new recruits to and from the airport, snicker and chuckle about what lay ahead of us. Trying to fight back my tears of fear, I just ignored them and looked out the darkened window. I began to hear the words of wisdom from my recruiter.

"Don't use the head, they need a urine sample."

When we arrived at the airport we were assisted with our check in and given strict verbal orders.

"You are not to leave the airport for any reason!" commented one of the petty officers, as the last recruit got their plane ticket. "You now belong to the United States Navy. Once this new recruit is finished getting his ticket I will take you to where you will wait until it is time to board your flight." *No doubt he was grandstanding to impress others who were not of the military adventure.*

As we waited in a military lounge for our flight, I got up to get a soda from a coke machine that was near the exit door. Suddenly, a petty officer jumped in front of me.

"Where do you think you're going recruit?" He said, trying to sound official.

"I need to get a drink and was going to get a soda from the machine over there."

"Oh…uh, here is some change get what you want…hey I didn't mean anything bad about what I said in the van. We were trying to scare a couple of new recruits in the back."

"Why?" I asked rather puzzled.

"They showed up yesterday and had the attitude that life was one big party."

Needless to say, two of those three recruits never made it through week two of boot camp.

I felt rather relieved after speaking with the petty officer who finally introduced himself to me as Stucky. It was a nickname that the others in the M.E.P.S. had given him as he was always stuck trucking recruits to and from the airport. *It fit.*

* * *

We finally boarded our flight, which didn't leave until deep into the afternoon. I sat beside Bill, who was also headed to boot camp. He seemed rather nervous about the whole situation, especially the flight. This was to be only my second time flying. I had flown once before with my father to Orlando, Florida to a Towing Association Convention and was not afraid of flying then and I wasn't afraid now.

I was pleased to know that I was sitting by another soon to be active duty Navy member. We got seated, buckled in, and prepared for take-off. As the plane started down the runway my life as a small child passed before my eyes. I was leaving behind my youth and I had nobody watching out for me. I would not be able to run to mom when the chips were down. I had to face responsibilities and challenges on my own. I never thought that the unknown challenges that lay before me would have such a physical and mental impact on my life.

As our flight made its way down the eastern coast, the sky was a true work of art. The brilliant colors of blue, gold and hue of magenta were breathtaking as the sun made its descent to give birth to an evening sky filled with stars that sparkled like an illuminated display case of new cut diamonds scattered across black velvet. We flew over New York City and were captivated by its dazzling marvel of lights. To view the World Trade Center from an evening sky was a moment in my life that I will never forget. That day means more to me than ever since its demise on September, 11, 2001. I will forever be haunted by that day as I felt a personal loss as well as the loss of thousands of innocent lives.

I looked at my watch and realized that the plane was going to be arriving at our final destination in about two hours. It seemed like all we had done all day, was to sit and wait. To help time move along, Bill and I decided to entertain ourselves with a game of tic-tac-toe on the only paper, which was an airsick bag, with a blue crayon that was dropped by a small child beside us. We enjoyed our meals and felt like we were on top of the world. All of our fun and freedom soon came to a halt when the plane landed. Two representatives from the recruit training facility waited impatiently as we made our way to the end of the gateway, while three others waited in the background to escort us to the USO office at the end of the terminal. It was there we continued to play the hurry up and wait game as we were awaiting the arrival of two other flights with new recruits heading in the same direction as ourselves. It was about 11:00 PM when I had an incredible urge to use the ladies room. In fear that if I did, I would not be able to give a urine sample during processing, I once again gave it my all to hold it so that I would be prepared. *Who would have ever thought that to look back in my life now, I'd be wishing for this kind of bladder control.*

Finally we were accounted for and were off to a waiting bus at the front entrance. I honestly do not remember if our trip was one of luxury or a nagging part of our past from our elementary school days. We were ordered to remain silent and that if anyone was talking it would result in 100 push-ups as soon as we arrived. That was enough for me to keep my mouth shut, and so I enjoyed the view of small houses, some with their Christmas lights still on and the shimmer of the street lights as they reflected on the palm trees swaying in the night breeze.

We arrived at 11:45 PM and slowly made our way off the bus. In the distance we witnessed baggage strewn all over the lawn and a bus full of new recruits doing their share of push-ups and we all knew why. As we were filing off the bus the men and women were immediately separated from each other.

"Women, in a straight line on one side of the sidewalk, men on the other!" A guard shouted that was standing next to our bus.

We stood in a single file and waited for what seemed to be hours staring at the back of the person's head that was in front of us. Then we were marched over to a small dark brick building. A sign posted over the doors, in yellow lettering on a navy blue background read, Recruit Processing Center, building number four.

"RECRUITS, HALT!" a stout woman, in a blue military uniform, shouted.

Her uniform had a gold rope that started from the top of her left shoulder and went under her arm and back up to her shoulder. Clearly she had to have been of some importance, but I didn't want to find out how much.

"Single line formation ladies, you will enter the building going to the first front table and chair available and fill the spaces one after another until all the seats are filled. You are to sit in silence and do not touch anything that is on the table in front of you."

On the tables were copies of the Blue Jackets manual, given that slang term for the color of its cover. *How original.* Its official name is the Military Regulations Guide. Also on the table were black and white permanent marking pens, a small soap dish, a small mesh laundry sack for washing socks and undergarments, a toothbrush with dental floss, a notebook and last but not least a number two lead pencil. We were called up to the front of the room to receive a stencil card that was the last four numbers of our social security number and a pair of dog tags that had our name, social security number and religious preference. I started to think about when they would ask me for a urine sample.

"Someone must have read my mind" I thought to myself as my mind registered the next command that was ordered throughout the room.

"When you are done getting your stencil card and dog tags, you will go back to your set and wait to be called into the head to give a urine sample." another Officer snapped, that was sitting in the back of the room picking at her fingernails.

I was told about this moment over and over before my journey here, but my recruiter failed to tell me on little detail for those dealing with being modest.

"Okay, recruit?"

"Lake" I replied

"That's Lake, Ma'am!" Company Commander Johnson, responded in a hostile voice.

She was a large women of African American descent, and boy, did she mean business. She handed me a cup with markings on the side, one yellow top and one sterile wipe to be used before I went to the bathroom.

"The head is open, after you recruit Lake."

I was confident that I would be able to fill this container with plenty to spare and was very proud of myself for having the ability to hold it for so long. It wasn't until I was informed that I had to perform this task without a door on the stall that I entered, my confidence diminished. To add to the humiliation of it all, she stood before me and watched to be sure that I filled the cup and that I didn't try to use a sample from another person. The urine sample would be used for drug testing.

After holding every bit of liquid that I could consume from Portland, Maine to Orlando, Florida something terrible happened. It was if my bladder went desert dry, nothing would come out, yet the urge was dreadful.

"I don't know what's wrong, I know I have to go," I said completely shaken.

"Two minutes recruit, or you are walking and drinking until you go!"

It was the fastest two-minutes of my life and before I knew it I was walking around the entire room and forced to stop at the scuttlebutt (water fountain) for a drink every once around the room. I felt bloated and in extreme pain, now I knew what a dairy cow felt like just before milking. After five trips they would let me try again, giving me a new cup, top and wipe, but still there was nothing. This went on through the night and between the pain of being so full and my newly added rash from the sterile wipe, it was hard for me to walk without looking bull legged. Finally, the uncontrollable urge came upon me, as though Niagara Falls had relocated in my body and the drainage system was too small for it all to come out at once.

"I can go!" I shouted across the room.

"Show some respect! Others are trying to sleep," said a voice from a temporary barracks room filled with bunk beds, we would soon learn to call them racks. I swiftly got myself over to the head and prepared myself, but when I sat, once again there was nothing. All I wanted to do was cry. Finally Company Commander Johnson, turned on a water faucet and before I knew it, Niagara Falls was present.

"A-huh yes...yes...A-huh," I moaned as my eyes rolled back in my head. "It's about damn time!" It was like having the most intense orgasm a woman could have. It felt so good, I forgot Company Commander Johnson, was still there as I wiped the sweat from my brow.

"It's about time!" shouted another CC, "Get over here and get your gear then you can hit the rack."

It was now 4:15 in the morning, I had been up almost twenty-four hours, and I felt totally exhausted. I lay there in my rack looking up at the many pipes that covered the ceiling and slowly drifted off to sleep.

Crash! Bang! Crash! was the first sound I heard and it was only 5:00 AM. I had only been asleep for forty five minutes. The sound was a metal garbage can that used to be in rather good shape in its day, being kicked across the floor of our barracks. I honestly think that this can was used on a daily basis for raising the dead. At least that is how we all felt.

"Rise and shine ladies! You are in my Navy now!" said an unfamiliar voice.

"Oh shit," I thought to myself, "here we go."

Chapter Four

In the Navy Now

I never thought that I would be sharing, showering, sleeping, eating and exercising with eighty other women during my eight-week training. I had a neighboring bunkmate with whom I would share my feelings and fears. We would help each other get through the emotional stress that we were under. There were many nights we would lay awake and listen to the different sounds that filled the barracks we all occupied. Along with the stress we also found much humor. During our late evening talks the room would be filled with the sounds of snoring and sleeping bodies passing gas, which eventually created a saying that found its way into our conversations every night, "there's that smell again." The hardest part of our day was trying to keep a straight face when speaking to the girls who would rattle the windows with both ends of their bodies. *Boy, if they only knew.*

Now to sum boot camp up in a nice little package-it is a total mind game. If you can keep your nose clean, have some athletic ability, do what you are told, fold and iron your clothes, make your bed and march as a group, you have it made. But if you are missing any of these key elements, you, my friend, are just setting yourself up for a big reality check and will be wishing that you had listened to your parents all those years.

My company was called K026, but shortly evolved in K zero too sick, because it seemed that every day there was always someone going to medical for a cough or a scraped knee or dehydration, something. Our days were filled with training, reading, exercise, and barracks inspections. I did rather well with keeping my Company Commander's Petty Officer Franklin, who was a man and Petty Officer Hill, who was a woman, out of my face. But that didn't last long when I folded a shirt a quarter of an inch out of place and kept my company from getting a perfect score during an inspection. We were told this after our morning run. The funny thing about it, was that when he said we missed a perfect inspection I knew it was because of me. I don't know how I knew, I just did. I didn't mess up intentionally, I had always had my gear together perfectly. It just happened to be one of my off days. I messed up our perfect inspection and would have to make it up with extra physical training. Something I was not looking forward too, as it wouldn't be easy.

Later on in the week after the inspection when I least expected it, I was sent to D.S.I.T. (Division Sidewalk Intensive Training) which I found to be a joke at first. I was not the only lucky recruit attending this wonderful workout, several others from adjoining barracks in our building were also there for something they had done. For example; failing an inspection or even an attitude could get you into some hot water and you would end up here. We did crunches, sit-ups, push-ups, and jumping jacks. Chief Fields was in charge of making us sweat. He did a rather nice job of it and he too loved to get right in your face and yell as loud as he could. He decided that I was to be his next victim and started going off. He had gotten so close to my face that I could taste his breath. This was punishment alone.

"Do you think you're good enough to be in the Navy...Recruit?"

"Yes Sir!" I responded sharply.

"Do you know how to follow orders?"

"Yes Sir!"

My Company Commanders both stood in the hall watching through the glass doors to see if I would break under the pressure.

"Do you have what it takes to be in my Navy...Recruit?"

To which I responded with a stern voice and a determining look straight into his eyes, "It's now my Navy too, Sir!"

You could see the whites of his eyes turning red to match the color of his angry red skin, at any moment he was going to blow. In a matter of three whole seconds he was yelling at the top of his lungs that attitude will get us nowhere and that we were all going to pay.

He then ordered all of us to make a quarter turn toward the front of the building. I was first in the line and could look directly at my Company Commanders. I never once looked away from either of them and I knew that they knew I was not going to break and that this was actually making me stronger and stronger inside. After an hour workout I was ordered to double-time it (run) back to the barracks. To my surprise when I entered the barracks, many recruits were waiting to ask me what D.S.I.T. was like.

"A joke," I responded as I made my way to my locker.

There was a lot of tension building within many of the recruits of K026 and it was creating major stress throughout the company. My being sent to D.S.I.T. only made the stress worse. That night I took out my journal and began to compose a new poem as a way to release my own inner tensions and hopefully of those around me as well.

"Boot Camp Blues"

Who would have ever thought,
that we all would be.
Here in sunny Orlando,
dreading upcoming PT.

We all have lost our privacy,
we all came here alone.
But if we pull together strong,
in a few weeks we'll all be home.

This room is filled with feelings,
so bottled up airtight.
Let's at night express these feelings,
and make the next day bright.

Deep within our bodies,
there's someone we want to be.
And in eight weeks we'll prove it,
right here in the old US Navy.

Keep you heads up ladies,
and don't be ashamed to cry.
The only thing they ask of us,
is to prove to them we'll try.

January 1991

* * *

I was the second oldest of all the recruits, only myself and one other person had lived outside their childhood place of residence before joining the Navy. I was shocked to learn that there were people in our group that didn't even know how to iron clothes. One day at a time we learned to help each other so that the remaining weeks would not be filled with hours of endless inspections and exercise. The only day that was truly ours was Sunday. We would march to morning chow (breakfast) then immediately following chow, we would all go to the church at the chapel across the courtyard. I had not been to church since my early childhood years, but found that it was something I was missing. I learned to enjoy and appreciate the music of the gospel. It was the only place that a recruit could show their true colors. I was given the honors of being the R.R.P.O. (Religious Recruit Petty Officer) for my company.

There were several times throughout the morning to attend the congregations and I found that by becoming the R.R.P.O. I was able to spend most of my Sunday mornings at the church. This meant I got out of washing and waxing the barracks floors every Sunday. Being the R.R.P.O., I did have to undertake the responsibilities of helping the other ladies get through their own personal struggles of being away from home. By helping them, I never understood that I was also helping myself become more connected with God. There were many tasks and events that I had to endure during my training that did not hold my interest. This however was indeed one task that I looked forward to and it made a permanent impact on my inner-self throughout my military career.

I slowly found ways to avoid specific events that I had no interest in; morning physical training was first on my list. I found that if I took my barracks watch from four to six in the morning, I could straggle (go alone) to morning chow and miss morning training. I also think I was the only one who gained fifteen pounds because of this. The most annoying part of being in boot camp was wearing Boon Dockers. Whoever invented these hideous things is in desperate need of psychological assistance.

It was a black leather boot that only came to mid-ankle that had no padding. Now we all know what leather does to the skin if it is not treated on the edges. It rubs and makes quite the monstrous blister. Now take the equation of eighty women marching in ranks of three abreast at arms-length away from each other. Does it sound to you like this idea works? If you said yes, you are so very wrong. My location, when marching in ranks, was seventh row back and the middleman. We were all placed according to height ranging from the tallest to the shortest. Going on, we were into our fourth week of training and probably marched from Florida to Alaska if you were to tally it in miles. My feet had just about enough and were covered in blisters on the backs of my heels and ankles, all of a sudden the girl behind me accidentally went out of step and tried to give me, what we used to call a flat tire, when wearing sneakers. Because these boots are tied around the ankle they never come off, but cause some major problems when this happens. I felt these horrendous pains, but kept in tempo with the company. My foot began to feel raw and excessively wet. I could not imagine what was going on.

When we arrived back to our barracks I immediately went into the head where no one could see what I was doing. I removed my boot and found it to be filled with blood. By her stepping on the back on my boot, it broke all the blisters and because it kept rubbing on the same spot no matter how much I tried to walk a little different, it began to bleed. Recruit Cappy, came in to see if I was alright, she was the one who stepped on the back of my boot. We promised one another not to ever tell anyone about this as we didn't want to keep the reputation of being K zero too sick, but always referred to story as the "Bloody Heel Incident."

It finally came time for our company to take on more advanced portions of our training. We had to participate in classes on the use of firefighting equipment, handling and firing a pistol and also to be able to float fifteen minutes then swim the length of an Olympic size pool.

I remember a day that I am sure one day will find its way into the history books for the most embarrassing moment. It was the day we were issued our black one piece bathing suits. What a contrast between this Lycra suit against my Yankee white skin. There was absolutely no doubt that Orca the whale was part of our family tree. If you could only picture this, as my husband says, "Not without slides." The suit had a sewn in bra, that unless you were an A cup, which I was not, was not going to hold any DDD breasts like mine in place. I took it upon myself to cut the bra out of the suit, but this only resulted in the look of long endless breasts heading south. I was about thirty pounds overweight and adding my long breasts, it gave me the look of a Weeble with legs. I also experienced this problem when faced with running track. I truly believe that a girl running with such large breasts as mine, would not live to tell about the experience. I was certain that some type of head trauma, broken nose, or black eyes would result. As I ran I used my arms for supports as if I had just stolen a twenty-pound bag of potatoes and was trying to make my get away on foot. To add to my suffering my shorts were so tight that I was forced to run with permanent wedgies. What a sight I must have been for others to watch. A real life freak show.

The worst of all trainings, and the most feared, was going into the gas-chamber. I am pleased to say that I never participated in the gas-chamber training due to a case of bronchitis at the same time. For those who did, they got to wear gas masks, but then found out the hard way, that it was not going to be that easy. One by one, recruits were told to enter a large metal room until it was packed full. When the steel door shut you heard a whistle from inside, exactly five minutes went by when suddenly the door flew open and recruits quickly tried to exit. They were not wearing their masks. All were experiencing excessively watery eyes and the worst was the big strands of snot coming from their noses. Others could not hold down what they had eaten at the chow hall, but then again most of them couldn't on a regular day. The grounds were a complete mess, suddenly out came the fire hoses to wash everything away. That was one day that I was glad to be ill and was even happier to learn that I didn't have to make up that class. *There is a God.*

Eight weeks seems long, but the weeks quickly passed. I looked back upon my time to review what I had accomplished. During work week (seven days of assigned jobs) I was assigned the job of painting the company flag. I planned it just right, it took me three days to paint and the other four days, I listened to music and slept in the lounge.

During our weekend liberty, which were the last two weekends of our training. I enjoyed some of the sights in Orlando. I went to Disney World and Epcot the first weekend and Wet and Wild Water Park and the Cheyenne Saloon the last weekend we were there. This much fun should be illegal, but all good things must come to an end.

On a cool sunny morning in March we began preparing for our graduation ceremony. We had finally made it to the most important day of recruit training. The hardest part for me on that day was that I didn't have one family member there to cheer me on. This was a very symbolic moment in my life, I finally followed through with something, yet no one was there to share this experience with me. I felt rewarded for what I had done over the past two months, but at the same time felt a deep sadness. It was time for another change. I was moving on and prepared for the life of an active duty Seabee member. When I returned to my barracks to pack my sea bag, I took a personal moment to put in words a way to mark this momentous occasion.

"US Troops"
-I'm in the Seabees now-

This life of many changes,
challenges still ahead.
No one ever told us,
no one ever said.
We walk a greater distance,
there's so many, but so few.
We hold our heads up to the sky,
and believe in what is true.
Patriotic, strong and bold,
Some people say it's crazy.
We support America,
we are the US Navy.
America the Beautiful,
we love the old and new.
And keep our flag a flying high,
the Red, the White, and Blue.

Graduation Day March 21, 1991

Time was getting away from us rather rapidly. We had all received our orders and our graduation information. Most of my things were packed, but how I obtained so much to fill one large size sea bag, I will never know. Now as I had explained before, the lack of common sense was part of the turmoil our company dealt with each and every day. For example; the laundry details that washed 100% blue cotton jeans in hot water with all the white T-shirts. Better yet was when one of the recruits tried to plug in an iron that had water on the end of the cord. There were some major sparks that day, both from the iron and the CC's. How we managed to get through all this I will never know. I have to honestly admit that what happened next was just sheer stupidity and was simply caused by adrenaline and the fact that we were going home. *Some lost their ability to use common sense.* For those of us that know some basic science all know that what goes up must come down. For some reason, a few of them forgot what happens when an item is pushed from a significant height.

Recruit Adams, just couldn't seem to get her belongings together to make it to her bus on time. So several of the other recruits took it upon themselves and helped her get organized and packed her sea bag, which at that point was the best for all of us, as we couldn't leave until everyone was ready to go, but she was always the last to get ready.

Our barracks were located on the third floor and we always had to use the exterior staircase to get to and from where we were going. In our full dress blue uniforms and lugging a seventy pound sea bag, we began filing out onto the stairs one by one. A lot of us bought luggage carts to make it easier to get from place to place during our travels, but we also knew that they couldn't function well on stairs. Recruit Adams, convinced that it would easier to keep her sea bag on her cart, tried to make it down the stairs. This resulted in the loss of one of the plastic wheels on her "Not made for heavy loads" cart. Believe it or not, other recruits actually felt saddened by what had happened.

I wanted so badly to say to all of them *"Come on ladies it wasn't like someone had just ran over a cat or something, it's a wheel on a cart."* I kept my comment to myself when I heard a recruit make a joking suggestion that resulted in the next event that is now known as the big bag blowout.

The advice that she was given was to throw her sea bag over the railing and pick it up when she got to the bottom, that the padlock on it would keep her stuff inside. Before I could interject, it was as if life went into slow motion as Recruit Adams, without hesitation, picked up her sea bag and threw it over the side rail from the second highest platform. I watched in amazement as the bag fell to the ground followed by a sound somewhat like a cannon filled with wet towels being fired. The stitching in the bottom of the bag failed and clothes were blown all over the courtyard. It looked like the end of a day at a bargain basement store. At that same moment I burst into the most uncontrollable fit of laughter that I had not experienced since my high school days. This was a laughter that had been kept under lock and key all through basic training, and I just could not hold it any longer.

Tears streamed down my face and I had to focus on one step at a time. When I arrived at the bottom, Recruit Adams had been surrounded by several recruits that were not leaving the training grounds until later in the day. They all were wearing the same look of loss as though it was an animal still suffering from its injuries after being hit by a car. A recruit from another barracks, saw what happened and double-timed it to the Navy Exchange to purchase her a new sea bag.

I am saddened to have to report that Recruit Adams was to be on one of the buses heading to the airport and didn't make it on time. For those of us concerned we all wondered what would happen if she missed the bus, thankfully our concerns were addressed when we were informed by our driver that she would have to go by taxi and that his was not the first time someone had missed their bus. I sat in the front seat and took in all the sights since this trip was during the day. I got over to the airport and checked in without any major events. Shortly after my arrival my plane was called for boarding and I took one last look behind me and then boarded my flight. I was headed home for two weeks on leave that fell over the Easter holiday. I found my window seat, got settled in and put my head back and let out a big sigh of relief. I had made it through boot camp. Phew!

CHAPTER FIVE

GEORGE

I was happy to finally be home after what seemed like months, but had a hard time dealing with the disappointment that I didn't have any family members attend my graduation. Yes, I was acting very selfish. What I didn't realize is that I was about to be taught a very hard lesson of life.

* * *

In the months before my departure into basic training, my mother, who had been divorced for about four years, had finally found the perfect man for her. His real name was George and my reason not to change his name is because he is and always will be very special to me and his legacy will live on forever. He reminded me of the old saying "Never judge a book by its cover." He was not the most handsome man, but he knew just what our family needed, pure and unconditional love and attention. He never had to buy our love with pricey gifts. He enjoyed listening to our stories, jokes and just tidbits of our daily lives. But the best of all, the fact that he would take time out of his day to spend it with us was more than enough.

George and my mother were like two pieces of a puzzle and lived for one another's heart and soul. Many people of the town looked at these two as being a perfect pair. They would stay together forever. Little did everyone know time wasn't on their side. During the month of September 1990, he began experiencing a chronic cough that would not offer any relief or comfort. At one point the doctors diagnosed it as the flu or cold and gave him medications. Still the cough was persistent and showed no signs of going away. Evenings tended to be the worst, but he'd never let it get the best of him. During a routine doctor appointment it was discovered on George's chest x-ray a small dark spot on one of his lungs which had the doctors suspicious of some type of cancer.

It was confirmed through an exploratory procedure that their suspicions were correct, lung cancer. The choice of care was to have the lung removed on January 5, 1991, which was at George's request. He didn't want to take away the enjoyment of the last Christmas we would have together before my military career began. Being prior military himself, he knew that trying to get leave, especially holiday leave, was a hard thing to get. None of us, including George, knew how serious his heath really was.

Our Christmas was simple and yet, very memorable. A small Charlie Brown tree was decorated with ornaments from our Christmases of yesteryears. It stood proudly in the living room window of our third floor apartment that overlooked the town of Hillsborough, New Hampshire. It was an angelic sight to drive down through the town and look up at its shimmering beauty. I remember a moment on Christmas Eve that feels like it was just yesterday. I woke to see the streetlights display the grace of waltzing snowflakes falling to the ground. How beautiful it was as it accumulated on the undisturbed roads of our little town.

To know me, is to know that my favorite thing to do is to take in nature's aromatic perfume while sitting in front of a partially open window. Something about the occasional gentle breeze tickles my senses and brings a calming inner peace.

With only the illumination of the tree and a window I had opened to smell the crispness of the air, I sat wrapped in a quilt and gazed out the window to take in the beauty. *A true Currier and Ives scene.* Thoughts passed through my soul during this private interlude. Most of them, the special someone needing me and the love I had to offer them. Slowly visions were in my mind and I began to have a sense of direction. I asked many questions out loud to myself, but not so anyone would be woken.

It is a man? Yes. But how do I know this? Who is he? He lives out west. How will I know who this person is? I will feel him in my heart, I will help him heal. We will heal as one.

My soul felt renewed and I couldn't help but smile through my tears. This was indeed the best Christmas present that I have ever received. To have this happen on Christmas Eve made it very spiritual to me. I never told anyone about what happened to me. That night I slept so peacefully and felt rejuvenated when morning was upon us. My mother also received a special gift that day. She got her wish for everyone to be together. We laughed and enjoyed the day together as a family.

As for George, it was a day of worry, yet he never would let on that he was scared. I felt rather selfish for enjoying the day, as his cough grew more and more unbearable. I can still see him sitting in the arm chair across the room exhausted from a long night of discomfort. We all agreed that he should lie down and get some rest.

"No…I am fine." He replied as he took in all the joy and laughter while we opened our gifts to one another.

This was the last Christmas that my mother, George, my brother Oliver, and I would spend together.

The holidays passed swiftly and soon it was the day for George to have his surgery. My mother, Ken, who was dear friend of the family, and myself impatiently waited in a gloomy sunless waiting room at the Manchester Veterans Hospital. The wait was maddening and I was certain the clock on the wall in the room was broken or had dead batteries. Every time I looked up at it to see how long we had been waiting, the hands just didn't move fast enough. Finally the surgeon slowly walked into the room. Just coming straight from the operating room, he walked over to my mother and dropped his head.

"Can we go into another room and speak for a moment privately," he said without much tone in his voice.

"Is he going to be alright?" fearing George had died during the operation.

"Please, ma'am…come with me."

My mother and Ken, agreed, but I chose to stay in the waiting room. It was such a surreal feeling, like being suspended in the middle of the room without any sense of stability. Something was wrong. I could feel it. I could see them both sitting in a room with a big glass window, yet was unable to hear what the discussion was.

When they came back into the waiting room, it was Ken that told me what the surgeon had discussed with them, my mother was speechless. The surgeon had told them that he was very sorry, but he could not complete the procedure. When they had opened his chest, what they thought was just a small spot and grown and was taking over his body. The surgeon then remarked that his illness was terminal and that George would need to get his final things in order. That he estimated approximately five months to a year of life remaining.

We all just sat in disbelief. The man that had done so much to bring our family back together was going die.

"How could this have gotten so bad so quickly?" I thought to myself.

Deep down we all knew the answer, we waited too long.

* * *

I had prayed that while at basic training, he would somehow be graced with a miracle. When I had finally arrived, I was shocked to find that what used to be the living room was now their makeshift hospital bedroom that was equipped with medical supplies and intravenous carts. My mother sat next to his bed as he savored every breath that he could. I was speechless and felt so bad for thinking my family didn't want to be at my basic training graduation. It was then I finally learned the actual reason why. The man my mother loved more than anything was dying before her eyes and there was nothing she could do to stop it. As I stood there before him, he smiled and told me how very proud he was of me. *Something my own father had never said to me until just before his dying day.* It was truly the best gift that George could have ever given me. We now shared a new bond as George had also enjoyed a career in the Navy. He stood 6"2' and was a cook on various submarines until he retired from the service.

During his years of retirement he worked as a mailman for the Peterborough area. *I never realized that it would have a significant impact on me after his passing.*

I made the most of the two weeks that I had before heading out to California for my builder A-school training with the Seabees. My mother never once showed any signs of breaking down. She was as solid as a rock, and kept moving forward to aid him with his every need.

"I only hope that I can be as strong as her one day," I said to myself as I watched them from the doorway to their bedroom. She sat in a chair next to his bed and just held his hand. They would talk of good times and bad, it didn't matter what the topic was, they were happy to be in the presence of each other. Occasionally she would stand up to lean over and kiss his forehead ever so gently and would say,

"I love you honey."

"I love you too" he'd respond in a frail voice.

During my time at home, I found it very hard to sleep. I felt guilty knowing that the days I would be living while I was home on leave, were the few that George had left of his life. That it was inevitable, the angels would be coming to take him home. Each day ended with my face deep in a pillow so that I could drown out the sounds of my sorrow.

What would his journey up to heaven be after his departure on earth? Would friends and family that had passed years earlier be waiting for him? Would his suffering end?

While I wanted to see everyone during my visit, I found that just sitting and talking with my mother and George was all that comforted me.

The day came and it was once again time for me to leave. It was one of the hardest days I was forced to face. I knew in my heart that someday soon, the call would come and the voice would say George has left us.

CHAPTER SIX

BETWEEN TWO WORLDS

On Thursday, April 4, 1991, I was driven to Boston's Logan Airport by my mother's friend Ken. He stayed with me until it was time to board my 11:05 morning flight on American Airlines to Los Angeles. Our entire conversation to the airport and then again while we were there, always revolved around my mother and George. That made my leaving a bit easier as he was a very special person to my family, and I knew he would keep their best interest at heart.

"We will now begin boarding flight 279 to Los Angeles," said a voice over the intercom in the terminal.

"Well kiddo you have to go," said Ken.

"Yeah, I guess so," I said trying to fight the rush of tears that were trying to overcome me.

He gave me a hug goodbye and told me not to worry about things here at home and to have a great time in California. If anything went wrong, I would be the first person he would call. I knew he meant every word he said.

As I walked up to the gate to give the attendant my ticket, I turned and took one last look at Ken.

"Take care of them for me." I said as I wiped the tears from my eyes and then headed towards my plane.

* * *

My arrival to LAX was overwhelming, people and luggage everywhere. It was just how it looked on television and so much more. I was amazed and star struck to know that I was on the other side of the United States. I immediately found the nearest phone and called home. It took a few minutes and to my surprise, it was George that answered the phone.

"Hello" he said in a shallow voice.

"Hi George, It's just me, Fallon. I am in California, it's beautiful."

"That's wonderful."

"How are you feeling?"

Knowing that his answer of "Great" was his way to keep my spirits up and that I would not worry. I told him to get better and kept our conversation as positive as one could, given the circumstances. I could hear in his voice he was getting very tired and so I decided to talk with my mother so he could rest.

"Is mom home? I'd love to talk with her too."

"Yes, she is in the kitchen getting me a drink. She will be right in."

"Great, hey George before I say my good-byes, I wanted you to know, I love you."

"I love you too. Here's your mom."

I heard some rustling over the phone and soon I heard my mother's voice.

"Hello?" she said.

"Hi mom, I made it in one piece, I am in California. You should see this place!" I said with so much excitement. Forgetting what was happening back at home.

"What time is it?"

"Only one o'clock, we are three hours behind you."

"You have a good time, and don't worry about us, everyone is fine. I love you Fallon."

"I love you too mom, tell George to get better and that I love him too, have to go, I'll call again soon." I said in a hurried voice.

"Bye, we love you Fallon."

"I love you both too."

We only talked for about five minutes for I feared I would miss my connecting flight to Oxnard, California.

As overwhelming as it was, I loved every bit of the experience as I walked through LAX to my connecting flight. People of all nationalities were wearing a multitude of various fashions that I had only seen inside the covers of magazines. I had to keep stopping to look around, I felt as though I was in a dream. When I finally reached my connecting flight location and check in, I was shell shocked when I looked out the window behind the check in counter and saw the tarmac.

"Good afternoon, are you checking in?" said the ticket agent with a big perfect California smile.

"Yes…I am. Is that the plane that I will be flying on to Oxnard?" I replied trying to hold back the fear in my voice.

"Yes, we call them hoppers as the flight is only approximately fifteen to twenty minutes tops and can only carry eight passengers at a time."

"Oh…great…"

"Have you ever flown on a plane this size?" She replied, sensing my fear.

"No, never"

"You will be fine and it is a lot faster than driving in LA traffic" she said trying to convince me that I should always take this mode of travel. "Here is your ticket. The plane will be boarding momentarily."

I had never been in a plane that was so small that you had to slide in on your knees. It reminded me of the old Fisher Price toy airplanes that had the door that opened into a set of stairs and tiny round windows. This one was built to an adult scale. It was also equipped with the best turbulence softener a flight could have. *Not!* It held about six people and a pilot comfortably. It was a brief and very beautiful flight. What a total rush it was to be flying so low in the air over the hillsides with the view of the land to one side and the Pacific Coastline on the other. *A small bit of advice for those who are claustrophobic: Consider renting a car and drive, this flight is not for you.*

We landed in a small airport that only catered to single engine planes. I got off the plane and walked into the building to get my luggage. There were several military members in uniform waiting to catch the same plane back to LA. They gave me instructions on calling for a taxi, what gate I should enter to get on the base and where the school was located. Once again I wasn't given the proper location of my final destination. I was unaware that this was a prank played on new students, by those who just graduated. I got a taxi, found the entrance gate and had the driver drop me off at the building called the 31st regiment. Unfortunately, this was not the correct building and it was located far from where I needed to be. I walked into the building to find someone to assist me. There was a man dressed in a real Seabee green uniform sitting behind the check in desk watching a small black and white television. I was amazed to know that someday I would be wearing the very same uniform, and I couldn't wait.

"Hello? Can I help you with something?" Petty Officer Brown rudely commented as though I inconvenienced him in some way.

"Ah yeah, hi, I am recruit Lake." responding completely lost and confused, but still eyeing the uniform.

"Wait…Don't tell me, you have orders for 'A' School right?" He said rather cocky, "You're a Wannabe."

"A what?"

As he got up from the desk and leaned over the counter, he started laughing.

"Never mind, wow, why so much luggage?" he said trying to control another burst of laughter and a few more nasty comments.

"I'm trying to report to the barracks for students that are attending 'A' School training.

Just then another Seabee came from around the corner.

"Hey what are all these bags?" asked Petty Officer Rodgers.

"They're mine. I am trying to get to my 'A' School. From the directions that I was given from some of the military guys at the airport, this is where I ended up."

"Another sucker" said Petty Officer Brown and he sat down to finish what he was watching. He could have cared less if I got to where I needed to be.

"Did you call someone to come and get her Brown?"

But there was no reply.

"Never mind him, I will help you with your things and take you where you're supposed to be. What's your name?"

"Recruit Lake"

"Well Recruit Lake, this here is Seabee country, so from now on dropped the recruit title. You're CONSTRUCTIONMEN Lake. Don't forget it."

"I won't, I promise."

We tossed the luggage into the back of his olive drab military issued pick-up truck.

"Hop in." he said with a kind smile.

Yes he was cute.

"Thank you, I really appreciate it," relieved to know that someone was willing to help me.

"So you're gonna be part of the Bee's?" he asked proudly.

"Yes if I can get through my schooling."

"What is your rate, which trade did you choose?"

"Builder, how bout' you, what is your rate?"

"That's great! I am sure you will like the instructors over there in Charlie Company, they are cool. My rate is an Equipment Operator, but I have been in over three years. Hey, I am not sure, but I think they just had a group of builder's class up, so you may have to wait a few days until they get more students in for your trade. You know what that means… liberty in civilian clothes on and off the base this weekend."

"I can leave the base?"

"Sure when you not in class and have a liberty pass, you can do what you want."

"Wow, I learn something new every day." I said pondering what type of wonder world was outside the metal fencing.

Petty Officer Rodgers was very nice and personable which helped ease my fear of what Seabee life was going to be like. He also catered to my endless session of, twenty questions. But the biggest surprise was not only did he drive me over to the barracks, he also helped me get my things over to the quarterdeck or otherwise known in the civilian world as a check in counter.

"Thank you so much for helping me Petty Officer Rodgers I really do appreciate you taking the time to assist me."

"Not a problem, I may even see you around sometime." He said with a smile and a wink of an eye, then turned and out the door he went.

I handed my orders to the officer on duty and he signed me in and gave me a key to my new barracks room that would be home until July 3, 1991. He also had informed me that my group would not be forming a new class until Monday, so I could have the weekend to do whatever. *It was the best weekend one could ever imagine for their first time in California.*

During those first few days I met a guy in the courtyard that was located in the center of all the barracks. His name was Tom, he was from Omaha, Nebraska and was attending 'A' School, but was only a reservist. He was going to be a Construction Mechanic and only had a few weeks left of school. He became a great friend and we hung around together during most of our spare time. Everyone claimed that we were an item and they we were dating. Hell, I had only been there two days and didn't have a clue what was going on. I was just living in the moment. I think the others were just jealous, as most of them were always too drunk to enjoy the adventures around them.

By Monday morning I was finally classed up and could only see him after school and on the weekend. I eventually did go on a date with Tom. He introduced me to a special wonder dinner for people on limited means, corn dogs and curly fries with mustard and ketchup. I had never tried either, but one bite and I was hooked. As the sun set down behind the ocean, we finished eating and decided to take a walk on the Hueneme pier. My eyes grew wide and a streak of fear raced through my body as this bright mass hung over the ocean horizon. At first I thought it was some kind of Hollywood movie set. It was huge!

"What in the world is that?" I said with the urge to run and hide, "What is that?"

"It's the moon, strange huh, it look much bigger on this side of the world." Tom said with a hint on laughter in his voice.

"It's amazing. I want to just sit and look at it, can we do that?"

"We can sit here all night if you want too."

Hand in hand we sat, looking at the moon and talking about our dreams for the future.

I had never been subjected to the moon in this magnitude. It was like watching an IMAX theater screen standing only a few feet away from it. I couldn't take my eyes off it as it moved through the night sky. The color was bright silver that reminded me of a set of high-beams on a dark country road. It lit everything around us as if it were the break of dawn and still to this very day I do not believe that I was really there among such a splendor of nature. If I do recall correctly, I never went back to my barracks that night. I sat with Tom on the same bench and gazed upon the moon until the dawn of a new day. What a breath taking experience, it made me feel like I had been given another chance to follow a new direction in my life. I made a wish and said a prayer, and you know, God was listening.

He was a very nice guy and I was saddened to see him go when it was time for him to return home. I have never forgotten the crazy things we did and I still have the letter and pictures, he sent to me, in my cedar chest. Not because I hope to one day look him up, but more as a memory to myself of the people I have met and the places I have been. There are just some people and things that are good to think about, but are better left in the past.

Although he touched my heart and was very special to me during that part of my life, I knew that he was not the one I was searching for that needed my help. He was the one who introduced me to the simpler parts of life. Long walks on the beach, corn dogs with ketchup and mustard, with a side of curly fries. *Thanks for the memories of a new beginning to my new life.*

*   *   *

I was now officially stationed at the Naval Construction Training Center, aka N.C.T.C. in Port Hueneme, California and a student in class number 90190. The weather was always perfect, just made you want to grab your swimsuit and hit the beaches. Unfortunately, moments like those had to be earned. If you didn't have a weekend liberty card in hand, it wasn't happening.

During a morning inspection on a huge parking lot made of pavement that was known as the grinder, my attention was drawn to a guy pulling into the adjacent parking lot beside us. He drove up in an old reddish van and was wearing his Seabee green uniform. *God he looked HOT!* My heart jumped into my throat and my palms began to sweat profusely, but he never noticed me and kept walking over to where his battalion buddies were gathering.

"What a guy," I thought as our inspection proceeded. *"Wow."*

"Constructionmen Lake, would you like to join us now?" said our instructor. "Inspection is over and we are heading to class, are you with us or do you need a moment to freshen up?"

"Yes Sir" I said so that all eyes would stop looking at me. Then as with every day for the next twelve weeks, going to and from class, we marched in perfectly straight ranks of three abreast to the rhythm of Constructionmen Franklin singing cadence to keep us all in step. *I LOVED IT!*

I was the only female in my class, and that was just how I wanted it. We learned everything a builder in the Navy needed to know to get the job done. Our days were again filled with the same concept as boot camp, schooling, marching, and physical training. Builder 'A' School, as it was known, had its good points and bad. Although the class was fun and rather easy, it was very hard to be accepted by the men of the military. To them this was not a place for women. Trying to gain the trust and respect of the men around me, a class all its own.

During field training while working on our huts we were building, I had fallen off the roof because my safety rope was not tied correctly. I never once went crying off too Medical, I just brushed myself off and got back up there to finish the task at hand. They all stood there, including my instructors, watching in amazement. They waited in nail biting wonder. It was if they were waiting for the water works to begin. I actually expected for someone to start placing bets that I would cry. Feeling an excruciating pain in my right hip, I bit my lip and showed no emotion.

"I refuse to give them the satisfaction." I said under my breath while tying the rope correctly this time.

It was from that day on that they finally accepted that I was there to work and learn a trade, not just stand around and try to be a beauty queen.

I loved learning how to hot tar a roof and lay block. I hated drywall and putting up ceramic tiles, but I persevered and continued trying to learn all that I could. One of my major struggles was understand the math that was required to becoming a builder. Trying to figure the pitch of a roof and the rise and run of stairs just wasn't getting through to me. I lost weekend liberty at one point due to a failure on a math exam. I had to stay after class to get extra help and was also given numerous math problems to do over the weekend. One way or another they were going to drill this into my brain. I am happy to say that this strategy worked and I was allowed to continue with my class, otherwise I would have been held back. And yes, I got my weekend liberty back the following weekend.

Now fitting in with the men and learning math were some of the obstacles that I had overcome. The biggest obstacle never mastered, ways to get out of physical training while attending 'A' School. My DDD breasts and I wanted no part of the mile run on the grinder. What a circus act that was, and very embarrassing. The men loved it. *Of course they would.* I was never the lucky one to figure out how to skip PT, and the men were not eager to share this information with me. This became a small competition between me and the men in my class. I recall a day when I knew I had the answer to this and I thought I was being really smart. The Red Cross was looking for blood donations from people who were O+. Our instructors told us, that anyone who gives blood would not have to participate in physical training.

"*YES! I'm O+. No physical training for me today!*" These were the words that filled my sneaky thoughts. "*I'm such a master mind.*"

Well…I had never given blood before and didn't know what it entailed. *Words of caution to those of a sensitive stomach…beware.*

Shortly before class had ended Petty Officer Marlin excused me so that I could head over to the temporary Red Cross facility. I walked into a vacant classroom that had been turned into a blood depot. I felt my legs begin to turn to Jell-O and my body became hot and tingly as if someone had coved my body with fire ants.

"Good afternoon…Constructionmen Lake." A nurse in a white lab coat said with a smile.

"Ah…Hi"

"Come with me and sit down over here, have you ever given blood before?"

"Yes, during a doctor appointment when I came into the Navy."

"No dear, this is not like that, we will take a pint of blood from your body with a butterfly needle." Her voice was calm and she made the whole concept sound like it was a piece of cake. "It will take a bit longer as well."

"Oh…that's fine." Keeping in mind if I didn't do this, it was an hour of physical training. Something I didn't want to do on a gorgeous sunny Friday afternoon.

The procedure created the strangest feelings and did not help my already sensitive stomach. They had to lay me back several times when I reported the room was growing darker and darker. The entire process took approximately fifteen minutes and before I knew it, I was done. I was forced to drink three cups of orange juice and eat two whole Twinkie's before they would let me go back to my barracks. I was proud to know I had finally found a way to get out of physical training. I stood outside the building, after I was done, thinking that I had just pulled a fast one when I heard Constructionmen Alders' voice from across the way.

"Hey Lake, physical training has been cancelled for today because battalion 5 is having a full inspection on the grinder. There won't be enough room for running the mile." He and the rest of the guys began to snicker and laugh as they marched towards the barracks.

I just sat there shaking my head with a shocked look on my face as if they had said to me,

"Hey Lake, is Mother Nature in town? There is something red on the back of your pants."

I hung my head in defeat as I slowly walked back to my barracks several yards behind the men of my class. Over and over in my mind I kept thinking.

"Men…nine. Women…Zilch. They win…again!"

CHAPTER SEVEN

THE CALL

There was a lot of excitement during the last few days of the month of April in 1991. Our school was going to be inspected by the Captain of the base and his guest, the Admiral of the Navy. We all had worked very hard polishing every nook and cranny of the school and our barracks as well. We were given a five day weekend liberty, yet I just didn't feel much like going out on the town. I decided to go to the Military Welfare & Recreation center, which in short was known as MWR, to watch their featured movie on the big screen television in the gathering room.

Everyone in their right minds where headed to LA or some exotic place to make their own memories of a long liberty. I sat alone and watched the movie "Flatliners". During that time I had this anxious feeling that was accompanied by a sense of extreme loss. I knew it then, something had happened to George. I walked to my barracks, saddened, confused and missing home.

When I got there, on my barracks door was an urgent message to call home, a call I had feared for many weeks. It was at the very second I knew that George had died. At first I felt as though I couldn't go home since I didn't have much leave time or money left. Petty Officer Cook, who was the Officer of the quarterdeck that night, knew that the best place I could be right now would be with my family. He helped me get travel assistance from the Red Cross and then personally took me over to the Oxnard Airport on the day of my departure. The only thing I really knew about him was that he drove a beautiful red Chevy pick-up truck, was married and had the most captivating blue eyes, yet looking past the material things, he was truly sincere.

My flight, an early morning red-eye, was leaving on the same day as George's funeral. I had made some special arrangements with a friend from Hillsborough. He was going to meet me at the airport and was instructed not to tell anyone of my coming home. I was going to be at that funeral no matter what I had to do to get there.

We made it with seconds to spare. I was glad that I had worn my full dress blues, as it was a military funeral. The funeral was just ending and people were coming out of the funeral home. The American Legionnaires from Post 59 were all outside waiting for my mother so that they could carry the casket to the hearse. I could hear my mother crying out George's name all the way across the parking lot.

"George, don't leave me! Please!" she cried over and over.

I gathered the nerve to come out from behind the truck I was near and walked towards the funeral home. As I came up the walkway I heard the command,

"Hand Salute"

They saluted me as I walked by and into the funeral home. My mother was kneeling before George's casket and she would not let go of his hands. Two of my mother's good friends were telling her that it was time to let him go. She was slowly and emotionally breaking down when I said to her,

"Okay lady it's time to let him sleep now."

She knew the voice. She turned at looked at me in disbelief she could not believe I was standing there after I had just got done telling her, two days ago, that I couldn't come home.

"It's time to go," I said as I helped her to her feet and putting my arms around her. I gave her a big hug then helped her to the door.

"Good-bye George" we both said simultaneously looking back at him.

"I love you honey." Mom said, with what strength she could gather and gently kissed her hand and with a single soft breath, blew him a kiss good-bye.

Once again the command for hand salute was called as we exited the funeral home. I got into her car with her and rode over to the cemetery following the glossy black hearse that carried George's body to his final resting-place.

During the ceremony a strange and wonderful thing happened to both a friend, whom we shall keep nameless as this event this haunts him to this very day, and myself. As the bugle began playing Taps, I looked up. Up on the hillside in the distance next to a set of mailboxes was mail truck parked backwards and a tall slender man in a uniform got out and stood beside of it and looked down upon our fair well gathering. At first my instinct was to wave, as if I knew him. My heart told me, I did know him and as I continued to look at him upon the hillside, I felt wrapped in a feeling of warmth that was enriched with peace, like a giant hug. It was then I knew who the man was on the hill.

We never heard or saw the mail truck pull up. To make this even more haunting, during the twenty-one gun salute and never once taking our eyes off this man, he and his mail truck just simply faded away.

"Sleep in peace George, I will miss you." I thought to myself.

* * *

I was allowed to be home for four days so that I could attend the funeral and spend three additional days with my family. My mother and I just sat and tried to enjoy the days by filling it with long overdue girl chat. I told her about what I had seen so far while being in the military and all the new and exciting things I had experienced. Aside from the final days of George's life, we spoke of what life was like living in California. It was a wonderful place and I fell in love with it as soon and the plane landed. I was happy to be back in Hillsborough, but my heart was growing more attached to the new life I was living.

She took me to the airport one bright sunny Thursday morning so I would get back to the base before midnight. She gave me a long hug before boarding my flight and told me to call her as soon as I got back to the base.

While I flew across our great nation, I took out my journal and began reading over some of my entries and poems that I had written while I was traveling. I came across one that was written while I was at church during boot camp.

"To My Mother"

To you, my only mother, you do so much for me.
And helped me through the thick and thin, in my life you are the key.
You are so very special, and there's so much that we both share.
Like our mother-daughter secrets, that no one else will ever bear.

Inside I hold such feelings, for you tend to be alone.
Just hold on to your Georgy, and soon I shall be home.
You know I had to do this, though sometimes I wonder why.
And when I had to leave that day, all I did was cry and cry.

Just hold your head up, mom, someday you know will be.
Your long and awaited day, a true life's fantasy.
Dear Mom, I may not say this much, but I know deep down you know.
I really truly care for you, and that I love you so.

February 1991

Reading this, there was no doubt that I was lacking a college education as the words were so elementary, yet it marked a time in my life when I wasn't able to speak about my feelings out loud. It was a way that I could have never expressed myself verbally, yet was so hard to find the right words, and so I left the words the way they were written on that not so long ago day in February.

Chapter Eight

Living a Dream

My training took me through the months of April, May, June and three days into July, which was perfect weather in my book. No humidity, sun warmed sand and surf, although still saddened of the past events, I kept my promise to my family I would do my best.

It was a time of my life that was filled with new and exciting encounters. The battalions were just coming back from an ending war in Saudi Arabia, and there was happiness and adrenaline in the air. Outside of school work and training, I mastered the art of making a little extra money on the weekends that I didn't have duty. One thing you learn being on a base, word travels fast. It was an excellent strategy for running and stimulating my business.

Trying to rent a car in the Oxnard and Port Hueneme area was a task not easy to achieve. If you were a student, your chances were slim to none due to many bad experiences in the past with local companies. In LA however, opportunities were golden and they didn't care who you were. If you purchased their insurance, were over the age of eighteen and held a current driver's license, you were driving. With this known, many of the students, come hell or high water, would make the journey via bus, taxi, or hopper just so they could have a set of wheels for their final 'A' School days.

By getting the word out that I dropped off rental cars for students that were graduating N.C.T.C., I had myself a small business. My charge was $100 dollars cash, for my time and a hopper flight, for myself, back to Oxnard. Making that kind of money, I got over my fear of flying, in the small planes, immediately.

Strange thing about it, a hopper flight one way was only $15, yet still without hesitation they would pay me to take their cars back. I always wondered why they just didn't drive the car back to LA themselves and catch their flights, as all the rental companies offered free transportation to L.A.X. I guess it was the excitement of graduation that cluttered their brains, but filled my wallet. *Uh yes, I'm smiling.*

At times I did fell a little guilty for not making the suggestion that they could save money, but chose to remain silent. *Wouldn't you if you were making $100.00 bucks?* But I fell that with my lack of the truth to make money, I made up for it with a few good deeds to ease my guilt. Knowing first-hand about the dreaded wrong directions and information prank on new students at the Oxnard Airport, I decided to do something about it when I could. On the days that I was flying after delivering a rental, I would ask both at L.A.X. and then again at the Oxnard Airport, if there were any new N.C.T.C. students heading to the base. Nine out of ten times there was always someone. I would call them a taxi, pay for it and ride back with them to be sure they knew where they were going. I personally think that not only did it please the new students of N.C.T.C. I bet it also made the desk clerk on duty at the 31st Regiment happy as well. He could watch all the television shows he wanted without any student interruptions.

With the extra money I made, one thing was certain, I enjoyed as many of the landmarks of the West Coast that I could. I encountered the thrill of my first adult roller coaster at Six Flags Magic Mountain in Vilcena, California. It was called the Viper and it was indeed the ultimate rush. I learned to enjoy and appreciate the finer tastes of real Mexican food and found that my body delighted in processing this food without any warning until the pain suddenly arrived. It was best to walk up wind from me and all my friends heeded this advice if Mexican food was on the menu.

I went to Disneyland with a tour group from the base, but was rather disappointed when I saw how tiny the castle was, it just couldn't compare to the one at Walt Disney World in Florida. Don't get me wrong, the rides were still fantastic!

One of the biggest events of my weekend liberties was getting lost in Hollywood with another student from school. We stumbled into the opportunity of a life time while trying to find the ever famous historic Hollywood sign in the hills. We were lucky to find a place to park our car because traffic had been stopped due to the "Welcome Home Parade" for some of our troops that had returned from Saudi Arabia. Not passing up a single opportunity to be a part of history, we found a great place to stand and held up a huge American flag that Constructionmen Kirk still had in the car from a purchase he'd made earlier in the week. We waved to movie stars as they passed in old model T's. Yelling at the top of our lungs, we cheered our troops as they marched and sang cadence. I was both humbled and honored to know what these brave men had done for us and I was proud to know that I could someday be part of their team. What a moment to have been a part of.

Now even though I mastered the art of making money, I had not mastered how to save it. When money was low, my roommates and I still found ways to have a great time; we took in as many two-dollar movies as we could. *Can you believe it, that was all it cost to see a new movie on the base. The good ole days.* Other days we would just go and sit on the beach and watch the world pass by.

My world was spinning around me and I could feel a special magic igniting inside my soul, I had to have more and more. At times all was so surreal, like a sense of floating into a life that years past would have only been part of a daydream or two. I remember a comment made in the movie "It Happened One Christmas", how the touch of one life, changes the lives of so many.

All these people that shared these moments with me will never truly understand the permanent impact they have made on my being. I would like to take this time to extend a sincere thank you and that even though we have grown apart and are no longer in touch, the memories are etched forever into the very foundation that makes up my soul.

* * *

While I was in Port Hueneme, I was in a situation that deserves the saying, "If I only knew then what I know now," I never would have been so hard on myself. One day specifically, I never realized that this one moment, was a link to my destiny and as I lived it, a door to my future was opened before my eyes and I couldn't see what awaited me on the other side.

By this time I had been at the training center for about five weeks, and during that time I made new friends and enjoyed my weekend liberties to the fullest. My friend Linda, who was another builder in training, and I went to Hueneme Beach to take in the summer sun and fun, while I tried to tan my Yankee white skin. *Burn to a crisp was more like it.*

Our day was relaxing and conversations overflowing with our hopes, dreams, and sorrows, while lying on the warm sand. Time always flies by when you're having fun, and like with any day that we were having fun, it would come to an end. Something we hated, but all good things do. While walking back to the naval base Linda mentioned that she knew a guy that lived in one of the condominiums close to the beach. She insisted that we stop in to say hello to him. Feeling very self-conscious and hesitant about my terrible beach appearance, I still foolishly agreed to her request.

He was home and with a little uncertainty invited us in to talk. They moved off into the kitchen and left me standing on my own. I was not close enough to hear their topic of conversation, but I think she was asking him for a ride, who knows. I was more worried that if we still had to walk the remainder of the way back to the base we would miss dinner at the chow hall. As I waited for her in the front hall near the stairs, there was a man sitting in a chair with his feet up drinking a beer, watching the sexy body of Denise Austin in her work out gear and smile, while still in his Seabee green pants, socks and T-shirt.

"Fallon…that's Frank's roommate…go say hi," said Linda, with a wink of an eye.

What a strange feeling it was to be standing in this apartment. I also couldn't help but keep looking at Frank's roommate. He looked familiar to me, but I just couldn't place the face.

"Hello" I said with my best friendly voice. "So you're a Seabee too?"

"Yeah.. whatever," he responded sharply as though he would rather not be bothered.

There was absolutely no doubt and no way possible, he was interested in this chick. Honestly, with the look I was sporting at that moment, nobody in their right mind would be. I had a round extra-large upper body appearance and was not smart enough to purchase a more flattering bathing suit with a cup support for my dropping triple D's. Once again, a perfect illustration of not being the sharpest tack in the bunch, I honestly thought I had to wear my military issued bathing suit for as long as I was in the military. *Can we say gullible? Yes we can.*

To best describe my appearance in one full sentence, a freshly beached whale with a sunburn and sand-covered body. I looked like I had just been harpooned and had washed up on shore. I was such a sight that I could even make medusa look like Miss Universe.

I just stood there fidgeting until Linda and I left. I wanted to get away from the awkward moment as fast as I could.

"You ready Fallon? Frank can't take us back tonight," she remarked, with a hint of discouragement in her voice.

I nodded my head in agreement and turn back to Frank's roommate.

"Well I guess I'll see you around the base sometime," trying to smile my way past my disappointment of not making a lasting impression on Frank's roommate.

"Don't hold your breath" was all I heard in his beer drenched voice.

It was a relief to know we were out of there, but bummed I'd be going without dinner, as we still had to walk back to the base.

"What a total asshole!" I said to Linda, who was still looking back over her shoulder constantly as if Frank would come running after her.

"I thought I felt some chemistry, I was only trying to be nice to him." I said, as I was slowly being consumed with tears of loneliness. "I know I'm not some California bred beach babe, but still, how hard is it to be nice. What a dickhead."

"Someday you find Mr. Right, Fallon, someday when you least expect it...he'll be standing right in front of you."

"Really...God I hope so Linda...I really hope so."

*   *   *

I have always believed that all things happen for a reason. Over the coming weeks Linda, was still feeling bad for what had happened and that she tried her best to make it up to me. I kept telling her it was not her fault I just needed to do something about the way I looked when I wasn't wearing make-up or had my hair done.

I just could not seem to get over the way Frank's roommate, Mr. Anti-social, had treated me and made me feel ugly and unwanted. I knew that I didn't look my best coming from the beach, but his actions kept me from going out as much and did a number on my self-esteem. She and her friends never gave up and went out of their way to include me in many of their weekend adventures.

The most spiritual adventure was a day trip to Ojhi cliff diving with Linda, and two of her male friends, Jay and Alex, from battalion 4. This was something that I had never done in my life and was a risk that I was willing to take.

It's so hard to use words to describe what happened to me and how it made me feel. Music however is my life and my life has its own sound track.

Music is the best way to share this moment with you. With your eyes closed while sitting in a dark cool room, listen to the melody of Silent Lucidity by Queensryche. *This is playing on my CD player at this moment, as I put my thoughts into print.*

Silhouetted by a back drop of a golden sun and blue sky, I stood upon the cliff side and extended my arms out to my side as if I was bird ready to take flight for the first time. I was scared to death as to what I was about to do, but nobody knew. With one deep breath I closed my eyes, emptied my mind and threw myself into the wind. For one brief second, time had completely stood still. My body felt weightless as I hung in the atmosphere before falling into the water below. When I pierced the water with my body, I opened my eyes to take in the water world around me. Green plants danced gracefully with the sun's rays in the underwater world. It was so heavenly and the urge to breathe was not instantaneous as I relished in it beauty as long as I could. It was all so dreamlike and energized a power within myself. When I slowly came back to the surface of the water, there were cheers mixed with concern. They had been worried something had happened to me when I didn't surface right away.

"Fallon…Fallon…you okay?" said Linda panic stricken.

"I'm fine, wow! Can I do that again!?"

"I can't believe you did it! Awesome!" cheered Alex.

"Here Fallon, grab my hand, I'll help you out of the water" Jay remarked gingerly as he reached out to me. "You know, I am also surprised you did it. I was sure you would back out. You have changed my whole perception of you."

"Thanks Jay" I said still trying to catch my breath while using his strength to help me to my feet.

'Fallon, do you mind if we go and sit somewhere, just you and I?"

"Sure Jay, just let me dry off."

We enjoyed ourselves and had long talks while we sat on the rocks basking in the warmth of the sun. He seemed rather nervous and fumbled over his words as he explained that he was feeling some type of connection between us. I guess his reasoning for talking alone was because he didn't want to be overheard by Alex or Linda. As for myself, he was fun to hang out with, but my feelings were not the same. Something inside told me that he was not the one I was looking for, but I never said anything to him and I decided that I would let time tell the story if we were to be together. We saw each other on and off during my schooling, but being a student and with him in battalion, it was inevitable that we were going to be forced to say our good-byes and long distant relationships usually ended up with someone cheating or hurting the other in some way. It was possible that our paths may never cross again, so I never took it as anything more than friends with benefits.

As we got closer and closer to graduation, base gossip and rumors were on the rise, especially around the school. The rumor this time was that the majority of the female students were being transferred to Adak, Alaska following graduation. The problem was, this rumor was true and I learned, just before graduation, that I had been turned down for the position I applied for at Camp David, and that both Linda and I were going to be two of those rumored females heading north. My job would be a builder in the Public Works Department. My transfer day was July 29, 1991. Jay and I were really excited to learn that he was going to be there on deployment from July 1991-January 1992. Maybe he was my future and I was being given more time to figure things out between us.

My twelve weeks in California went by as if driving through a desert town with only one building. Blink and it was gone. Our final day in 'A' School was here and it was time to embark on another new and exciting journey. All the special times with friends that I had made were now going to be memories in time. *This is the hardest part of military life, just when you make a good friend, or two, it's time to transfer to a new duty station.*

At ten in the morning, following our graduation, we would be forced to say our good-byes and head out into the world to consume any leave that we had on the books or if we chose too, we could go straight to our next command. I decided to take more leave so that I could go home to make sure my mother was ok.

My reason for not writing about my graduation is that I don't recall anything more than standing in a small parking lot mid-morning in our working whites as if we were in an inspection. There was some small talk about the accomplishments of a few students. Immediately following the small talk babble, we were handed our certificates of completions as we walked forward to the podium when our names were called. From the beginning to the end, the entire informal event was no more than forty-five minutes at best. Once the certificates were passed out, we were told good luck and then dismissed. *Cheesy!*

*   *   *

I had earned some extra leave time and had made the choice to use it rather than wait until my next duty station. For some reason, I felt a pulling that told me that I should go home to mom and spend as much time with her as I could. With my next duty station in Adak, Alaska, getting leave off the base was harder to do, so I was told, with the limited number of flights on and off the island. Going home first was the better choice.

My flight was not leaving until 6:45 that night, which I had planned that way. I wanted the extra time following graduation to take some last minute pictures and video of friends that I had made while I was there. All my things had been packed, with the exception of my uniform and some personals, the night before.

My heart sank as I made my way into my barrack room #209, for the last time. I walked over to the window and opened it, just a crack, so that I could listen to the students in the courtyard engulfed in conversation and smell the breeze of the ocean air. This was something that was a daily ritual while working on homework or writing in my journal.

"Well Fallon...it's time to go." I said out loud to myself. "It's time to go."

With my bags in hand I turned and took one last look at the room which had been my home away from home.

"I'm so going to miss this place," I thought to myself while trying to hold back my tears and swallowing the tightness growing in my throat.

I left the window open so that I could hear the voices from the courtyard, as I turned off the lights and slowly closed the door to another chapter in my life.

I made sure I walked through the courtyard on my way to get my taxi. I said my good-byes to students that were still waiting for their graduation day and then met up with Constructionmen Jackson, on my way to the parking lot.

He and I decided to share the expense of the taxi to the airport and at 5:30 PM, as ironically as this may sound, we were both heading back to the east coast on the same red-eye flight. In no time at all we were loaded and underway.

I felt an emptiness as the taxi made its way across the base to the gate. I loved California and I didn't want to leave, there was something here for me and I had not found it yet, but whatever this feeling was to find the person who needed me, it felt very strong here. When we got to the gate we had to wait for the red light to change, which I found odd as this light was always green. At that same time, it was then, I saw him…the man in the reddish colored van coming onto the base. I felt my heart jump into my throat and I could barely breathe.

"OH MY GOD! IT'S HIM…IT'S HIM!" I shouted out as I spun around to look out the rear window as he passed by.

"It's who?" replied Jackson puzzled at my loss of control.

"I don't know who he is, but I have to meet him, somehow I have to meet him!"

"Girl, you're crazy he's just another guy and you're leaving, or don't you remember? You're going home and then off to Alaska. Good luck finding him in this huge world. You don't even know his name."

But, I was so focused on the van that what Jackson said to me had no effect. I had to meet this man.

As the taxi finally had a green light my heart broke again, leaving me feeling emotionally exhausted. I sat back in my seat speechless and continued on my journey homeward.

Why God! Why! Who is he? Why do I have this need to meet him? How can I meet a man if I don't know who he is? Are you playing a joke on me? TELL ME! SHOW ME! What am I supposed to do! What are these feelings! What do you want me to see! HELP ME!

CHAPTER NINE

TRAVEL TO HEAL

Mom seemed to be doing somewhat better dealing with the loss of George. Yet the pain still remained in her eyes when she spoke his name. Friends and family kept their promise to make sure that she was doing ok. They all believed that what kept her spirits up was that she was really looking forward to my coming home. She had concerns that with my love for being on the West Coast, I was going to choose to stay in California until my transfer to Adak.

My mother has always been a great one to sense when something is wrong and she knew that there was something wrong with me. I had only been home two days and I was going stir crazy. Even my love for the Fourth of July was very quiet and subdued. I was lost and confused and just felt this need to search for something, but what? This time was as though Hillsborough was a vacation and my home was California, which made me homesick, I had to go back and she knew this. Our discussions were always centered on traveling and my days in California. We talked about how she had only been to Florida during a drive with George and that she had never flown before. It was her next comment that put a twinkle back in my eye and a hop in my step.

"Someday I would love to fly somewhere and see new places."

Enjoying my new found personality that I found after my cliff diving experience, being spontaneous to try new things, I jumped up and grabbed the phone.

"I can change that, are you willing to try something new?" I said trying with all my might to hold back my sheer excitement.

What?" She asked, fearing the worst.

"Yes or No?" were the only answers I gave her to choose from.

With some hesitation, I heard her say the words, "Yes."

"GREAT! That's what I wanted to hear."

With only two phone calls, I made reservations for my mother, her friend Paul and myself, for two rooms at the Navy Lodge on the base where I was stationed in California, and three plane tickets. In less than an hour our itinerary was complete and we were leaving from Logan Airport in Massachusetts, the very next day.

* * *

She was indeed scared of what a flight would be like as she buckled her seat belt. As for Paul, he couldn't wait to get to California. You see we had promised him that we would take him to Tijuana, Mexico to get plenty of tequila and a new pair of Mexican leather boots. You could see their adrenaline rush as the plane taxied down the runway with incredible speed and with the tip of the nose pointing towards the crystal blue sky, we were airborne. I couldn't help but smile as the realization that I was going back to California set in. Not only was I happy about my return, I relished in the thought of knowing that what my eyes had seen before, were now going to be enjoyed by the most important person in my life, my mother.

As we flew through the sky, my emotions were blanketed by a sensation, someone seriously needing me to be part of their life, but whom? I relaxed into a tranquil sleep, as the clouds gathered around the plane like the stuffing of an over-sized pillow. Dreams that were more like visions so real filtered before my eyes and kept me wanting to see more. I could see a man walking towards me in a green Seabee uniform, yet I was never blessed with the knowledge that revealed his identity. His hair was dark, his skin was sun kissed and his smile was hypnotizing.

"Who are you?" I remember saying, "Please tell me who you are! Do you seek me as I seek you?"

As the vision slowly darkened, there was a brilliant flash and I saw the reddish van on the base I had seen so many weeks ago and then again as I was leaving to go home. As I watched the vision slowly faded as a voice became very loud that me feel very confused and then it suddenly woke me.

"Please put your seats and tray tables in their upright positions as we prepare the cabin for our arrival into Los Angeles." said the stewardess.

I opened my eyes and looked around unsure if what I had just seen was really a dream. It was all so real.

What does all this mean? Maybe I will see the van again when I get back to the base? Maybe? How beautiful, I am home again. Help me find him Lord, help me find him.

I filled with joy when I looked out the window of the plane and gazed upon the Los Angeles city skyline. I was back where I wanted to be. My mother and Paul were seated in the middle of the plane and were unable to take in the sights that the West Coast had to offer from the sky.

We landed, got our luggage and proceeded to the place I knew so very well, Dollar Rental to pick up our car.

"Hello Fallon, are you dropping off another car?"

Yes, they had gotten to know me personally.

"Hi Lisa, it's so nice to see you again. This time I am picking up a car for myself. I brought my family here to show them the sights of the West Coast."

"Welcome to LA," Lisa said to my mother and Paul in her usual cheerful voice. "Fallon the only car I have available is a medium sized car, will that be ok?"

"Not a problem what is it?"

"A red Dodge Dynasty, you're going to love it, low miles and velvet interior."

"Wow, that's great! Better than the economy cars I was bringing back here, don't ya think?"

We both started laughing as she shook her head, agreeing with my last comment.

Still unsure as to why the man in the van would filter into my thoughts. I smiled as I recalled the feeling I had when I saw him, then pushed the thoughts aside to continue filling out the paperwork for our rental. With the car all loaded, all of us belted in and the car in drive, away we went to the adventure that awaited us. I couldn't help but chuckle throughout the day at the thought that our red Dodge Dynasty was the same color as the reddish-van that I saw on the base.

"Maybe this was the sign I had asked God to show me?" I wondered with a sigh "Just maybe."

I was so excited to be driving up the highway towards Oxnard and Port Hueneme with my mother and Paul with me. The strawberry fields were green and lush with fresh ripened fruit. The hillsides were of striking blends of copper tones. It was even more beautiful to me than when I was here during 'A' School. To them it was as if they had stepped into a dream and tried to take in as much as they both could. There were still many of my classmates and friends on the base when we arrived. They all addressed my mother with hello mom, and because she had seen them on a tape that I had made, she felt as if she knew them all.

Over the week that we were there we took in many sights. Universal Studios and driving up the Coast to Ventura was very enjoyable to them. We can't forget when we got Paul on the Free Fall at Magic Mountain. *You had to see it to believe it.* During the evenings we would go to the Whales Tail for drinks, hor d'oeuvres, and to enjoy the setting of the sun from a covered balcony over a yacht filled marina.

The biggest of all the trips was going to Mexico, what fun we had. We had always been told during our 'A' School days, that we were never to spend the night over the border. I had asked my friend Josh, who was still attending school, to join us. I assured him that we would be back that night. I also built up the trip as an opportunity of a lifetime; he'd be a fool if he passed up the chance. Besides that, I was thinking more about myself. I would have someone to dance with and Paul would have a male buddy to chat with if the girl chat got to be too intense, needless to say, he said yes. We drove down the coast of California to San Diego to the train station that would take us to the border. Because the train could only take us to a point about a quarter of a mile from the customs center, we had to walk across the border. I got a great picture from the overpass of the Mexican border auto check in center.

Immediately as we passed through the steel gates, we felt like we had walked into a new dimension, that didn't smell the greatest and was excessively busy, but we made do. There were people of all walks of life everywhere we turned. Vendors blanketed the sidewalks in front of small rundown shops insisting they had the best deals in town. The most popular items that sold were Mexican blankets, T-shirts, Tequila, baskets and leather boots. Paul was ecstatic when he purchased a pair of black leather boots for only ten dollars; *it wasn't until he was back in Hillsborough some many months after our trip, that he realized that the reason for such a deal was because the stitching on the boots didn't match at all.*

We walked up and down the Tijuana strip enjoying the sounds of Mexican music that filled the air and the array of lights that began to illuminate as duck came upon us. Billboards with the words "Free Drinks" and "Live Nude Women" appeared from the rooftops of many buildings on the strip. Prostitutes of all nationalities solicited sex for less than a case of soda.

If you were the type of person who enjoyed getting completely intoxicated, this was the place, and beautiful women at the doors of competing nightclubs advertised house drinks as being only one dollar. I know this was a gimmick to get you through their doors and then the more you drank, the more it cost since you were not in a frame of mind to know your money was burning a hole in your wallet. Paul and Josh, without a moment of hesitation, fell into this money making scheme and drank their way from place to place. My mother and I walked along side of them making sure that their choices would not put them into the luxury of a Mexican Jail cell. *I mean that in the most sarcastic way.*

With the nightlife never ending, Paul and Josh became extremely intoxicated and the choice to go back over the border was no longer an option. Border patrol was known for giving their share of grief to people that were military and to anyone who was intoxicated beyond any recollection of knowing what was taking place around them. My mother and I always joked about wanting to stay in the sleaziest place in Mexico, just to say that we did. Well you know what, that is exactly what we chose to do as that was the only type of hotel rooms that were available. Josh was in desperate need of a place to crash and so I took him to our room that I had next to my mother and Paul. I was speechless when I opened the door to our room and turned on the light, it was just what my mother and I wanted.

"What a hell hole," I said as I helped Josh into the room.

He passed out as soon as he hit the bed. Not a care in the world that he was going to sleep in the same clothes he had worn all day. The room was so hot that I decided to open a window. How shocked I was to find when I opened the heavy drapes that the window had been removed and solid brick was in its place. I decided that if I couldn't open a window, and there was no air conditioning, then I would do the next best thing, take a shower to try to cool off. The water was colored with an orange tint and had the scent of old rust. That soap could not even lather it was so bad.

There was not a doubt in my mind that tiles in the shower were held in with used chewing gum. *Ok, how did I know this? A few of the tiles in the shower fell off the wall and guess what was on the back of them? You got it…gum.*

To make matters wonderfully worse, I didn't have anything to dry off with or change into after my rust rinse. So to be resourceful, I grabbed the old and worn out bedspread and made myself a toga to sleep in. I then lay down on the bed next to Josh, who was snoring so bad I could see what was left of the paint on the ceiling coming off.

The night had been uneventful until sometime after two in the morning. I was awoken by the sounds of a shuffle of people in the narrow, dirty and dim lit hallway just outside my door. All of a sudden the disturbance got really loud and wham, the door that I thought that I had locked to our room, burst open followed by the light being switched on. In the doorway stood a man of African American descent that could hardly walk upright through the door because he was so tall. My first thought was that he was going to rape me or maybe kill me due to the pained look on his face.

"I should have listened to our instructors at N.C.T.C. What was I thinking, oh God please…."

"I need to use your pisser," he said interrupting my train of thought.

"He needs to use my what? He needs to use my pisser? Needs to use the pisser?" I said to myself over and over as I watched him standing over the toilet with the bathroom door wide-open relieving himself. Then tucking himself back into his pants with one hand, he flushed the toilet with the other. *At least he flushed.* Then he came out of the bathroom, turned off the light and went back into the hall closing the door behind him. Josh never moved one inch of his body; he was still dead to the world. It took a few hours before I was able to get back to sleep. I was not sure if they would ever go away, but eventually my adrenaline shakes slowly subsided back to a reasonable level. It was indeed an eventful night and feeling completely exhausted, I too, became dead to the world.

The next morning there was a light knocking at the door, unsure of whom it was, I asked first before opening it.

"Fallon…It's mom, let me in."

As I opened the door, we both burst into an uncontrollable laughter; we had both used our bedspreads for a nightgown. I told her about Mr. Pisser, and she told me about the giant cockroaches that also got a room with them for the night. How we laughed at the stories we each had to share about the night before. Josh and Paul finally came back to life and were in total disbelief of the many adventures we had endured during our over-nighter in Tijuana. We all got ourselves together and went out to have a little breakfast and finished our Mexican adventure with a taxi version sightseeing tour.

With the smells of the city becoming so intense in the summer heat and the fact that the windows would not go down, we decided it was time for our trip in Mexico to come to an end. We went through customs to claim what we had purchased and then headed back to the train.

We made it safe and sound and no one went to jail or was raped or murdered. That was a good thing. It was the complaints of the new found headaches that Paul and Josh were sporting, that we wished they had stayed in Mexico. We made it back safely to the base and told everyone that we stayed in a hotel in San Diego so that Josh and I would not be in any type of trouble. We decided that the last few days of our stay, we were just going to keep it very simple. Our remaining days were spent at Hueneme Beach by day and the Whales Tail by night.

On the morning of our departure my mother, Paul and I collected our belongings and loaded the car to make our way back to the airport in LA. I was saddened that not once during my time here with my family, did I ever see the man in the reddish van. I guess it wasn't really meant to be. We all said our good-byes to my friends from my 'A' School and then headed back down the Pacific Coast highway. I wanted to see the coastline one more time.

My mother and Paul were returning home on American Airlines and I was leaving on Continental Airlines heading in the opposite direction for Anchorage, Alaska towards my next command in Adak, Alaska. We shared tears of happiness and sadness as we said our good-byes before going to our own terminals.

"I love you mom," I yelled out as I watched her disappear into the crowd.

"I love you too, be good," she yelled back as she waved her arm for me to see.

With a heavy heart I turned and began my new journey to another stepping stone in what my destiny had planned for me, both good times and bad.

During my flight I took advantage to write a few lines that told of my inner most thoughts and this is what it read;

A drifter, alone on this road I roam. I don't know what I'm looking for. My mind, rushing madness wanting oh so much, if I had more time. A friend, one love, romance, I long for. Where does this search begin or will it ever end? I strive for much success, how will I know I made it?

I am waiting, waiting for a sign. I feel the power inside me, it's deep, it burns, energy! Someday I will show so bright. The courage to go on, I will, I can, I shall. I'll fly to the highest point and stay afloat forever. Feel my madness, feel the strength within.

Come fly with me to yonder blue skies, to meet the earth, to feel the sun, I am human I am one. Just show me the way. July 1991

CHAPTER TEN

HEADED NORTH

It had been only six months since my journey had begun and already God had bestowed so many precious moments to aid me in my growth and development to be one with myself. To view the changes of the landscape while flying over the United States heightened my understanding of how big this world really is. I had only seen the great cities of New York and Boston and the lush green countryside throughout the New England states along with a brief visit to Disney World in Orland, Florida.

It was in November of 1989, I was awoken from a crazy dream, and in my mind I could hear the words that someone needed me. It was as if I woke into a life of another person, and the person I used to be could no longer be found inside me. I struggled with the questions of who this someone was that needed me. Before long, nothing else mattered except to fulfill my quest to find the answer. With every attempt I made while living in New Hampshire, the result would always end in heartbreak, for I knew that what I was looking for would not be found here, which resulted in my joining the military.

As my flight landed in Anchorage, Alaska on July 26, 1991, I felt that my quest for an answer was gaining ground and that someday soon, God would show me another sign. I got in about 4:00pm and collected my bags and then called for a taxi to take me over to the billeting office. Billeting is a military term for overnight accommodations for military personnel that are traveling with orders. I was to go to Elemendorf Air Force base to check into the billeting office until my next flight to Adak. Several of us that were traveling from Port Hueneme had not been instructed to call the billeting office in advance to arrange for a room for the night. *Yes, another military practical joke. To me the jokes were getting very old.*

When it was finally my turn to check in, Boston and Portland flashed in my head. I handed the check in clerk my orders that indicated that I needed to report to my new command on the island of Adak, but also noted that I was only enlisted personnel. The desk clerk gave me a familiar look.

"I know that look! No, No, No! What if this turns out like my first day in the military?" I thought to myself, trying to put the image out of my head, so that it wouldn't come true.

I was dazed when I head the following words from the clerk, "I am sorry, but we don't have any more rooms available, you will need to find accommodations off the base. Here are some of the listings that you can call." She said in a monotone voice.

I knew that this was something she was tired of saying over and over on a daily basis. But honestly, this was something that I was tired of hearing over and over.

I knew Constructionmen Hall, who was also in line for the very same reason. He and I were from the same 'A' School class and we were both in the same situation. I knew that he didn't much care for me or for any of the female species for the matter, other than his girl he left back home. I gathered the nerve to confront him with the dilemma we were faced with and I went on to share how my money situation was becoming grim and would he be willing to share the cost of a room off the base, no strings attached.

Not being pleased with my suggestion, but he too was having financial problems, agreed to my proposal and we got a cab and stayed at a rundown Days Inn. There were two small full size beds, so my fear of having to share an immediate space with him receded. As I soaked in a hot bath behind a locked bathroom door, I overheard his phone conversation back home. He spoke with his girlfriend to explain the situation and that I didn't mean a damn thing to him, I was just a financial aid to help find a place to crash for the night. Hearing those words hurt, even though there was nothing between us, but I still felt rather used.

I had a very hard time sleeping, not because I was sharing a room with a guy, it was due to the overwhelming amount of sunlight filtering into our room through the drapes. It was two in the morning and the sun was still high in the sky as if it were noontime on a sunny summer day back in New Hampshire. I finally fell into a light sleep with the same visions, of someone, maybe Mr. Wonderful who needed me, taking my twilight thoughts on a wild ride.

When morning finally came, we made our way back to a small base terminal. There was talk amongst the passengers if our flight would land or not this time.

"What's wrong with the plane?" I asked nervously.

"Nothing hon, the winds have been very gusty and makes landing on the island impossible, that is why they call Adak, the birth place of the winds."

"Huh, I've never heard that before. So what happens if we cannot land?"

"Then you fly all the way back here until the weather gets better out there."

Believe it or not, I suffered through three long days of repeated attempts of flying out to the island, only to see it from the sky, but due to heavy winds we could not land and would have to return to the mainland each time. Now granted, I liked the thought of having extra leave time, but by the end of our first day I was out of money and could not afford a hotel for another night. There was a first class petty officer that was on his way back to Adak after a couple days of rest and relaxation in Anchorage. He was in the lobby of the billeting office and over heard my pleas to the desk clerk to check and see if there were any openings for the night. Again, her reply was no.

"Excuse me miss," he said interrupting my groveling, "these two are with me I'm checking them in." said the petty officer.

"Oh, I am so sorry Petty Officer Kendall, I was not aware that they too were part of your group."

I had to have been in the presence of a miracle. *A deal with the Devil is more like it.* She turned around, tore a sheet of paper off the computer and handed us both our own room keys.

"Thank you sir, I just don't know what we would have done without you." I said with a smile of relief on my face.

"Hey, I've been in your shoes before and it's no picnic when you are not informed of the headaches the military will put you through. It is all about rank and there are only a number of rooms slotted for each particular rank. First Class had four extra rooms tonight."

"What a pain in the ass," said Constructionmen Hall.

"I heard that you two were also a bit hard up for cash and you know if the weather doesn't clear again tomorrow it will be the same situation. So here is the deal, I will spot you guys some cash, you can come with me to the Chief's club for some dinner, and you can pay me back when you get your paychecks. *I didn't realize the cash pay back was for men only.*

"That sounds great, I am so hungry. I haven't really eaten anything since the flight yesterday and a bag of chips this morning." I still couldn't believe someone wanted to help us out.

Thanks to Petty Officer Kendall, we ate great food and had a place to sleep for the next three days before we finally arrived on Adak. Unfortunately this arrangement for me would not be allowed to be paid with money like Constructionmen Hall. My payment was expected that night, with sexual favors. All I will say, is when I arrived on the island and his wife was there to greet him, I pulled him aside and said my thanks for all to hear, and then quietly whispered that I promise that if he ever tried to make me feel guilty and decided he wanted me to continue paying, I would kindly call his wife and explain his bad practices.

* * *

Now what is Adak, Alaska and what is it like you ask? Well here is some information that I retrieved from some current websites that may answer some of your questions as to what things were like during my tour from August 2, 1991 to April 6, 1994. The word Adak is from the Aleut word adaq meaning "Father." Adak is located in the Andreanof Islands, 1,300 miles southwest of Anchorage and 350 miles west of Unalaska/Dutch Harbor, in the Aleutian Island chain. If you were to travel from Adak to Anchorage by airline it would be a flight of about three hours. Adak is the southern-most community in Alaska. Aleuts historically occupied Adak as well as the other Aleutian islands. In the early 1800's as the Aleut hunters followed the Russian fur trade eastward and famine set in on the Andreanof Island group. However, they continued to actively hunt and fish around the island over the years, until World War II began. Adak was developed as a Naval Air Station after the war, playing an important role during the cold war as submarine surveillance center.

Adak has always been known for its share of earthquakes. Three of the largest in history rocked the island in 1957, 1964, and 1977. Since World War II, the U.S. Navy developed outstanding facilities and recreations opportunities at Adak. As a military member on Adak, there were many places to go and things to do on the island. My favorite was the movie theater and the night clubs. But the island had so much more. Other facilities included, but were not limited too; roller-skating, swimming pools, ski lodge, bowling alleys, skeet range, auto hobby and builder shop, photo lab, racquetball and tennis courts, and we even had our very own McDonalds and Baskin Robbins.

During its peak as a Naval facility, roughly 6,000 naval personnel and their families lived on the island. It was during the year before my transfer in 1994, while sitting in a base wide meeting, located at the Bering Theater where we were told of the severe cut-backs and that eventually the base would be shut down. Family housing and schools were closed and the Naval Air Station officially closed its operations on the island on March 31, 1997, and now only houses 30 Navy personnel and 200 civilian caretakers.

To describe, what was once called home to many, Adak is a beautiful and rugged terrain. Adak is not only known for marine and wildlife, it's also known as the "Birth Place of the Winds." Adak lies in the maritime climate zone, characterized by persistently overcast skies, high winds and frequent cyclonic storms. Numerous winter squalls produce wind gusts in excess of 100 knots. Tunnels were constructed underground that connected the Bering Galley, the Barracks, and the Bering Hill building, which was where the movie theater, mini mart, and a few food shops were located. The Bering hill was the barracks location for all single military enlisted personnel stationed on the island and temporary battalion units on deployment for six months at a time.

During the summer, extensive fog forms over the Bering Sea and North Pacific. The average temperature ranges from 20 to 60 degrees, but wind chill factors can be severe. Total precipitation is approximately 64 inches annually, with an average accumulated snowfall of 100 inches, primarily in the mountains. Adak only being 28 miles in length has its own special meaning to each and every person who has been there. I find that as I find old friends or someone who has been stationed on the island, all respond in the very same way – They still have dreams they are on the island, they miss it so much, and would go back in a heartbeat.

CHAPTER ELEVEN

ANOTHER NEW HOME

I finally arrived on Adak, August 2, 1991. It was a whole new world that lay before my eyes to explore. The land looked like rolling grassy hills with blackened mountains of razor sharp rock penetrating up through the land along the coastal waters.

I was immediately taken in by its splendor and enjoyed every place the island had to offer. Unfortunately, I would not be able to begin working for public works until after I completed 90 days of a Temporary Assigned Duty or otherwise known as T.A.D. You see it is required that all new active duty personnel that arrive on the island have to do their share of T.A.D. For example; the galley was usually where everyone did their 90 days, but I found a way to get out of that duty by saying I had chronic bronchitis, it worked. I was one of the lucky ones and was assigned a T.A.D. job with the barracks maintenance team, which I enjoyed to the fullest. It was a great way to keep up with my construction skills. I was the one always patching and repairing holes that the battalion guys had punched in the walls during their drunken free for alls. With each repair I also had to paint the walls, so I had to make many trips to public works for paint. It was during these trips when I realized that after my T.A.D. was complete, I wanted to work in the paint and sign shop. I knew what I wanted and knew just how to get it.

One of the guys that worked there said if I wanted the job, I had to go out to dinner with him. *Just dinner, he was a nice guy.* He didn't like the idea of me possibly hooking up with a battalion guy, that I deserved a nice guy like himself. Many of the public works women always seemed to want to date a guy from battalion and that only made the men from public works very resentful. I had no problem going out with him. He was a cutie and looked just like Elvis Presley. Although our relationship never blossomed outside of a great friendship, he kept his promise and by the end of December that same year, I was working as a sign maker in the paint shop. It was my job to do work orders for area departments that needed specialized signs made. The most memorable ones that I made were for Base Security on Bering Hill and the Adak National Forest sign that I made with Petty Officer Henley.

*   *   *

It was during my T.A.D. that Love, so I thought, found its way into my life again. Jay, who was the man I went cliff diving with in California, was stationed there for a six month deployment with NMCB 4. I was awestruck when I bumped into him at just outside the mini mart, after coming back from a maintenance job I was working on. Just like our times in California we had our share of fun and made great memories, but still the nagging feeling of something missing plagued me and the more I tried to understand and talk with Jay about how I was feeling, the further apart we grew. I don't recall the exact date when our relationship ended, but I do know, I was the reason, and it was for the best.

I do however recall a night at the enlisted club called the "Husky", that Jay introduced me to Jim. He said all the right things and had a way of making me feel special. I did not know until later, that it was a pre-planned joke that was being played on me. Guess a few of Jay's friends had the wild idea of getting me to participate in some wild sexual fantasy. *Womanizers!*

Jim was also part of NMCB 4 and unbeknownst to me, he was also a good friend of Jay's. Our relationship really took flight. We enjoyed going to movies and going to the exchange to look over the newest selections of music and stereo equipment that the barge had brought in. Overall, most of our time was spent at the enlisted club. He was always nice to me and we got along great until he let his womanizing side rear its ugly head. He decided that I had a weight problem that was turning him off. During our relationship he had made several comments that my weight was becoming an issue and he felt it was affecting how I was feeling about myself and it showed in my clothing and my personality.

Since when did he become an expert on the mental thinking of a woman?" I thought to myself, as he went on about how I could improve my body, *"baby…you need to take a long look in the mirror yourself,"* I wanted so much to say this to him.

He was a body builder, but had a hard time getting his waist area to look like the rest of his muscles.

I knew the real reason for his negative comments, things were getting serious and he didn't want any part of it. I was losing control over my weight and didn't know what to do. I slowly fell into a deep depression that would not grace me with any signs of recovery. I found myself sitting at the bar on paydays trying to soothe my problems with alcohol and Jim's visits were fewer and far between. I was tired of always going to the club alone and drinking my money away. With my love for music I decided to redirect my attention to the one thing that made me happy, the melody of song. I would sit in my room for hours after work and put my mind through a series of dramatics. My favorite thing to do was to act out what I would like to say to people, that pissed me off, but was afraid to speak my mind. It was during this long span of solitude, that I realized that here I was feeling sorry for myself again, because of some shit a man had said to me. He had control of me, with just one damn comment.

"NO MORE!" I screamed out loud, with determination in my voice. "NO FUCKEN MORE!"

I collected what little money I did have left and gave myself a complete makeover both inside and out, which included losing the weight instead of talking about it. The hardest part about living on an isolated island, we didn't have all the luxuries that are offered on the mainland, but I made do with what little resources I had and began a grand transformation. Hair, makeup, clothes, shoes and my attitude got a complete overhaul. I had been away from the club for about a month, I stayed out of Jim's sight, and worked on things for me, and that was just how I wanted it.

I was looking for the right moment to present my shock and awe. It wasn't until the end of October 1991, that I felt confident enough to be back in the public eye wearing something other than my Seabee green uniform. The look on the faces of both strangers and friends when I walked into the club wearing a black leather mini skirt and a hot pink angora pull over, it was priceless. Jim and I got back together that night and agreed to start over and give our relationship another chance.

We made the best of the remainder of the time he had left on the island. Our nights were spent at the gym working out together or a movie here and there. We attended holiday events that were planned across the base and it seemed that our friendship was trying to turn very serious.

Over time I fell more and more in love with him and knowing he was to return to California in January of 1992 increased my fears of being alone once again. It seemed that the more I let my fear take over me, the more I was slowly losing sight that this was the reality that lay before us and to make the best of the time we had left. It had the same powerful feeling as when I was told George had only a short time to live. Make the best of every moment, as you don't know how many moments you're going to get in life.

Only once did Jim ever tell me that he loved me, which was about seven days before his departure on January 14, 1992. I knew that things would never be the same after he left and that the distance would eventually break us apart. Even though I had made a promise to take some leave from the island after he had been back in California and got settled, that would be a promise that I would never keep. Deep inside me, I knew that when his battalion was done with their deployment, I would hear from him, but it would be the last time that I would ever see him again. *I was right.*

Ill-natured and irate I stood alone looking out my barracks window down upon the makeshift airport as he boarded his flight with the remainder of his battalion. The sad part about it, I never shed a tear and that hurt me more. It wasn't until after he left, that I realized I wasn't in love with him, it was merely infatuation. What I loved was that fact that he helped filled the emptiness of being alone.

* * *

On the same day that Jim had left with his battalion, NMCB 5 arrived. Jim kept in touch with me and made it a point to talk about all the parties and fun he was having on the mainland. To say he missed me sounded like only words, no honesty. Just say it, to make me happy kind of thing. Little did he know, I had gotten good at being alone and ok, single. I got a job with MWR as a Disc Jockey for the clubs and parties on the base. I loved it, getting paid to play music, FANTASTIC! I could go to the club without having a man by my side and it was a great way to get to know new people.

I had finally gotten a roommate and hoped that things would start looking up, but she was frequently moody like a dog without its distemper shots. We got along as best as two women, living in a room the size of two large U-Haul moving trucks, could. I credit my ability to keep what sanity

I had left, to my love for music and working out at the gym. On nights that I wasn't working at the club, I was working out.

While at the gym one night, I had a strange sensation when I saw a new guy that I had never seen before. He looked familiar but I could not place the face and tried shrugging him off, but I couldn't resist watching him, well as much as I could without being noticed. The room was wall to wall mirrors so while I went from one piece of training equipment to another, I could keep my eyes on this familiar stranger. What happened next as I watched him from the other side of the room, deserves the award as the best show off moment of the world. He puffed up his chest like a new cock in a packed hen house, and walked with the attitude as if he were the macho body builder of the decade. *Somehow I knew better.* While laying down on the bench press he had his two buddies that were at least a foot shorter than he was, help put the bar, with at least three hundred pounds of weight, in his hands.

"This should be interesting." I said just loud enough to make a guy beside me take interest in what was going on.

"They have got to be joking…right? He's gonna get hurt."

I chuckled and nodded my head with agreement.

"Put more weight on the bar guys," he said as he curled his upper lip.

"Hey man, I think you better watch yourself, it's heavier than you think." said one of his buddies that appeared very concerned.

"I'm fine, just do it!"

"One, Two, Three…lift!" they all yelled together.

"I can't hold it, help guys!" he exclaimed as his arms slowly lowered the overweight bar onto his chest.

It took two of his little buddies, that couldn't have weighed more than 200 pounds between the two of them while soaking wet, and Mr. Muscle himself to remove the weight bar off his chest by pushing it off to one side. It wasn't until later in the night at the gym that I would look in the mirrors and catch him looking back at me. There was absolutely no doubt he was trying to get my attention. He succeeded, with a performance like that, and as entertaining as it was, I couldn't help but watch and wonder what the next stunt was going to be.

*   *   *

Since Jim had gone back to his homeport in California, things were going as best they could with what was left of our long distance relationship.

He would call me just to catch up, but really was more interested in knowing if I had met or been sleeping with any new guys. He seemed to have somewhat of a hang up, or who knows, a sick fetish about it. It got rather bothersome to have to keep reassuring him that I was being faithful. I often wondered, was he? I took this as a serious development that this relationship was gaining speed to end in an abrupt halt. It wasn't until I received a call and pictures from one of his friends in California, that my gut feeling that he had found someone new and was unfaithful was confirmed. I was done with men! I was tired of all the bullshit drama and just want to focus on work and making money. I went on with my daily activities and got my work done to keep up with my perfect evaluation. But honestly, life likes to throw a punch when you least expect it. All I can say is that if I knew what event was on the horizon for me, one special day in the galley, I would have never had gotten out of bed. I would have faked a sick day.

It was during chow one Friday evening that I grew very angry over what I had seen. Some of the new battalion guys were laughing and enjoying themselves while constantly looking over at me as I sat alone at my table. I assumed that I was the brunt of their jokes and finger pointing, but I kept my head down as much as possible and ate as quickly as I could so that I could get out of there.

When I looked up, one of them caught my attention.

"No it can't be?" I said as I shook my head, "Son of a bitch!"

I realized that the one guy at the table was the roommate of Linda's friend Frank. Yes, it was Mr. Anti-social in person. I looked directly at him with my best glare, then stood up, grabbed my tray and went on my way.

"First crap with Jim and now this guy…what next? I am not going to let the next six months get me down because that asshole is here." I said while clenching my fists as I walked briskly to my room to prepare for my DJ job at the "Husky Club". "No way is he going to cause problems, you wait I'm going to make myself look hot! He is going to realize what he passed up! He passed up a good thing!"

This is really where it all began. - Bering Hill Barracks, Adak, Alaska

Chapter Twelve

The Special Someone

There has always been a special quote that I want to share with you. Its had a deep and significant meaning in my life, since I met my husband of now nineteen years. Singer and songwriter Stevie Nicks, was inspired by it and wrote it to Joe Walsh. The entire quote appears in the insert of "The Best of Stevie Nicks Time Space," cassette.

She writes, "I guess in a very few rare cases…some people find someone, that they fall in love with the very first time they see them…from across the room, from a million miles away. Some people call it love at first sight, and of course, I never believed in that until…that night."

* * *

While working as a DJ at the "Husky Club" on January 28, 1992, I decided to take a break from my booth to wander around the still empty areas of the club. As I walked from the dance floor into the bar area, my eyes were drawn to a man standing with a pool stick in his hands waiting for his turn to sink the eight ball.

He was wearing blue jeans with a pearl snap red and beige cowboy shirt, a red and white Nebraska ball cap and a pair of snake skin cowboy boots. I was simple awestruck.

"I have got to get a closer look at this hunk," so I went into the pool room to pretend to be watching some of the games that were going on.

He was simply to die for, 6'1", eyes as blue as the ocean waters accented with sun kissed golden skin, dark brown hair with an auburn shine, a great build and a smile, oh how that smile gleamed, it truly made my toes curl. I had never seen or met a man as handsome as this. *Well except for the man in the van, but I never got a close look at him.* Before I could realize what was happening to me a tingle began to radiate from deep within me and my mind was racing a mile a minute. I found myself playing the ever popular high school game of 20 questions, with the men around him, while attempting to play a game of pool.

When I was awaiting a turn, I would make conversation with some of the guys in the room that were waiting for their time on the pool table as well. There was no hiding my interest in him, and his friends could see it.

They told me his name was Don, and that he was 100% unavailable and a married man too.

"What a disappointment, figures, the good ones are always taken," I thought to myself. "No…I am not going to listen to them, what if these guys are lying to me. I am going to find out for myself."

Before I comprehended what was happening, my legs took control over me. I found myself walking over to where Don and his friends where leaning against the pool room wall. My intentions were to say hello, how are you, yet the only words that come out of my mouth were,

"Do you know what time it is?"

What time is it? OH MY GOD…I am such a bonehead…come on girl say something intelligent.

"It's after seven," he replied with a smile of interest.

"Many thanks, what's your name?" Knowing perfectly well what it was already,

"Don, what's yours?"

"Fallon…hey…ah…I am working as the DJ here tonight. I have a table with some of my friends up near the booth. If you would like to come and sit with us, you are more than welcome." I remarked, trying to hide the fear of him saying no to me.

To my surprise his answer was not no, yet even better he put his pool stick away and said he wanted to go sit down and talk before it got really busy. As we began to walk over to my table, with a grin and a chuckle he turned to his friends and simply said, "Told Ya!"

"Told Ya?" I asked rather puzzled.

"It's nothing, let's go sit down." He said with a big white smile that immediately changed my thoughts to just him.

During a conversation with Don, while sitting at my table with my friends, they were all taken in by the way we kept our continued eye contact with each other, as we talked. It was the eye contact that helped me seek out the answer about him being married or not.

Letting the outgoing person, of a dual personality, push my inner shy girl to one side, I found the nerve to ask the ever pressing question.

"So Don, tell me, are you married or what? I don't see a ring on that finger and your friends tell me you are. Is that true?" Inside I was praying that his friends were lying to me.

His response was jumbled and filled with several pauses. "Yes...well no...well yeah...kind of, I'm...I'm." Pausing again with what seemed almost as if it had been too private of a question to be asking. "I'm engaged to a girl back home. Her name is Jessie."

"Are you happy with that?"

"Yes, I am."

"Well there ya go, doesn't mean we can't be friends." I was content with it, disappointed, but he was honest and I was not going to be a one night stand. But that didn't keep him from wanting to sit and talk with me, so I was not bothered by his response. It was just friendly conversation that's all.

He loved music as much as I did and that made our conversations even more interesting. It was as if we were long lost friends and had years to catch up on.

"Too bad I have to work, what if he leaves," I wondered.

My fears quickly changed throughout the evening, he would spread his time between playing pool with his buddies for free beers and talking with me. He would bring me sodas and fries from the food counter and point to the guys, while with me in the sound booth as if to say, I got something you don't. I didn't mind him coming in the booth with me, it was great to be talking to someone and doing what I loved...playing music. We laughed and shared stories of things we had done while being Seabees in the Navy.

He was an equipment operator and a third class petty officer. He joined the service in 1988, just a few short months after graduating high school. He told me he would have gone in sooner, but his family owned a 3,500 acre dry land wheat farm, and they needed his help for harvest. He had always been in battalion 5, which had its homeport in Port Hueneme, California, but he didn't live on the base. He had seen places like Puerto Rico and was part of the disaster relief team in North Carolina after Hurricane Hugo. He had been in Saudi Arabia during Desert Shield and Desert Storm then came back to California for a six-month homeport before arriving here on Adak. As he spoke, I wished and hoped our time together would never end. He spoke of his home as a child and that he'd someday want to return to the wide-open plains of Nebraska. That his true love was farming.

The evening quickly passed and I knew that I was not ready to let him leave. But I didn't know him well or if he enjoyed my company, maybe he was just being polite. Either way, just knowing he was spoken for was a hard reality for me.

How would I find him again if I wanted to hang out with him and his friends again?

When the evening ended and the club closed, Don and his buddy Mark walked with me and a friend of mine, Christine, back through the halls that led back to all the barracks.

"Well Don, I want to thank you for making my night a great one. You're a sweet guy. Maybe I will see you around again sometime?" praying he would say that would be great.

What was funny is that I had a feeling that Mark and Christine had also had a great evening together. They danced every dance they could, including the slow ones. There was definitely love in the air between the two of them.

"Goodnight guys," Christine and I chimed together.

"We'll see you around, you can count on that!" Mark said, accompanied with a wink of an eye towards Christine.

We parted in the hallway and headed down to the tunnel to the location of where I lived in the Longview-A Barracks. As Christine and I shared the stories of our night, we heard the sound of someone running down the tunnel at a very high rate of speed. It was Mark. He was running towards us with a smile of relief that he caught up to us. He and Don wanted to know if they could come to my lounge and talk.

"Sure, that sounds great!" I said trying to hold back my excitement. "Great! I get to see Don again."

My heart pumped harder and harder and then I felt it jump into my throat when he came from around the corner walking towards us.

"Hey, let Mark and I carry those music cases for you, Fallon." Don said with a smile as he looked into my eyes. Of course I didn't refuse. Mark and Christine also seemed very excited and together we all went back to my barracks lounge and talked into the early hours of the morning.

By four o'clock Mark and my friend Christine said their good-byes and went back to their rooms. As for Don and I, the night was in no way over. How we laughed and enjoyed the company of each other. I wanted so much to touch him in some way. To feel his warmth that he generated as he spoke of his life as a child to when he joined the Navy. What really had me very intrigued, were his comments on what it would be like if we still knew each other when we got back to the States.

Although our eyes grew tired and heavy, we could not say goodbye. We promised that we would get together later in the day since it was now Saturday. We planned to go to the club again since I didn't have to work that night and we could play pool. Then he did something that I never expected. He stood up and walked over to me, extending his hand to mine, he pulled me into him and embraced me with his loving arms. He never said good-bye, he just simply said, "I promise," in the most loving and tender voice. Then he went on his way back to the battalion barracks quarters.

I went into my room, closed the door and without getting undressed, I just lay there on my bed in a peaceful stare at my ceiling. It was Don, without a doubt, I felt he was the man in my dreams.

"What kind of help could this stranger possibly need from me, if he is the one?" I wondered.

Over the weekend the evenings ended the very same way as our first encounter ended, long talks into the morning after returning home from the club. We both hated the thought that we would have to return back to work on Monday after spending most of our time together over the weekend. Eight hours without seeing one another was going to be hard, as we felt inseparable. As sad as it was for me, Don helped me realize that my fantasy to be with the man in the reddish van was just that, a fantasy. Though I never did tell him about how I felt and left the wonder of the mysterious man my little secret. It was time to move on with my life and I was so happy to be sharing it with my new found friend Don.

CHAPTER THIRTEEN

LOVE OF A LIFETIME

Now being a Seabee was something more important to me than anything. *So I thought.* It was a job that I could have done for years, but with Don now in my life, all I could think about was how wonderful it would be, if we could be a real couple. I had a permanent smile that would not leave my face and focusing on the work task at hand was mind boggling. What I thought was going to last only days, or a week or two, like many guy friendships before him, became weeks that quickly turned into months. What was even worse was not telling anyone how I was feeling. Knowing he was to marry another, that didn't stop my heart inside from falling deeply in love with him.

During the day my personal life was the number one topic of conversation at public works. How upset many were to learn that I was spending time with another battalion man, but they didn't know who he was and I was not about to tell them. I honestly believe that some spoke out of envy or jealousy. Either way I wasn't affected in the slightest. I realized things were changing for Don and I when he first started calling my shop at the same time every day just to say hi. He even began making up strange excuses, false names and convinced some of his buddies to call my shop, and hand the phone over to him after I got on the line, so that my supervisors would let me talk. The most creative idea was when he started showing up at the paint shop where I worked in various construction equipment and vehicles.

The secretaries upstairs above my department used to bet on what he would drive over to public works each day. To add to their bets, they wondered, *who was this good looking guy coming to see?* He was coming to see me and little did he know he had me hook, line, and sinker. But still I never let anything show that I loved him.

We would also meet at the galley on a daily basis to eat lunch together with the rest of the guys that were working with him on the rock crushing crew. I was heart-broken when he told me that his hours were going to be extended to work the night shift from six to twelve, and that he would not be able to go to the club as much.

There was no way that his new schedule was going to steal our together time. Suddenly I was stricken with a bad case of "open mouth insert foot" disease. Not knowing a damn thing about running equipment, I blurted out, "I'll help you guys, if you want me to!" Yes, a very desperate attempt to be with him as much as I could.

They all just looked at me with their mouths wide open as if I had just suggested naked scuba diving in the icy waters of the Bering. Don and a guy whose name was Richard, were the only two working this shift, quickly said that it sounded great and to be in front of the galley at 5:45pm. I know they didn't think I would really show up, especially knowing I was going to be working.

"You got it!" I said, speculating on what I had just committed myself to.

Sure enough, at 5:45pm on the dot, Don pulled in front of the galley driving a duce and a half truck.

"Wow, I didn't think you'd show up?" Richard remarked with surprise.

"You're not wearing your inspection boots for this job, are you?" Don said in a worried tone of voice while I pulled myself up into the truck.

"This is the only pair that I have. I can polish them when I get back to my room."

"You have never been up to the rock crusher area I take it?" said Richard.

"No Why?"

Laughing with a smirk on his face he responded, "You'll see."

Because of the wonderful weather that was 90% of the time, rain, the mud in some areas would be deep and I found this out the hard way. Not only did I sink up to my knees at one point in this wet muddy mess, the job I was given required me to shovel it. Don had given me the job of running a shovel to keep a bearing clear from any debris as they ran the equipment gathering large boulders to be placed into the crusher to make various sizes of aggregate. I didn't realize that they were testing me to see if I was a worker or that I used my tools as a place to lean on and rest. I was indeed a worker, trying to show off in front of these men to prove that I would do my share, whatever the job may be, even if it meant shoveling mud for six hours.

After six hours of going to work with them following a full day with my own command, I would still show up at the galley to be picked up at 5:45pm and head to the quarry with them. I never once complained. After the fifth day I finally moved up in my job details. Don decided to give me instructions on learning how to operate the John Deer 844 front-end loader that he was operating to select rocks for the crusher.

Now ladies, this was like no other driving class. (Not only was I sitting inside the biggest piece of machinery that had the best vibration that a woman in her right mind would not pass up). Add the fact that Don, the sexy cowboy equipment operator, was standing against me with his hands on mine to teach me how to use the levers. Just feeling the warmth of his strong body against mine was an absolute turn on. *I know he did this intentionally, but I wasn't complaining.* As cold as the weather was outside…I was getting hot.

I have always been a quick learner, but this time I was taking full advantage of my acting skills and played the dumb card as long as I could. Unfortunately, he caught on quick and said you're on your own. Show me what you can do. Without hesitation I was off to enjoy digging into the dirt and rocks with the guidance of Don by my side.

As I went from one rock to another, Don began making comments that he was unsure about getting married. *Was he serious or looking for a way to up our friendship to friends with benefits? I continued to listen.* We started having a long talk about what was he going to do about his fiancée back home. It was then that I also told him of my relationship with Jim that was in battalion 4. *Yes, I should have just kept my mouth shut.*

Don became rather silent after my comment as if I had lied to him. I didn't lie. I just didn't know where my relationship stood with Jim. I was afraid to talk about it as I knew how bad the riffs get between each battalion. It was no secret that for years, battalion 4 and 5 were two units that could never get along, and I knew this after dating Jay and Jim. I wanted my relationship with Jim to work, but at the same time, I was falling for Don. The sad reality of it was that Don had another woman and

I had another man. I did feel a sense of guilt for falling in love with Don, but I felt worse when I thought of a day when Don would be gone. My heart would ache every time I thought about him leaving the island, and leaving me. There was no way that I would be able to let Don out of my life, but I knew his wife to be would have no part of that. No woman wants their man's best friend to be another woman. It's just trouble waiting.

He seemed rather upset that I was seeing another man, but did not wish to talk about it when he learned Jim's last name. He then continued with how he did not like the way his fiancée seemed to nit-pick the things he did. He had met her when his mother was in the hospital, she was her radiologist. Not getting into the full details of how he met her, he went on to say how he felt obligated to marry her because his parents got them together and they really liked her. I was bothered by that comment and it actually pissed me off.

When we finished with our work, he drove me straight back to my room without any conversation. Thoughts rushed through my mind as we neared my barracks.

He's a grown man that was sharing his inner most thoughts and dreams with me, but he was going to marry someone else because he feels obligated, and that his parents got them together. What the hell is that? He is 21 and his parents are still running his life? Foolish!

What made this situation worse is that I actually said to Don, how I felt about it. I was angry and jealous that I didn't find him first. I could not look him in the eyes as I didn't want him to see that I loved him. He still gave me a hug and what was worse, this time he said good-bye. My heart shattered at that very moment into a million shards of irreplaceable glass. I feared that he would see my anger and jealously and mistake it for hate and disappointment. I worried that he would never understand my emotions were to hide how much I truly loved him and how much I was hurting inside. But I didn't want to be the one that split him and his fiancée up. It would have to be his choice to decide what he wanted to do with his life. He left that night feeling a cold and distant part of me. As I watched him slowly walk back to his barracks from the doorway to my barracks, the tears began to stream down my face, and with all the fight in this world I could not stop them.

"I love you so much Don. So much and you will never know." I said under my breath and went up to my room.

* * *

Over the radio the next day while I was at work there was a song that was dedicated to me from him. The song was "I Can't Make You Love Me" by Bonnie Raitt.

BUT I DO LOVE YOU! I love you more than my existence on this very earth that I walk. Did he really not see how I felt? He consumed my every thought, every step, and every breath. I have to tell him, but how? We come from two different worlds, yet we are the same.

He knew that part of me that could not express what I was feeling with words when it came to love. For me, the best way to person's heart, was through song. My life had always been tamed or fueled by the passions of music and lyrics. There was always a song that could say what I was feeling and this moment was not any different. My dedication said all the words that I wanted him to hear, but feared saying to him. I decided to send him a song by Vanessa Williams called "Save the Best for Last." When my dedication had finished playing, he immediately called me.

"I am so sorry Don for the way I acted yesterday...I was just hurt."

"I understand now, really I do."

"Friends? I asked, hoping his answer would be yes.

"More" was his reply.

Our dedications of these two songs went on for days. We were becoming not only the talk of Public Works with the way the radio DJ's were talking. We were now quite the talk of our isolated island. People wanted to know who these two people were and why they were denying their love for one another.

As the music played each day at the same time, our friendship grew. We spent many moments together helping each other through the trials and tribulations of living on an isolated little island that didn't offer much in the way of entertainment. I enjoyed hanging out with him and his friends playing pool at the club or just kicking back watching programs on the television. Oh and I can't forget our 'Sunday Oink feasts." We would buy all kinds of junk food Saturday night and never leave my room all day Sunday. We would just lie on the bed all day and do nothing except making sure the television remote and the food was always within arms-length. *Still, neither of us made the move to sleep together.*

He also assisted me with studying for my astronomy class that I was taking through the University of Alaska Adak. He would pick me up after class in a shop truck so that I would not have to walk up the hill in bad weather. He was a sweetheart. If you saw one of us, bet your bottom dollar that the other was only two steps away and we loved every bit of it. Our relationship was new, exciting and sex free.

One evening life changed for both of us when Don arrived at my door sad and all alone one Friday night late in the month of February. It was obvious that he had been drinking, but no so much that he was not aware of what he was saying or doing. Worried and concerned, I asked him in.

"What's the matter?"

"It's my birthday," he said, beginning to cry.

In my entire life I had never seen a grown man cry. I was unsure as to what to do. I sat down beside him on the edge of my bed and comforted him.

"Don, did you get the memo? Birthdays are supposed to be a happy time," I said with a smile. "So tell my, why no smile?"

"Not mine, they never have been,"

"Do you want to tell me why?" Worried that he may think I was interfering.

"I want to find my birthmother; I was adopted as a baby and always felt like something was missing."

"Wow…and your family doesn't know who your birthmother is?"

"No." He said trying to collect the pieces of his broken heart.

"Look, if that is something you really want to do, I can find her, trust me I have connections."

"Yes, I have to find her before it is too late."

"Don, are you sure this is what you want"

"More than anything."

It was at that moment as I held him in my arms, my heart began to change. What feelings I still might have had for Jim, I no longer questioned. I could feel Don was in need of real unconditional love and my heart wanted to give so much to him. As much as I wanted to believe we were just friends, this too had changed and I wanted to tell him I loved him. I was afraid to say the words and so I made him a promise. No matter how much of my life it took, I would find his birthmother. He just needed to always stay in contact with me, so when I find her I could give him the information he needed. I felt sad, happy and scared of the obstacles that lay before us, but I would find her. I knew how and that I would.

He looked up at me with his tender eyes and leaned towards me.

"Can I kiss you?" was all that he said.

"But…I don't know…I…" without finishing my thoughts, I kissed him.

How tenderly his lips touched mine. His hands began to caress my back and shoulders. Afraid of wanting to feel this way I paused before putting my arms around him to pull him closer to me. I was becoming lost in the moment. Our kisses became more erotic as we became open to explore each other. We wanted this to happen. We wanted each other.

We had kissed before in fun, but never so intense that we found it hard to stop before anything got physical. Our breathing quickened as I felt hot and weak in the knees when he put his hand underneath my blouse and then pulled me tightly into him. This time, things were different and we let our guard down to live in this passion filled sexual moment.

This was the first time that I actually felt the difference between sex and making love. It was a true stress reliever as I began to cry as we both reached the peak of ecstasy. This was something I had never felt before with any man. It was perfect, passionate, tender, loving, mesmerizing, it was all so right. I was filled with so much emotion, I wanted this to happen, but at the same time I worried that it would hurt him, that it would hurt us, and the facts were still the same, he still was to marry another. How would he tell her what happened or would he ever tell her, were the words that kept coming into my thoughts along with my wanting him in my arms forever. I was so overwhelmed with a multitude of feelings that he didn't understand my reasons for crying and I could not find the words, or my voice to explain.

He felt bad as if he had done something wrong and decided he should leave. I broke down completely when I heard the door close behind him. My love of a lifetime was walking out the door and I didn't know how to tell him how much I needed him in my life, but I knew that I would find the right song, little did I realize it was playing on my radio when our special moment took place. It just summed us up so perfectly.

"Loving Arms"
Written by: Tom Jans
Sung by: Dobie Gray

If you could see me now
The one who said that he'd rather roam
The one who said he'd rather be alone
If you could only see me now

If I could hold you now
Just for moment, if I could really make you mine
Just for a while, turn back the hands of time
If I could only hold you now
I've been too long in the wind
Too long in the rain
Taking any comfort that I can
Looking back and longing for
The freedom of my chains
Lying in your loving arms again
If you could hear me now
Singing somewhere through the lonely night
Dreaming of the arms that held me tight
If you could only hear me now
I've been too long in the wind
Too long in the rain
Taking any comfort that I can
Looking back and longing for the freedom of my chains
Lying your loving arms again
I can almost feel your loving arms again

The intense pain of knowing that he was promised to someone was as if someone had ripped my heart from my chest and left it on a table for anyone to destroy. This was not just another one of my crazy infatuations. I could feel the power that this was truly God's sign. An answer to the mystical evening dream and thoughts that followed one November morning back in 1989 when I suddenly, without any warning, decided to leave a five year relationship because of a dream that someone needed me. My whole life turned upside down to find a faceless mystery military man in a dream.

It is you that I have been searching for all these years. It is you. I feel it. He won't understand why I know he is the one. Please God, bring us together forever. I can't live without him. I know he is promised to someone else, but I can't live without him knowing that our souls have now become one for eternity. I love you Don. Always and forever.

Don, it was Don, the faceless mystery man that needed my help...I couldn't let him slip away. He is the reason why I have come this far, the reason for my journey for an answer, he needs my help to find his mother.

We are the missing connections that our souls needed to be complete. I could not sleep that night. I just wanted to find him and bring him back to me. I don't know what it was, but a miracle brought us back together later that night, my prayers had been answered.

From that instant on a union of two hearts began to beat as one and we did everything we could to see each other every day. He spent many nights in my room and the feeling of waking, with his arms wrapped around me – Heaven. We no longer hid our feelings in public. Our friends were in total awe each time they would talk with us about how Don and I felt, and only knowing each other for such a short amount of time. All I could say was he was my right hand, without him, I couldn't function.

Still some were disappointed that I had chosen to spend my time with a battalion man. They knew that the Battalion deployments were only on the island for six months, then what? Would it be a long distance relationship? I already had one of those and that didn't work. My choice remained steadfast; Don was the man for me, yet I still questioned, was I the woman that he wanted to spend the rest of his life with?

*   *   *

My command had asked me if I would design the backdrop for the pictures to be taken at the 50th Anniversary Seabee ball. I was honored and I also received many special treatments and fringe benefits for accepting the task. I painted a beautiful sign with the Seabee logo and had it framed in oak. It was a work of art and unbeknown to me was also very valuable. Everyone would stop in the paint shop to see my masterpiece, but they would also ask the burning question, who was I going to the ball with?

"You'll have to wait and see." Was all the information I would offer them.

Now I must tell you, Seabees are like family and they really know how to party and protect one another, but within this large family are smaller ones. They are categorized as Battalions, Constructions Battalion Units, Public Works, Dive teams, and Reservists. I know I must have missed others, but I was only part of a PW and a CBU during my career. Each group lives by an unwritten rule that we stick with our own group where we work unless it is a drink fest. This is why it was so important to my command at public works to know if I would be attending with a guy from our division or my battalion man. I knew that my upper chain had a problem with my current decisions, and I felt they were doing all they could to sabotage my future plans, but for me, it was none of their business and they would find out soon enough.

What a shocker it was when Don and I attended the Seabee Ball together. I had gotten to know his supervisors and battalion friends rather well, so Don and I sat with them all to enjoy dinner and the musical entertainment of the evening. The biggest drama filled fiasco during the ball was that my sign had been stolen several times during the evening after the pictures had all been taken. I knew that my command wanted it to display it on the quarterdeck of Public Works. I was convinced that it was stolen by someone in Public Works that wanted it all to himself.

"Someone stole my sign, I can't believe it, someone stole my sign!" I was outraged as the ball ended.

"It's ok Fallon, someone will find it." Don said in a very calm voice.

"Don, something as big as that can't just walk out of a crown of people and not be noticed," said Tony, one of the guys that I didn't know.

"You sure about that?" said Mark with a bit of a snicker.

Tony glared at Mark and mouthed the words "Shut your ass."

I believed that one of them knew something, but they all claimed that they had too much to drink and didn't know what they were talking about. Don and Tony just looked at each other and chuckled.

It wasn't until two weeks later following the Seabee ball, Don had called my office to tell me that he had made the sign reappear. He asked me to come over to the battalion work spaces so that he could explain what happened. Come to find out, it was an already planned situation by his supervisors and many other guys from Don's unit. They were going to make sure this work of art stayed with its rightful owner, me. I was speechless, and humbled to know that they went to such great lengths and took some serious risks for me. *Do I have the sign to this day…come to a future Seabee get together and we'll discuss it.*

By the end of an eventful night out, we found ourselves embraced by a soulful connection when he took me back to my room. I think it was this moment that he had been waiting for since our first encounter. He took hold of me and held me close to his heart. I looked up into his eyes and he cupped my face in the palms of his hands and gently kissed me. I knew that he could reach right down into my soul, as I stood face to face with him. He held me in his arms and while looking in my eyes he spoke ever so gently, the words I longed to hear.

"I love you. I want to be with you forever."

Blushing as I spoke with tears in my eyes, I replied, "Forever is a long time."

He simply said, holding me tightly, "No, it's not long enough."

As the moment gave way to a pause of silence, I found the strength within me and with every ounce of my heart and soul, without hesitation, I told him what I had longed to say since I met him.

"I love you too." Then I smiled and wrapped my arms around him. He made me feel safe and I never wanted to let go.

"I knew you did," he said with relief as if it had been something he'd been waiting to hear for a very long time.

It was now no secret to anyone on the island that Don and I were getting closer and closer with each day that passed. Our favorite thing to do since that night was to spend as much time together as we could. We also loved to go to the club and slow dance to a song that he would always request. "Love of a Lifetime" by Firehouse. We had finally found the love of a lifetime. What I was not prepared for, was an unsolved mystery that would find us later in our relationship. *We knew each other more than we thought.*

CHAPTER FOURTEEN

DID SOMEONE MENTION MARRIAGE?

Interesting as our little island home may sound, there is a lot that you need to know about adapting to its lifestyle, especially if you are active duty. Like with any small town, it was not uncommon for everyone to know your business. It created a negative saying throughout all the departments on the island. *If I fart my neighbors knew about it two days before I decided to do it.* This is how our base life was. No privacy. It was the same with people arriving and leaving the base as well. There could never be any surprises, inspections by upper echelon from the lower 48, or guests, because everything had to be cleared twenty four hours before any arrivals and you couldn't leave the base without the approval of the command you were attached to.

This friends, was the reason for the increased tension that began to build during my tour. Many things that were happening on Adak went undiscovered by the outside world. The local commands took it upon themselves to play, as one would say, God. It was because of this God complex that my life with Don, found its way onto one hell of a roller coaster ride. There are still those to this very day that insist that they did nothing wrong. My response to that, they simply did NOTHING!

* * *

Our plans were to get married while we were stationed on Adak. Most of our friends were extremely excited and very supportive to hear of our plans. Word traveled like the speed of light throughout Public Works about our plans to be wed. *Gossip was a bad disease that eighty percent of the population suffered from.* Unlike our friends that were happy for us, others made it rather clear how they disliked the news and what they had to say was not good. Though these comments are all hear-say, the extent of it was that if they could have any say in the matter, this wedding would not take place. And they meant it. We followed all the proper procedures so that we could be married on the island for all to see. The date that we had chosen was May 26, 1992.

We never thought we would run into any obstacles, yet many were ahead of us and one by one they appeared, both with my command and telling his family back home. Don, had not told his family or fiancée of his choice to call off the wedding at home and my command would not approve our marriage without going through counseling. We decided, before calling his parents and getting everyone upset, to attend the counseling that was given by the local chapel. We wanted to make sure we were making the right decision. On March 30, 1992, I made the call to schedule an appointment.

"Good Morning, Bering Hill Chapel," said a friendly voice on the other end of the receiver.

"Yes, good morning ma'am. My name is Constructionmen Lake; I am calling to schedule an appointment to attend the marriage counseling class."

Pausing as if she knew the name, she replied, "Class? Are you already married?" she asked rather inquisitively.

"No, we want to. My command said that they would not approve my request to get married on the base until we attended the counseling classes."

I could hear the sound of a pencil tapping and papers rustling around.

"Ma'am, are you still there?" I asked somewhat impatient.

"Yes, you work at Public Works right?"

"Yes, how did you know that?"

"Your command called last week to see if you were planning on getting married here at the chapel."

I was rather puzzled when I heard what she had said. *My command called her already? Why would they do something like that? I just filled out the proper paperwork this week. I followed my chain of command, why, why would the call the chapel?*

"I need to get some information from you so that we can put you on the schedule…First thing, the name of the man you want to marry, his command, age, religion, and the date that you have planned."

"Oh…yes, I'm sorry I got sidetracked for a moment, please excuse me. You need information…sure I can give you that." I said trying to get my thoughts back on track.

I gave her all the necessary information that she had asked for, but when I gave her the date that we were planning for our wedding, the tone in her voice became very negative.

"That date is less than two months away. I can't get you into a class until the end of April."

"You don't have anything sooner? I am going on leave on April 18, and I won't be back until May 9. I am going on leave for harp duty with the local recruiting office back home. Are you sure we can't do this any sooner?"

"Well…" with extreme hesitation in her voice as if someone was prompting her on what to say, "we can have you take the pre-test to determine if you are a compatible match for one another, who knows it might be in your best interest if the test uncovers some problems."

I could not believe my ears. "A What? A Test? Like when I joined the Navy kind of test?" I was flabbergasted but did not take the discouragement; she was trying to get in my mind, seriously. I agreed to take the test, anything to get our classes earlier than when she had told us we could begin.

Now, I don't know what person in his or her right frame of mind wrote this horrendous test, but it was definitely someone who had never been in love. Don and I found it to be very intrusive into our lives. This had nothing to do with love and how we felt for one another. It felt more like an application. We were put in separate rooms to answer fifty questions that ranged on various topics of infidelity within our families to how much money we make. I was so pissed off I could have spit nails.

This was none of their business as to what my family life was like. So my dad was unfaithful, does that mean that I would be the same way? HELL NO! I actually learned something from my dad's infidelity all those years as a child. I knew the signs and what to look for. That didn't mean that I would be just as heartless! I also knew that Don would never be like my father. This test was just another one of those with a God complex, and for Christ sakes of all places, right in our own church!

I completed twelve of the fifty some odd questions, then just started marking any answer just to get out of there. When we both finished we waited for the Chaplain to come in and collect our papers. Once collected he simply instructed us to come back the next day at the same time for our score. That was it.

"OUR SCORE!?" Now I have heard everything. My command had indeed been a part of this little diversion to get us to change our minds. "IT'S NOT GOING TO WORK!"

I wish you could have seen the Chaplain's face when we arrived the next day. PRICELESS! He was indeed speechless.

The longest sentence that he spoke consisted of only seven words. "Your total score was only a 59%."

I am certain that my random selection of answers after question twelve had something to do with the total score, but I never said a word to the Chaplain as to what I had done.

Everything else he said was, gee, oh, and this, and you and so on. You get the gist I'm sure. He didn't really know what to say to us, only that he was convinced that we were not the perfect couple. We insisted that we were. His recommendations were to attend the marriage classes as soon as possible. He called over to his secretary and had us scheduled for the following Monday.

I couldn't help but chuckle when Don and I left the chapel and went back to the barracks for lunch.

"Don, I have to tell you something, please don't be mad at me," worried that he would take my actions the wrong way. "I only answered the first twelve questions. I got so mad at what they were asking on the stupid test, that I just checked off anything without reading any of the remaining questions. I am so sorry, do you forgive me?"

He looked at me with such a strange expression. "You did what?"

Feeling very ashamed I dropped my head and went on with an answer. "I purposely fudged the test."

"I love you sweetness." He said as he began to laugh uncontrollably.

"What? Any why are you laughing?" taking his remark the wrong way. "Don't you want to marry me?"

He tried to calm himself down so that he could talk. He gave me a big hug and said he had done the same thing and was totally impressed that we managed to still score a 59%.

"You did too?" I smiled sheepishly.

"Yeah, can you imagine how some of those questions would have made us look? I am sure that some of our answers would have been very inappropriate in the eyes of any church."

"Oh my God." was all I could say and then I too began to laugh with him, "too funny!"

We found our own special way to deal with the endless bullshit and madness of our newest night class, marriage counseling. We sat through many needless hours pretending to listen to the best way to balance a checkbook, keeping the line of communication open, and the emotional effects of an unfaithful spouse.

During our classes we played made up personal games to keep Don and I awake. He was very good at "I made you laugh first," "What's that behind you," and though not appreciated by the women of the class, this next one was truly a man's game. "I have gas, can you guess what I ate." When we could sit together we played tic-tac-toe all over the hand out sheets and Don loved the ever popular and definitely his favorite game, "Squeeze my finger until I cry," but because of this game we were usually separated. We were actually enjoyed by the other couples fearing to let their guard down and have fun with their significant other. Every time we looked up, someone in the class was trying to hold back their laughter as they watched us. We were the class clowns.

After attending three evening classes, we were asked by the instructor, before going home, why were we there? This class was for couples that didn't get along, yet for some reason feel the need to get or stay married. In her mind that was not a problem that Don and I had. We just simply explained what we did when we took the test that was required for this class. She smiled to learn that our score was because we fudged the test intentionally, that it had nothing to do with how we truly felt for one another. She told us that she would sign our papers that we attended all the classes. We would not have to return and finish the remaining classes we were scheduled for. We didn't need it. She congratulated us on a long and happy life together and sent us on our way.

How shocked my command was when they had learned that we had finished all the marriage classes that were required. *This was not what they were hoping to hear. They were adamant that this marriage would not take place now or in the future.*

Their response to this information was that they would put the request chit through, but it would not be fully approved until I got back from my leave. They had made up some excuse that one of the officers, that had to sign this, was off the base and wouldn't be back until I was back from my leave.

I never gave it a second thought. I assumed (Never Assume) they would do this for me. *Ok Yes, I was still a few sandwiches short in my picnic basket.*

Don's command with NMCB 5 was a command that one would dream of being a part of. They were always so supportive of Don's choices. They quickly approved his request to get married and never gave it a second thought. Their only stipulation…they wanted to be the ones to give him a bachelor party. *As I have said before about Seabees, if there is a reason, there is a party.*

We had overcome one of the obstacles with the command, completing the required classes, but little did we know we had a bigger problem to face. He had to call his family and fiancée back home to break the news to them about our plans. I had suggested to Don that he and Jessie needed to talk alone and that I would not be there while he made the phone call, but more importantly I was going to give him some time to truly think about what we were about to do and was this what he really wanted.

After several long phone calls home to his fiancée trying to explain to her that he was having second thoughts about getting married, Don finally made the decision that he and I were destined to be together and he called off the wedding. Don had always been the all-around guy, never made people mad and never wanted people mad at him, yet the information of his choice was not well received by those back home.

He came to my room to tell me of the conversation with his fiancée. It was during his last call he made to her, when he told her that it wasn't that he didn't want to get married, it was that he had met someone else. He told me of comments that she had made about expenses that she had encountered preparing for their wedding in September, which upset him to know that she went forward with ordering the invitations after being told that he needed time to decide what his true feelings were about marriage. He felt obligated to pay it, yet at the same time he didn't feel he was responsible for the bill after she started yelling at him about her rights and what her uncle had told her. Don just felt that she was trying to make him feel guilty. The only thing he was probably guilty of was that he loved her, but failed to tell her that he was not in love with her.

Not taking into consideration the devastation she must have felt when hit with the words "another woman" I did something that to this day I wish I could take back. I had absolutely no understanding, at the time, of just how much of a devastating impact this must have had on her spirit. She was already dealing with the facts that what was once a happy event being planned was now being tossed aside because Don and I fell in love with each other. No matter how I wanted to believe that I was in the right, the facts still stood the same, in her eyes and the eyes of his family, I would always be the other woman. I never meant for anyone to get hurt. The sad reality of it all was someone did and I should have understood this as my mother was in an awkward situation, when an intimate lady friend and my father made their relationship public. I may never be forgiven, but with all my heart, I am so very sorry. I am so much like so many other people in this world that do strange things for love and to be loved.

Now to add to the sadness of the situation between Don and Jessie, his parents also didn't take the news to kindly and assumed (never assume) that his reasons were because he had gotten me pregnant. *I just happen to be in the room during this call and it wasn't pleasant.* Their response insulted Don which resulted in him hanging up the phone on them. This I admit was not the smartest idea at the time, but goes hand in hand with the stress he was already under. He called them right back, and several times as well over the course of a few days. Eventually, but not with their full blessing on what he was about to do, simply said that it was his decision and his choice to marry me.

After only knowing each other for three months we made another life changing decision and took fate into our own hands. My mother bought Don a plane ticket, as a wedding gift, to travel to New Hampshire while I was there. We contacted our families to let them know that our plans were to marry in Hillsborough, instead of on Adak, and we wished for them to join us. I am happy to say, his mother, father and sister also flew out to be a part of our glorious day.

On May 6, 1992, during a small evening ceremony at the United Methodist Church on Main Street in Hillsborough, New Hampshire, Don and I exchanged our vows before our immediate family members and a few friends. It was a dream come true and we were truly happy. To get to this point in our lives, our love for each other had to endure many types of strengths working against us, little did everyone know, it was only making our relationship stronger.

CHAPTER FIFTEEN

A <u>GOOD</u> DOC, IS HARD TO FIND

It is because of the laws of our great nation, that as much as I would love to reveal this doctor's true identity during the events of which I am writing about and how they unfolded, the law states it could be looked at as a form of slander and that I must change the names. My philosophy is that it is malpractice and a uniform is protecting him. But this will not stop me from sharing with you the details even though his name is completely fictitious. That maybe someday you will find yourself in the same situation and keeping in mind, that the only person who will take care of your health matter is you! Only you know your own body. Don't be fooled by passive sentences to steer you in another direction as it could result in a matter of life or death!

*　*　*

During my assignment in Adak, Alaska my health was in reasonably great shape with a minor flu bug, a successful appendectomy, and an occasional yeast infection, that could be treated with over the counter products. It wasn't until sometime during the end of May in 1992 that my problems began. During one Friday evening I began to feel sensitivity in a lower molar. With it being of minimal pain, I took some extra strength Tylenol and passed it off as sinus pressure. By the wee hours of Saturday morning I was woken with a piercing pain radiating across my jaw and gums.

"I must have a bad cavity," I thought as I leaned over to turn a light on.

I then took another couple of extra strength Tylenol and tried my best to wish the intensity of the pain away. Unfortunately my wish never came true. I was unable to eat or drink anything hot or cold and I knew that as much as I feared the dentist, this did not come with any choices. Being so isolated our dental department on the island was extremely small staffed and they didn't take kindly to be called in over a weekend. Knowing that I could not get through another day I ended up with an emergency dental appointment that afternoon. With the extensive amount of pain that I was in, and the size of the infection, the dentist would only prescribe an antibiotic of Vibramycin (doxycycline hyclate) and Motrin, until the pain was more tolerable. Then they would do a root canal. When I looked at the name of the prescription that he wrote I told him that I was allergic to penicillin and several drugs with the penicillin family. He looked at me rather disgusted as if to say, I came in on a Saturday for you and your telling me you can't take this, but instead he simply said,

"I don't see it noted in your records. Take it!"

It was clearly indicated on my medical records, but for some reason was not noted on my dental records. I was given back the slip and told in a direct tone of voice, "Fill the prescription, NOW!"

Still very uneasy about following his orders, I walked over to the medical department that was just across the hall, to talk with the doctor who was on duty for that day. I only wanted advice on how I should handle this situation.

"Excuse me, who is on duty?" I asked Corpsman Avery

"Let me see," he responded as he carefully began to check a small hand written employee schedule he had attached to his clipboard.

"Commander Palmer."

"Oh no, not him again," I said rather disappointed.

You see Commander Palmer and I had not gotten along very well since a series of examinations that he gave me earlier in the year. I had been dealing with some rather uncomfortable hip pain that usually resulted during physical training, but was not in conjunction with my appendectomy that I had during Christmas of 1991. He looked at this as my way of getting out of doing the morning runs that we did on Monday, Wednesday, and Friday mornings. Now I understand his reasoning in the matter, as we did have several ladies within our command that took advantage of having a written note from a doctor stating that they were on light duty, which included no physical training. These doctor notes were known in the world of the Seabees as Whimp chits and was something you didn't want be accused of having too many of.

Yes, I hated doing physical training just like the rest of them who would rather sleep in on a cold windy Adak day. The problem though, if you did not condition yourself, in the long run it would have a major impact on our body during the physical readiness test, which could result in failing and being put on remedial PT. This special program was always after working hours, so it was better to just do physical training with everyone else during the mornings it was scheduled. Like bad medicine, just take it and get it over with.

It wasn't so much his attitude that bothered me; it was a comment that he made to me during my last exam that changed my perception on his credibility as a doctor.

"You're just like every woman in this world and this military; you just want to ride the shirttails of a man. Just a free ride and never work a day in your pathetic life."

Those were his exact words, and I am sure that he still will deny that he said this, but I have never forgotten this bastard's words and I never will. It wasn't as if I had a long list of other doctors to choose from. I tried my best to see someone else when I did need to go to medical and did my damnedest to avoid him.

Because of the extreme pain that I was in, I needed to take something and so I decided to talk with him in spite of how I felt about him. I wanted to see if he could find an alternate prescription, other than Vibramycin, that would have the same result in getting rid of my infection.

"Is that what you dentist gave you?" he said in a snide way.

"Yes sir it is...but."

"Yes sir but what?"

"I'm allergic to penicillin as it causes a hives reaction."

"Is it indicated on your record?"

"It's only on my medical record."

"Why isn't it on your dental record?"

"I do not know sir, but I do have allergic reactions to these types of medications!" I responded with a lack of respect, knowing perfectly well that he was an officer in the Navy, but I felt like I was talking to a brick wall.

"If this is what he gave you, you are to take it. Just like it's stated on the prescription slip."

"I can't do that sir. I am allergic to this medication."

"You can't or you won't?" He responded in a quick-tempered voice.

"Both!"

"Constructionmen Lake, I hereby order you to report to medical three times a day to coincide with the dosing instructions on your prescription. You will report at the same time each day until all medications have been taken. Do you understand these orders?"

I was known as a type not to argue, especially with military personnel, as I always feared that it would affect my ability to receive a perfect quarterly report that I had been working so hard for. When I got back to the barracks I had told Don about what had happened with this doctor. He was baffled when he read the dosage of my prescription. His suggestion was to see if I could talk to someone else, it just didn't seem right.

Thinking that would cause trouble I did as I was instructed, I would take two 100-milligram capsules, three times a day for ten days, until I finished my prescription. I did what I was ordered to do, even though deep down I knew it was wrong and somehow knew I was going to regret it later. My instinct told me this was going to result in something far more serious than a tooth infection.

The dental clinic made several attempts at a crown build up after completing the root canal, but would result in the same problem over and over, it would crack. After four long hours the tooth had been filed down to a nub.

In tears I pulled away from the drill. "I can't do this any longer. I need a break, please!" I pleaded, on the verge of screaming.

The dentist smoothed out what was left of my tooth. His recommendations, schedule an appointment for next week and he would try again. That's what he thought. I already knew I was in no way coming back. I was devastated when I returned to my room. I knew that there was nothing left of my tooth and it felt very strange on my tongue. While standing in front of my bathroom mirror, I pulled my lower lip down and to the left to look at the aftermath.

"I can't believe it, filed down to nothing," I said talking to the image of myself in the mirror. I was glad that the pain part of it was over, but the image of myself, seemed distorted. I never felt that I was pretty or attractive and now having this gap in the bridge of my teeth, didn't help. Thank God it wasn't a front tooth. I never said anything to anyone with the exception of Don, about the whole saga. I did an excellent job at hiding my imperfection and I resumed life as it was.

*   *   *

During the month of July 1992, my shop was getting behind and I had several orders to repair signs throughout the base. Don was still attached to his battalion and even though we were married we still had to follow the same rules of our commands until we got orders together. He worked at the rock crusher still, no longer the night crew, but now had to work weekends. So I took advantage of his being at work over the weekend. I decided to work over the weekend as well. I wanted and needed to get things caught up.

As I was working on a sign I felt my legs becoming very weak and I felt intensely dizzy. I had a strong iron taste in my mouth, but thought it was the sheet metal that I was working with. Maybe when I touched my tooth, as it still made me very self-conscious, that was how the taste got there. Don got a chance to get away from the job and as a surprise he brought me McDonald's for lunch. When he walked through the door to my office, he looked at me strangely.

You could see that he was concerned when he called out to me.

"Fallon! What's wrong? Are you feeling ok?"

"No Don, I don't feel very well. I feel like I want to pass out."

"Here sweetie, have a seat and take a drink, maybe you are dehydrated or something."

"Don, I think I need to go to medical. This strange feeling…it's scaring me."

He called up to the job site and explained to his commander that I was feeling very ill and he was going to drive me over to medical to be seen by a doctor. When we arrived, I was immediately sent to phlebotomy for lab work, then had to sit in Commander Palmer's office. Unfortunately, he was the attending doctor on duty again. *Didn't this man have a life other than medical?*

I was not worried about Commander Palmer this time since Don was going to be with me during my exam.

"I didn't find anything unusual in your labs, so change into this examination gown and we will do a physical." Commander Palmer remarked in a snide voice again as he was leaving the exam room so that I could change.

As I got undressed and was changing into my gown Don commented on my skin coloring.

"Fallon, what are all those red dots on your skin?"

"What red dots?"

"The ones all over your back."

"I don't know, I can't see back there," I said jokingly.

On my back were small red pencil point size spots on the back of my arms, around my ankles and on the bottom of my feet were big purple bruises. When the Commander returned and saw these marking on my skin he immediately escorted Don out of the room with him. They were gone for about ten to fifteen minutes. I sat there trying to figure out why my feet and ankles looked so bad. Both returned to my room with angered looks upon their faces.

"What's going on?" I demanded an answer from both of them.

"You don't know how you got these bruises?" asked Commander Palmer while he looked at Don very suspiciously.

"No, I didn't see them yesterday or this morning when I put my boots on."

Don just stood there with fire in his eyes and a very irate look upon his face, but he never said a word. I had never seen Don that upset, but I knew he was pissed about something.

"What's going on Don?"

"Nothing Fallon, don't worry about it." He responded sharply and quickly.

Soon there was a knock on my exam room door, it was Corpsman Avery and he was carrying, what looked like, a lab slip.

"Can I see you in the hall sir?"

Commander Palmer heeded to the Corpsman request and left Don and I alone in the room.

"WHAT IS GOING ON?" I demanded while at the same time feeling totally confused.

"Hold on Fallon, I want to hear what they are talking about." Don knew something was up.

Commander Palmer and Corpsman Avery were in the hall discussing, what I believed to be my lab results. In a loud voice I heard the Corpsman shout down the hallway to another Corpsman. "We are admitting her NOW!"

It was Corpsman Avery that noticed that there was a problem with one of my lab results. It revealed that my platelets were dangerously low and that I needed immediate medical attention that could not be provided on Adak. The staff began processing orders for me to go to Bremerton Naval Medical Center in Washington State, S.T.A.T.

"Don, I don't want to go alone, please come with me, I'm scared."

"Fallon, I am going up to see my commanders to try to get emergency medical leave so that I can go with you. I will stop by your room and get a few things to take with you. Don't worry everything is going to be alright, I promise." And he kissed me quickly to hide his tears before leaving.

I was prepped with an intravenous line in my left hand and given continuous saline. Don had gotten the approval from his command to go with me to Washington, but the medical staff had other ideas. They did not want him anywhere near me, and I didn't know why. Their continuous reply was that it would not be possible for him to accompany me. Don never took no for an answer. He was very insistent that he was going to go with me and he called his command once again. He explained the situation and that he needed their help. His Master Chief and assistant arrived within minutes of Don's call. They refused to let anyone harass one of their men.

*   *   *

It wasn't until the summer of 1998, that Don finally shared with me what had happened when he was asked to leave my exam room and why they didn't want him to accompany me during my travels to Washington State. They had accused him of abuse. They believed that he was tying me up and beating me. That was what they thought all the bruises were on my body. It wasn't until I was sent from Bremerton Naval Hospital to Madigan Army Medical Center, that I was diagnosed. I was told that I was suffering from a medical condition called Idiopathic Thrombocytopenia, or in short I.T.P. (Low Platelet Count). This condition can become very serious and even life threatening, as platelets are needed to make the blood coagulate. My blood was so thin it was slowly coming through the pores in my skin, which gave the appearance of a bruise, if you pushed on the skin hard enough. My work boots caused the marks on my feet and around my ankles and the marks on the back of my arms were from Don holding me up as I walked into the hospital.

This did not surprise me in the slightest. As I had said before, I've had nothing but problems with the medical clinic/hospital on Adak for a long time. It wasn't until some years later, that I made a horrifying discovery while looking through a Physician Desk References Manual on prescription drugs. This is what I read.

The adult dose of Vibramycin, which is also known as a doxycycline, as an oral dose is 200mg on the first day of treatment (<u>*Administered 100mg every 12 hours*</u>*) followed by a maintenance dose of 100mg/day. The maintence dose may be administered as a single does or as 50mg every 12 hours. In the management of more severe infections (particularly chronic infections of the urinary tract,) 100mg every 12 hours is recommended. Adverse Reactions in the blood:* <u>THROMBOCYTOPENIA.</u>

Don had been right to say that he thought the dose, that I was being ordered to take, seemed to be really high.

Reading the dosing information in this reference manual confirmed my perception of Commander Palmer's credibility as a doctor. I couldn't help but ponder the idea, that this could have been some type of premeditated murder plan. Not only did he know that I was allergic to this, he also knew the dose was too high and ordered me to take it anyways. *Did this doctor hate me that much?*

It was always a joke among people that knew about the ways that some people got orders to Adak. Military members that were known as screw-ups, got into trouble or didn't perform well in their rate, would find themselves isolated from the lower 48 on the island of Adak. I knew that didn't apply to the doctor staff of Adak, only Commander Palmer.

*   *   *

Don's quest to get orders with me were made easier with the assistance of the Commander of his battalion, who stayed by his side the whole time. He got the decisions of the medical administrators changed so Don could accompany me. Don was worried as to the seriousness of someone in my condition. I was not allowed to go back to my room to pack a bag, but they were going to have me travel alone? It just didn't make any sense, but then again, it was the military, it's not supposed to make sense.

They put me in a small private room at the back of the hospital and kept me on the intravenous line with saline, but no solid foods. I spent the night at the hospital with Don, as he never left my side once. It was early morning when I was notified of my travel orders. All my medevac arrangements were on commercial airlines.

"You've got to be kidding!" Don said at the top of his lungs. "You can't even walk without the bottoms of your feet turning purple!"

To make matters worse, they also decided not to remove my heplock, which is a piece that is attached to the intravenous line that is in the vein

"They were going to send you alone! No help at all! With that, that, that thing in your hand!" Don was losing his cool as he shook his hands in the air.

"You're going with me sweetie. Don't worry; nothing is going to hurt me." I said trying to help him stay calm.

As we started to get our things together Don just stopped and turned to me. He eyes were filled with tears. He picked up a small white bag and handed it to me.

"I love you honey, this is for you," he said.

"For me? Thank you honey."

It was a white teddy bear that said "Get Well Soon". It was a gift from the guys in Don's battalion; they too were worried about the situation at hand.

I stood up and gave him a big hug and told him that I was going to be fine, and with him being by my side, all was great. We got our things and rode over to the airport with a chief from his unit. He dropped us off and then found a place to park and then met up with us again inside. Some of the guys from his job were also there to say their good-byes and wished us a safe and healthy return. It was like being part of a family, but what really made me feel good, they were truly sincere and cared. *Thanks guys! We miss you all!*

At 11:20am we boarded Reeves Aleutian Airline and were under-way towards Anchorage, Alaska to catch a 1:00am red eye flight to Washington. Don was so exhausted from running around the day before, that as soon as the flight was in the air, he was sound asleep. I never understood just how much he had gone through to get everything organized. Being the patient, it's somewhat easy. Do treatments, stay in bed, and get better. But for family, the stress can really take a lot out of them. Either way I was happy my honey was with me, even if he slept most of the trip. Hearing him snore was music to my ears.

* * *

It was a humid and overcast day when we arrived in Seattle, Washington. Because our flight arrived late, we missed the last morning shuttle to the Bremerton area. Frustrated and confused, our only choice was to find a taxi driver that was willing to take us. Little did we know that in all this hustle and bustle we were about to embark on an eighty-dollar taxi ride to Bremerton Naval Hospital. The ride was not what one would call a scenic route.

"So many trees, don't you think so Don?" I said

"Yea, this is definitely not Adak."

The only thing covering our little island, tall grasses, wild flowers and sharp mountainous rock. The only trees to be found were in a small area that was the size of an eighteen-wheeler. I found it to be more of a joke when I heard what it was called. *What do get when you have thirty-five or so trees in a small cluster on Adak – the "Adak National Forest."*

As we watched the meter in the taxi increase dollar by dollar, and still far from where we needed to be, we had to ask the drive to stop at an ATM so that we could get more cash to pay for this little adventure. He was very cooperative; I think he understood our situation. We got more money and continued on our way. When we finally arrived at the hospital, the taxi driver was gracious enough to write a receipt so that we could someday be reimbursed by the Navy.

I checked in and was given a room. I was put on another liquid diet and they insisted that I had to have the heplock, in my hand, replaced with one of their own. The doctors would only use their own that was inserted by their nursing staff. I wish I had known, before they removed my heplock, that Bremerton was mainly a training hospital. After two hours and eighteen attempts later, the phlebotomy technician was still unable to insert a new intravenous line. The corpsman that was collecting my information from Don was called to the nurse's station and was informed of some overlooked, yet vital, information. It seemed that once again the Navy had processed my orders incorrectly and that I was to be sent to Madigan Army Medical Center in Tacoma, Washington. During my six hour ordeal in Bremerton, the doctors were still puzzled as to my true medical condition. Unfortunately, it wasn't until three hours after they had received the information on my transfer, Don and I got a free ride, by ambulance, to Madigan.

CHAPTER SIXTEEN

SAVED BY THE ARMY

My arrival room, at Madigan, was an open bay concept until the private unit across the hall was cleaned and ready for me. A female technician was sent up to try to insert a new heplock into what was left of my arms.

"We are going to take good care of you, there is nothing to be afraid of," said the technician taking my arm and massaging it gently. She was disgusted by all the bruises and needle marks on my arms from the technicians from Bremerton.

"My name is Amy, I don't believe in addressing people in a military manner in the hospital," she said. "Boy, hon, they really did a number on your arms didn't they?"

"She went into, somewhat of a state of shock after about the tenth time they attempted to insert that thing into her arms." Don couldn't hide his frustrations as he spoke of the whole ordeal.

"Please Amy, be gentle, my arms really hurt."

"You know what sweetie; I am going to put some warm towels on your arms to help them feel better before I try to put your line in. Just relax, you going to be just fine." Amy said with a very angelic voice.

I could barely keep my eyes open and my body felt very heavy.

"Fallon seems very lethargic. Has she eaten anything today?" asked a nurse entering the room.

"No, the doctors told her that she was to be on a liquid diet," explained Don.

"Liquid diet for I.T.P! That is ridiculous! I will call down to the cafeteria to have a tray brought up here immediately. Would you like something Mr...?"

"Bentley, but you can call me Don. Yes, that would be nice, thank you ma'am."

It seemed that the staff knew all about my case and already seemed to know exactly what the problem was. This made Don feel somewhat more at ease. My condition didn't seem to alarming to them and actually they seemed very confident that I would be up and about in a day or two. They needed to do a few tests to determine if their diagnosis was correct. The tests consisted of blood work and a couple of x-rays. All of this was completed during my first few hours on the ward. The next task would be relocating to a spacious private room with a grand view to boot. *A suite is a better way to describe it. I think they gave this to me to soften the blow when they told me what my next test would consist of.*

A team of hematologists dressed in uniforms covered with white clinic coats came into my new room first thing in the next morning. They had been discussing my situation during a staff meeting and all agreed that it was necessary to perform a bone marrow biopsy.

"What is that?" Don asked, once again worried.

"It's a procedure where we numb the area on her back so that we can enter through a small location in the hip. We extract some of the marrow in the area so that we can run tests too rule out leukemia or any other serious diseases.

"That doesn't sound too bad. It's the needle part that I don't much care for," I said confidently.

They decided to do the procedure that morning so that they could get started on whatever treatments that were necessary.

*   *   *

A bone marrow biopsy is a procedure that I wouldn't wish on my worst of enemies. As Don waited out in the waiting room, I was wheeled into a small procedure room. It was filled with large lights and lots of trays and carts that had four color-coded drawers and equipped with wheels for easy mobility in case of an emergency. I wore a hospital gown that was open in the back and a pair of hospital pajama pants. I was asked to lie on the exam table face down. I was given a shot of Morphine to try to relax my already nervous body. *One shot didn't do it.* The doctor told me at this point that I was not to move in any way or it could cause complications. That comment didn't make me feel any better no matter how much they wanted me to relax. The doctor put on his medical gloves and pulled three of the six medical tray carts, in the room, over to where he was working. He cleaned the area with a non-iodine cleanser, as I am allergic to Iodine as well, and prepared to start the procedure.

"Ok Mrs. Bentley, we are ready to give you a local and then begin."

"How long with this take?" I asked so that I could count time or something to get my mind off of what this was going to be like.

"Ten minutes tops, if you can keep very still."

Just then a very thin nurse wearing a surgical mask came into the room and held my hands and kept talking to me. I knew that she was trying to keep my mind off what was about to happen. The local was more or less a stick and a burn.

"That wasn't bad," I said relieved thinking it was over.

"You are going to feel some pressure, just remain very still," said the nurse in a very soft and calm voice.

I could feel the pressure, but very little discomfort. It was almost like an interior bone massage. It was when they used the syringe needle to draw the marrow fluid from my hip bone.

"OH MY GOD! STOP, STOP!" I screamed bloody murder,

"Just a bit more," said the doctor quickly trying to collect as much as he could before I started moving around. "We're almost done, count out loud."

"HOLY SHIT! One, two, three! ARE WE DONE YET? Four, five! STOP!"

"Yes, we got enough for our study, it is all over, you will feel very tender in this area for a few days, but we will give you some muscle relaxers to cut the pain."

The doctor left the room and the nurse then cleaned up the bloody area from my hip, dressed it with sterile gauze, and sealed the bandage with medical paper tape. I slowly got myself into an upright position and wiped the tears from my eyes. I looked over at the tray table that the doctor used during the procedure. It was covered with medical tools and a small cup, just like the one I used in boot camp for a urine sample. In the cup was a blackish fluid that could not have been more than an ounce. *I endured a lot of pain for that ounce.*

'What is that?" I asked, "It looks dirty."

"That is the marrow that he just extracted from your hip bone," replied the nurse as she helped me off the table and into my wheelchair.

"It's so dark," I thought as I was being wheeled out the door.

In the waiting room still sitting in the same place where I left him, was Don. He was ghostly white and looked as though he was feeling rather ill.

"What's the matter honey?" I was more worried about him, than what my results were going to be. Somehow I just knew that I was fine.

"I could hear you screaming all the way out here, are you ok?"

"I am now, let's go back to my room, but maybe you need the wheelchair instead." I said with a chuckle.

"No, I'll be fine." he replied while swallowing hard several times.

* * *

We laughed and joked as we sat in my room trying to find something on television.

"Pretty Woman, let's watch that." I said with a big grin, "Chick Flick."

We didn't watch much of it, but it added some happy sounds to the room. He sat in a chair that was made to fold out into a recliner as I lay on my side so that I would not make my hip hurt any more than it had to. I was given Tylenol 3's for the pain, which caused me to come in and out of a twilight type of sleep. Don would not let go of my hand and occasionally when he thought that I was asleep, I would catch him wiping the tears from his eyes. Not to embarrass him, I would just close my eyes and stir as though I was just waking to give him time to regroup and look as if all was fine and dandy, but I knew he was scared.

Later that afternoon there was a soft knocking at my door.

"Mrs. Bentley?" whispered one of the phlebotomy technicians, "Are you awake, ma'am?"

"Yes, come on in."

"I'm sorry, I know you don't like this, but I need to draw some labs again."

"That's fine. Would you please use my right arm that has the best vein," really I didn't want to let go of Don's hand.

"Sure ma'am. I want you to know, the doctors are on their way up here, word has it you don't have leukemia and that treatment is going to be easy if you respond well."

"Really!"

"You didn't hear it from me. I just wanted to make a stressful situation easier and if I can deliver good news…well I am all for it." She smiled.

"Thanks, we could use some good news."

She drew my labs and then went about her way to collect blood samples from her list of patients on the ward. It was shortly after her departure that Colonel Jameson and Dr. Faber came into my room. They were the head residents of hematology, I think. They told me that I didn't have leukemia and that my course of treatment was various levels of Prednisone. I would start with a high dose for a period of time to increase my platelet count and then eventually start a gradual taper to see if my body could maintain the proper levels on its own. I am happy to report that this idea worked very well. Each new day my levels came up very quickly.

I stayed on the ward for about five days, which was very hard for Don as he was having trouble getting a room in the billeting area on the base. The first night he stayed out in town and found the place was more of a No-Tell Motel, you rented rooms by the hour not the night. It was not a place to be for a long period of time. He only had to stay there one night, the next day the billeting office had a room and since he had orders, was able to stay as long as he needed.

I was released from the ward and placed into the medical holding barracks just down the road from the hospital. This was going to be my new home for about a month. This was great as I didn't have to stay in the hospital anymore. I got my own private dorm room with others, both men and women, who were also on medical hold. Don was only given two weeks of emergency leave and then he had to return to Adak so that he could assist with his battalion to get ready to turn their command over to NMCB 7. From Adak he would return back to his homeport in California. We made the very best of the days we had left together. We saw the movie "Far and Away" at the base theater, we went shopping for new clothes for Don at the PX, and we even ventured of the base and took a bus to the mall to look around. It was like old times again and the reality of my medical problems seemed to move to the back of my mind.

Time quickly passed and before we knew it, Don had to return to Adak. With all that had been going on in our lives, we came to the sad realization that we were going to be without each other for quite some time. It would be at least December before we would be together again. *One thing Don learned, never underestimate me, especially if it meant that him and I could be together.* Shortly after he had returned to Adak, I had an idea. My only hope was that my doctor would approve.

* * *

While I was on medical hold I worked T.A.D. in the Navy liaison office helping other recruits with their medical situations. Don had returned to the island and had to stay for another three weeks before returning to California. He called me every day like clockwork and never once forgot to tell me how much he loved and missed me. On August 21, 1992 he and his command would be packing their things and preparing to return to Port Hueneme. I asked my Supervisor, who I was working for, if I could take some leave to go to California to surprise Don.

"If your doctor approves it, it is fine with me, you've earned it."

"Great, can I go see him and get this approved?"

"Sure, go on, get out of here."

My doctor wrote the approval for my convalescent leave, but there were stipulations. I had to promise that if I felt bad, dizzy, sick, tired, anything, I would report to the nearest hospital. In a matter of hours I was packed and on my way. It felt good to be getting away from medical and back to the warm sandy beaches of California and into the loving arms of my sweetheart. *I could hardly wait!*

I was unaware, until I arrived in California that I was a day earlier than Don because his plane was delayed in Anchorage, because of a storm. I was sad that it wasn't Don standing at the gate waiting for me. Sally, who was the wife of Don's roommate, and her friend Rachel, came and picked me up at the airport. They knew that Don was supposed to marry Jessie, and they had even met her a few times. They always thought that Don and Jessie seemed happy, so they believed the reason their wedding was called off was because Don had gotten me pregnant.

The looks on their faces, priceless, when I got off the plane wearing a black leather mini skirt and a silky tight hot pick blouse.

"Well she's not pregnant." said Rachel under her breath.

I heard her, but she didn't know that.

During the ride back to Oxnard/Port Hueneme I played their game of 20 Questions. I knew they were trying to get something out of me, I just didn't know what, but I knew this interrogation would not end unless I came up with something. I decided to take control of the situation and asked them one question. Did they think Don and I got married because he knocked me up?

Both looked at one another somewhat embarrassed before responding. Because I had heard Rachel's comment earlier, when they both answered, yes, it was no shock to me. They apologized for thinking that way, but were pleased to hear me say how much I was in love with Don. To Sally, Don was like her big brother and she was rather protective over him. As for Rachel, any wise woman would know what her intent was, and she didn't hide it either, she was hoping to get Don into bed. Yes, she was married, but due to the drama in her life, *that is a story of its own*, technically she was single.

I really took to Sally, and I tolerated Rachel. From that point on we talked as normal people and enjoyed the rest of the ride up the coastal route. It was a strange feeling to know that I was going to see where Don actually lived. I didn't know anything about his life in California. I did all I could to hide my excitement and anticipation, but I am sure Sally and Rachel knew I didn't care about the small talk, I wanted my man.

I do have to admit, when we drove past the base, other thoughts besides Don, cluttered my brain. I was newly married, but I couldn't help but wonder about the man in the reddish van.

What if I see him while I am here? What if he wants to talk to me? What if I do see him and find I still have feelings for him? Don would certainly hate me.

I was so consumed by my thoughts, I never heard Sally say that we were back at Don's apartment. It was the slamming of the doors that brought me back to reality. When we arrived at the building, I was speechless and surprised. I knew this place; I had been here before. I told Sally and Rachel about the time that Linda and I had come here to see a Seabee guy she knew. They laughed and told me that 90% of the men here were Seabees. It could have been anyone if I didn't have a name.

"Wouldn't it be funny if it was the same apartment?" I thought.

We made our way up the same stairs and before I knew it, we were standing in front of the same door to enter his apartment.

"Maybe it won't be funny." I thought as I began biting my lower lip, *"what if that jerk is here again? This time I'll let him have it. I was now 100 lbs. thinner and I was feeling like one hot mama."*

It was a bad case of deja vu. I knew it was indeed the same place as I walked through the door. To hide my nervousness and fear of running into Mr. Anti-social, I took a close look at the all the pictures that were displayed on the walls. *The same diamond shape lay out on the wall. Same frames, same pictures.*

It was then that it dawned on me when Sally said that Frank wouldn't be home until later and that Don's room was upstairs, I felt a serious "oh shit" moment coming over me.

"Sally, does Frank have any other roommates living here?" I asked fearing the answer.

"Only Don, well wait, I take that back, Rachel is here while her husband is overseas."

"So you're telling me there is nobody else?"

"Just the two guys and now us girls. Why?"

I suddenly realized that the friend of Linda, Frank, was Don's roommate, and Frank was also Sally's husband. *Now don't get me wrong, there was no funny business between Frank and Linda. They were only friends as Linda had a boyfriend of her own while we were at N.C.T.C.*

But that wasn't the worst part. I was slowly finding out that the same person who sat in front of the television drinking a beer, while probably getting aroused as Denise Austin did her workout, and treated me like the scum of the earth, then totally blew me off...was now my husband.

It can't be? It just can't be? There is no way. He's too sweet to me. He can't be the same guy.

It was an odd feeling, but I kept my secret about being there before, especially since the 20 Question interrogation I got for marrying Don, I left well enough alone.

They showed me Don's bedroom at the top of the stairs. Rachel had been staying there while her husband was on deployment in Okinawa with Sally's husband, but her husband would not be returning with the rest of Frank's battalion, he had been extended for legal reasons. His room was filled with boxes of Rachel's things, and I couldn't help but notice that this apartment was only a two bedroom. I was pleased to hear that she was looking for an apartment, as the idea of her shacking up with Don while I was gone, was not happening. Her dilemma, there wasn't any available apartments, with affordable rent for people on their own. That was why she was staying with Sally and stored her stuff in Don's room. I was not too keen on the idea, that to add to my limited toleration of her, she and I also had to share his bed for the night, as she couldn't stay with friends until the next day.

The next morning I decided to do what any good wife would do to get to know her husband better. I checked out his room. He had a small wooden end table with a clear phone and a few pictures of his family in the drawer. On the wall he had a huge poster of a red Lamborghini over his bed. *Indeed this was the room, of a used to be, single man.*

I opened the bottle of cologne, he had on his dresser and dabbed some onto my neck. I pulled out one of his t-shirts, and put it on as I rustled through his dresser draws to see how he put his clothes away. I even looked under the bed to see if he was a clutter bug. Many thoughts began filtering into my mind as I took everything in. His scent was wrapped around me like a quilt, yet he was not there.

I am standing in a room that belongs to a man that I am now married to. I am married to, married to. Is this real, am I really standing here? Who are you Don? I don't know a lot about you. God is he really my mister right?

As I stood peering around his room, something caught my eye. On his dresser, sticking half way out from under a piece of paper that Rachel had forgotten, was a photo that rendered me absolutely speechless as I walked closer to it. My mind flashed back to everything I had seen and done when I first arrived in Port Hueneme for 'A' School. My hands immediately began to sweat and I could hardly breathe. What I was seeing had to be a joke Rachel was playing on me, but she didn't know, I never told her about the man. Don, must have set me up, but I never told him either. I began to panic and scream.

"SALLY…SALLY…SALLY!"

She came running up the stairs as fast as she could, she was sure my health was acting up. "Fallon! Fallon! Are you ok?"

Catching my breath I asked her, "Who is this man in this photo?"

"It's Don. Isn't he cute?"

"Sally. Whose van is this?"

"Don's, why?"

I felt my legs get weak and I sat down abruptly on his bed. It was him; it had been Don the whole time. I began to solve the mystery and put the pieces of my dream together. The photo was of Don working on a van, the same reddish van I had seen on the base to be exact. The mystery man, in the reddish van in my dreams, was in fact the same man who blew me off and the same man I married. I just couldn't believe it. All our time together and I never put any of this together. But my next worry was did Don know that I was the girl standing in his apartment, looking like a beached whale, that he laughed at and called names. I wondered. Would he still love me?

CHAPTER SEVENTEEN

CALIFORNIA DREAMING AND BACK

MWR and other military wives had put together a "Welcome Home Celebration" for the men of NMCB 5. I stood waiting impatiently at the MWR building surrounded by a multitude of colored welcome home balloons, wives waiting for their husbands and their children waiting to see their dads. That was where the bus was going to be dropping off the men of Don's battalion. My mystery man was soon to arrive. I couldn't wait to tell him what I had discovered. He knew there was a man I had seen when I was in Hueneme, but I never went into great detail about him. For all I know, Don probably thought he was someone I went out with. Maybe that is why we never put two and two together. I paced the walkway like an expectant father awaiting the birth of his first child.

"Hurry up bus!" I remarked loudly and others waiting could hear me.

"You must be waiting for your significant other as well?" said a lady waiting, with her two children, for her husband to return.

"You-bet-ya! We just got married only three months ago and we won't be stationed together until January of 1993. Time is very valuable to us."

"Wow, are you sure your marriage will survive? With all the cheating that goes on around here when the spouse is gone, not a lot of distant military marriages can handle the long separations."

"I'm not worried. I know ours will, we've been through a lot together and it is only making our bond stronger than ever."

Making a face she asked, "So who's the lucky guy?"

"Petty Officer Bentley. I met him on Adak."

"Don? Don Bentley?" She couldn't hide her surprise.

"Yes, why so shocked?"

"You're not Jessie. What happened to her?"

If I had a dollar for every time I'd be hearing that statement over the next two years. I'd be a rich woman.

As I began to reply, a beautiful sound filled the air. Air breaks of a tour bus that had my mystery man and his battalion aboard. I never did finish my conversation as Don was the only thing on my mind and the only one I wanted to talk to. One by one the men departed from the bus. I think Don purposely waited to be last, just to watch me squirm. He even had one of the guys say that he wouldn't be coming home until the next day. Not something I wanted to hear, but pretended that I didn't take him seriously. Thank God I didn't. There he was in his full Seabee green uniform, my husband and my mystery man. The other wives and girlfriends of the men tried to talk to him, but he was focused on one thing, getting me into his arms and locking lips.

"Hey Bentley! Get a room!" said the guys from his unit as they began to chuckle.

"I plan to!" he responded as he gave me a big hug accompanied by a huge mesmerizing smile.

We were the talk of the welcome home celebration. Don had married some woman and it wasn't Jessie. Talk about new gossip for the base. But he didn't care, he lived out in town. With so many wanting to know our story, we felt a little bit like celebrities. Within hours our story was out so that it could be told incorrectly to others. *That's what happens with gossip.*

* * *

Our days together in California were filled with an enriched and everlasting love. Endless talks while sitting on the beach and long afternoon drives up the coastline was how we filled our days. Every place we went, we were either arm in arm or hand in hand. It felt like a dream or a scene from a romance movie. I told him about my discovery, that he was the man I had been searching for and that my sign from God was when I found the picture of him and his van. That he was a gift that I had longed for. Unbeknown to me, my future had been in front of my eyes. All this happened before my transfer to Adak. I knew it when I first saw him during my inspection on that sunny April morning during 'A' School.

I had become obsessed to find my mystery man. I had even returned to California with my mother between commands just to find him. He was driving me crazy and I didn't even know him. Each time I spoke of this, his eyes lit up and he'd pull me into him.

"I love you sweetness. I really love you." He'd say just before our lips would gently touch.

"I love you too. Always and forever."

The biggest surprise to him, when I told him I was the girl in his apartment in the spring of 1991. I informed him of how badly he spoke to me when I was there with my friend Linda, who was there to see his roommate Frank.

"I don't recall it being you standing there, but I do remember someone. Not to be mean, but you've lost a lot of weight. I'm sorry and I'm sorry for the way I treated you. Jessie and I were having some problems and I just didn't want to talk to anyone that day. I was just having a bad day."

"It's over now and I have you. That was the past and ya know what, I still love ya." I said as I looked deep into his blue eyes.

He proudly smiled.

He enjoyed taking me to the homes of friends to introduce the new love in his life. He would always ask me to tell them about my journey that brought us together. Our relationship was accepted by everyone, well everyone but Rachel. Rachel had always had a fondness for Don and her hopes were clear, since her marriage was not working out, that maybe she and Don had a chance. She was always nice to my face, but when I was not around, like any devious woman, she would do her best to talk Don out of our relationship. I knew that her not having an apartment and Don's only being two bedrooms, I needed to do something fast before I left.

My time there was not only filled with romance, I also dabbled, a bit in a couple of secure business transactions. Finding ways to save money was my favorite strategic hobby. But finding the deals of the century was very exciting to me as well. I found Don a second hand Ford 4X4 pick-up truck at a great price, and he looked hot driving his blue F250 beauty. But the best find, a new apartment with three bedrooms, one for Don, one for Frank and Sally and their new baby boy, and yes one for Rachel too. *Don't ask me what I was thinking by adding Rachel to the equation. I trusted Don, and I knew Frank and Sally wouldn't let her pull and funny business or they would put her out on her ear.*

Another sign from above, that all was going to work out, when I saw the name of the street the apartment was on, Saviors Road. *It fit.*

My days in California were coming to an end and soon I would have to return to my life in medical hold in Washington. For the last two days of my stay, we did some serious talking. Our biggest challenge was only a few days ahead of us. Could we survive the separation and loneliness? We were going to be separated, not by choice, until his new orders went into effect at the end of the year. I would not see him again until December 28, 1992. My heart was breaking. I didn't want to be without him. I wanted to stay in California and start our new life together.

I also had some major decisions to make as well, did I want to get out of the service or stay in? I loved the Navy and being a Seabee, Don on the other hand didn't care for military life. Our decision, I was going to stay in and become an officer and he was going to be my dependent. I would continue my classes with the University of Alaska, Adak and pursue an officers training program. Don would transfer to Adak and work with Public Works finishing out his last four years. The plan was flawless. *So we thought.*

I was at a loss for words as Don and I stood hugging each other before they called for boarding on my return flight to Tacoma.

"I promise to be forever faithful to you Fallon," he whispered into my ear. 'I love you. You mean so much to me. I'm so scared that something is going to happen to you."

"Please don't worry. Nothing is going to happen to me. This is just a crazy test, both with my health and our love. We can do it. Fate brought us together. We'll be together for so long that we will be hired to do the Country Time lemonade commercials, and why, because we will be the perfect still in love, loving old couple."

I was hoping that my positive outlook would help soothe his broken heart. Yet, still he couldn't fight the show of tears and emotions.

"We will now begin boarding flight 262 to Tacoma, Washington." A happy check-in boarding attendant announced.

How could anyone be happy on a day like today, we were being forced apart.

"I have to go now, Don. I promise to write and call you as much as I can. Promise me you'll do the same?"

"I…I promise…Oh, I don't want you to go."

Quickly I was losing the battle to hid my tears and remain strong. I couldn't say anything as the lump in my throat kept me speechless. With my arms around him, I tried to make a mental note of what he felt like against me. I loved the strength of his arms, the warmth of his body, the feeling of being safe as long as we embraced each other, being pressed against him, I couldn't leave him. I didn't want to go, and couldn't get myself to pull away. Suddenly my strength was gone and I broke down into an uncontrollable cry. Finally the truth came out that I too, was scared of the unknown with my health. I was worried that something would happen and that I would never get to see my wonderful mystery man again. I would never look into those beautiful blue eyes again, I would never hear his sweet voice say my name and how we were meant to be together. Just having him by my side was the best medicine I could have.

"This is the final boarding of flight 262 to Tacoma, Washington." said a ticket agent that was looking directly at me.

"I'm not going!"

"What? Fallon what you are saying? You have to go, what about your doctor's orders?"

"I'll call him and tell him some made-up excuse. I'm going to stay with you. Then I'll have another weekend, I'll go back on Monday the 31st. I just need to stay with you. Don I'm not ready to go."

And this is just what I did. I changed my flight with the ticket agent. I told her I forgot to get some important papers and would she reschedule my ticket to leave in three days. She knew that I had not forgotten anything. She knew we were not ready to say good-bye and even said to me how beautiful it was to witness such a power of love between two people.

I called my doctor. He was fine with my extended stay, since my health was still doing well. That weekend we did nothing but sit on the rocks at Point Magu and watch the sunset. At night we slept tightly in a loving embrace and savored every second we had together. Yes, it was still hard to say our good-byes on Monday, but to have just those three extra days helped us in so many magical ways.

*   *   *

With each day that I remained within the military, my soul was broken down and I was forced to rebuild myself. Experiencing what I had so far, only made me more determined to succeed in everything I did. Many were not happy with the new image that had come over me, but it was not for them to decide. I wouldn't let my illness or my chain of command stop me from being an officer in the military. I was going to be the first woman to take charge of a battalion on the front lines. My motto was PMS Semper Fi that I would get the job done and done right! Looking back on that statement, I now understand that it was not healthy to let the hate keep building inside of me. On the outside I was building a better image, but on the inside I was building a stronger resentment toward those in my command and a specific doctor in Adak. I did the treatments and with each day I got better. I continue to refuse to let the military discharge me from the Navy. I was determined to go back to Adak as an active duty military member. A Seabee!

On September 1, 1992, I was asked to attend a meeting with the Chief resident of hematology in Madigan.

"Before you begin, doctor, I have something to say." Speaking in a determined voice, "I have been thinking seriously about my future over these past two months. I want to return to full active duty at my present command in Adak."

The doctor sat there stroking his chin with the look of disbelief that I wanted to return. He understood my wanting to stay in the military, but wanting to return to Adak, who in their right mind would want to go back if they could get their orders for state side West Coast.

"Are you sure that is what you're truly wanting to do?" he asked.

"Yes sir," I replied with a very stern voice.

"I will have to call the medical department in Adak. I won't let you return if you don't have a doctor to follow your health care needs."

I gave him the number and he made the call while I sat before him in his office. The agreement was made that, Commander Palmer; at the Adak Branch Medical Hospital department would be the accepting physician. With the knowledge of a bad doctor patient relationship, I honestly believed they truly thought I would refuse to return if he was my caregiver. I think the medical department did this just so that I would decide not to come back. *They didn't know that I was looking for a new fight. I fought an illness, now I needed something new to battle.*

Lt. Colonel Branzell, never mentioned who the doctor was until after the call. The plan was that he would follow me with the understanding that he would monitor my condition by performing routine CBC's and monthly physicals and watch for any unusual swelling. If anything went wrong with my health, I was to be immediately sent back to Madigan.

With the newly added concerns that were mentioned to manage my care, I still agreed to his recommendations, not knowing who my caregiver was going to be. Under all the conditions Adak Branch Medical Hospital still agreed to accept me into their care and Doctor Commander Palmer would be my primary caregiver. As he hung up the phone a long silence filled the room.

"They have assigned a doctor to care for you when you get back there."

"Do you know who it is?" I asked

"Dr. Palmer."

"What!"

"It's no mystery Fallon, that there is clearly a stressful situation between the both of you. I also know that you question his abilities as a doctor. It is up to you if this is what you want to do. It will also be up to you to do self-examinations and I will send you with plenty of extra medications. Please be careful as this medication can cause bone problems and breakage. No high impact sports or running. You will have to take it easy for the next several months. I will also send you with my recommendations on your care guidelines and light duty status. But in addition to all that I have told you, you must not, and I repeat, must not get pregnant. If that happens, you will not be able to continue your duty on Adak as you will need to be followed by our high risk OB-GYN team. Right now a pregnancy could be a serious situation that could be fatal for both you and the baby. Fallon, are you absolutely sure this is what you really want? Do you really want to go back to Adak?"

"Yes."

"What about your husband, what does he think?"

"He is fine with what I want to do and he had gotten orders for Public Works in Adak and will report in January of 1993."

"That's a long time to be apart, are you sure you can handle the stress up there on your own?"

"Yes, I know I can. I will be a form of closure for me."

"Well then I guess it is settled, I will call downstairs and have the Navy Liaison representative get your travel orders together and you will head out as early as tomorrow morning." Lt. Colonel Branzell stated with worry in his voice.

He couldn't stress strongly enough and constantly repeated to me, that if I developed any lumps, bumps, or swelling that if medical didn't help me, I was to get myself on the next available plane back to his clinic.

"I will take care of myself I promise. Thank you so much sir, you and your staff, you have all done so much for me. I am truly thankful. You saved my life."

* * *

My stay in Madigan was pleasant and I loved being back in the states, but I was truly missing my life on Adak, as the time passed by. I knew that as long as I had my loving husband in my corner fighting for me when I needed help, nothing could go wrong. On September 2, 1992, I made my way back to my island life and stepped back into my job as if I had never left. The hardest part now was facing a bigger challenge, the long lonely nights I would have to endure as I counted the days until I would see Don again.

Chapter Eighteen

Dealing with Uncertainty

Only being married for a short time this would be a true test of our relationship as an active duty military couple. Don was stationed in California and I was in Adak. I would not see him again for another four months. The days and weeks felt like years as each month slowly passed by. I found myself becoming even more depressed with my surroundings. My longing to have Don once again by my side grew worse as the lonely nights filled me up.

*   *   *

One evening in late September while trying to fall asleep, I found that when I would lay on my left side the feeling of breathlessness would come over me.

"That's strange," I thought to myself as I began to worry.

Each time I would try to lie on my side I would find myself with the same reaction. My first instinct was to go to medical.

What would my command think of me, I just got back from getting over an illness; maybe it has something to do with my illness? Maybe I am just over reacting. It's probably just a cold or flu trying to get the better of me.

I chose not to go to medical right away to see if it would go away. Some nights seemed better than others did and so I considered it just a flu bug and gave it no future thought. By the end of the month I knew that something was wrong, but still feared the negative criticism from my command, and said nothing.

I eventually called Dr. Palmer and after ten minutes of trying to explain what I was experiencing and wanted to make an appointment with him, he quickly diagnosed the problem as bronchitis and that I should drink plenty of fluids.

Still after a week of following doctor's orders, the feeling did not seem to go away and so I called my command and told them I wasn't going to make morning muster, that I had an appointment. *One thing everyone learned if you were active duty, if you said you had a doctor's appointment, you didn't have to go to your department first and you wouldn't be marked as UA. (Unauthorized Absence).*

I walked into the clinic without an appointment. *A true rebel without a clue moment.* Dr. Palmer was furious with my showing up unannounced. His way to deal with the situation, make me wait in the waiting room for three hours before seeing me. Finally his assistant called me into his examination room to take my temperature and blood pressure. As quickly as his assistant arrived, he too was gone. I sat again for another hour until Dr. Palmer finally came back into the room.

"So what's the problem now?" he said in a negative tone of voice.

Trying to hold back my cast iron bitch attitude I sweetly replied, "Sir, I just don't feel right, I feel very tired and sluggish and having problems breathing at night."

To my surprise I never anticipated that this bastard would take another opportunity to bash me.

"You know what your problem is Bentley? I've said it before. You're just like every damn woman in this world you just don't want to work. You want the men to do it for you! Stand around and look pretty, that's all you know."

I just sat there dazed, confused, and speechless as my little fire inside was become a raging inferno.

What just happened here? He didn't just say those words to me again! Was this a comment just for me? And then to say it twice in less than a year! Should I say something? Could they write me up if I did? He doesn't believe me!

I was filled with so much anger, but chose to remain silent. I took his useless advice to drink plenty of fluids and headed back to the Paint shop.

"He is going to pay dearly if something was seriously wrong with me," I muttered to myself over and over. "I guarantee someone is going to hear about this you piece of shit! One way or another, people are going to know what you have done!

* * *

The sensation of breathlessness now happened around the clock and interfered with my personality and performance in my job. It also sparked some major attitudes throughout my command when my condition caused me to faint during the run portion of my physical readiness test. My command wrote it off as a way to draw attention to myself.

They will never know the fear I felt as the world around me grew warm and dark. I had no control of my body as it went limp. When I woke, there standing over me was Jack, my supervisor in the Paint Shop who worked with me and was a very dear friend. He chose not to continue with the test and stayed by my side until the paramedics came. He stayed with me until he was assured I would be fine. Something nobody but Don and his battalion had ever done for me. He had known that I had not been feeling like myself and he was always there when I needed someone to talk to during working hours. I also knew he'd update Don if things were life threatening.

This was also something that my command frowned upon. I honestly believed that they wanted to do all they could to make it look like two married people were more than close friends, and that something sexual was going on. All it would take is some slip of bullshit gossip and we would have a problem on our hands.

They slowly made life very difficult for Jack and me, especially when it came time for Jack to make up the run portion of his physical readiness test. It was a long battle and many requests to see the captain of the base. Finally our command allowed him to make it up. If they had gotten their way, they would have failed him. They didn't want to hear, nor did they care that he stopped to help me. They didn't care one bit.

Over time after my collapse our friendship grew stronger. We were both married and always respected that of one another. Don held my entire heart and soul in the palm of his hands forever. There would never be another. Jack respected this and always wished us well.

Now, my friendship was made of laughter and tears, career dreams and career fears that we shared with each other. He spoke of the struggles of not having his son that he love so much. You could feel his pain as he spoke of how his son was getting older every day and he would never get those days back again. He would do anything to have him by his side again. He worked day and night to get orders to the East Coast so he could be closer to his son. This discussion had been over heard one day by a Senior Chief in passing, who then later, tried to get Jack's orders changed to the West Coast just to spite him.

When I heard this rumor, I knew who it was that did this and I had to do something. I couldn't help but feel responsible and the reason for this spiteful act. My Senior Chief was already mad at me for marrying Don, so why not hurt someone else that knew me, since Don was not here yet. One day while Jack was out getting supplies, Senior Chief decided to pay me a visit. *Not a very smart move on his part.*

"So how's the paint shop doing?" he asked uninterestedly.

"Fine" I responded with a bitchy snap in my tone.

"Where's Jack?"

"He's out getting supplies. Why do you ask?"

"What do you mean?" he tried to ask as I quickly interrupted him.

"Senior, do you understand what will happen if Jack's orders are cut for the West Coast? Do you know that he has a child on the East Coast? He's done just about everything to be able to see his only son that he has not seen for years. How would you sleep at night knowing that you had something to do with his only son never being able to see his father? That is a lot of guilt and pressure that I would never want on my shoulders. Can you handle it? There is no way I could. Think about it before you destroy what little hope they may have of being together."

I found it hard to hold back but kept my composure and kept looking straight into his eyes. For a moment I could see the aggressive side of him change and the reality of the situation hit him. The reality of what this could do to a child. That even though Jack was a military member in his command...he was also a father of an only son.

Although he never admitted to it, I do believe that Senior Chief thought this through and in 1994, Jack finally received orders to Gulfport, Mississippi. Jack did not get mad at me for telling Senior Chief about his personal situation. He seemed pleased that I actually stood up and said something. It was like I had repaid the favor that he did for me when he chose to stop and help me in my time of need.

* * *

After my talk with Senior Chief, I found that the pressure of the command lightened up on both Jack and I. Life on the island was finally feeling normal again. Unfortunately, I was still having problems with my breathing and started suffering from terrible headaches. I went to medical for check-ups to be sure that everything was fine with my health. My inner self feared a bad situation looming in the distance.

I always tried to make sure that I got to see someone other than Dr. Palmer. Their diagnosis was that I might have developed a slight bit of asthma or a thyroid problem from the steroids I was taking. By the later part of October 1992, I was given a chest x-ray that had many shaded spots across the neck and chest area. Dr. Palmer passed it off as gas bubbles and it was common to see that show up on an x-ray. Not only was there problems with my x-ray, I was also experiencing severe headaches. It was because of the uncertainty of my headaches and what they could be stemming from, I was scheduled for a series of tests and the medical center in Elemendorf Air Force Base and Humana Hospital in Anchorage, Alaska. I was going to have an ultrasound done on my neck and a C.A.T. scan on my head. When I got there, I was told that I would be there for about ten days. This would give the Air Force and Humana Hospital, time to gather all the results before my return to Adak.

Never underestimate the thinking of a woman in love! I was going to see Don.

"Ten Days," I thought to myself, *"I've got to call Don. I need to have him with me."*

His command in California had always been very supportive of my medical situation. Immediately they processed his request to fly to Anchorage to be by my side during my testing. It had been almost two long months since I had seen him last. It was only a matter of time and I would be back in his arms once again. He was flying into the International side of the Anchorage airport because the flight he was on originally began in China.

As I waited anxiously for his arrival, I felt like a child standing in the kitchen waiting for a fresh batch of brownies to come out of the oven. I stood and admired the many colors of the flags from the different countries that were hung throughout the arrival area. At different angles it looked like a palette of oil paints blended to create a form of abstract art. While looking at the many colors, a feeling passed over me. I turned around and looked toward the stairs where passengers were descending into the terminal. A man wearing blue jeans, a denim jacket and a red Nebraska cap captivated me.

"Don? Don? Don!" I shouted and ran to him.

I had to have been dreaming. To be inside the clutches of his arms and the warmth of his face pressing against mine was sheer heaven. Don was really holding me. It was him, against me.

"God I missed you." He said in a soft whisper into my ear.

I began to melt into him. "I missed you too." I replied as he met his lips with mine. We were together again and nothing else mattered.

We got his luggage and made out way to the car. I wish I had a camera to capture the surprised look on his face when he saw the rental car that I had.

Now picture this, he's 6'1 and I am 6' trying to get into a Geo Metro. I am sure to the outsiders watching, we must have looked like one hell of a circus act, two clowns getting into their miniature car in the center ring with everyone watching in amazement. It took a lot of maneuvering, but we managed to fit the luggage and ourselves into the car.

"It would be a lot more comfortable if we pulled the front seats out and used the back ones. Don't you think?" said Don, laughing at how silly we looked.

With our knees practically up beside our ears and his luggage forced in the back we made our way to the Black Angus Hotel in Anchorage. Don was right. It would've been more comfortable if we could have pulled the front seats out and used just the back seats, but we made the best of it and to this very day still laugh at our adventure.

As time always does, it was quickly passing by. During our time together between medical testing and doctor appointments, Don and I made the most of our mini adventure. We enjoyed doing donuts in snow covered parking lots with the windows down and the music playing as loud as a standard model Geo Metro radio would allow. We took in many movies, played pool; ice skated on the huge rink inside the mall, and our favorite, watching television. On the night before Halloween the area was hit with a tremendous snowstorm and by morning the grounds were blanketed in a winter wonderland of white. Don, who also enjoyed the cold as much as I did, did not object when I suggested, that before going to bed that night that we wrap our naked bodies together in a huge blanket, open the window to our room, enjoy the beauty of nature illuminated by the street lights, and inhale the freshness of the crisp wintery air. It was a little bit of Heaven on earth.

We didn't sleep at all that night. We stayed wrapped together tightly, talking about our dreams, our hopes, and our plans for the future.

For being such a happy time during the occasional medical worries, we knew that he was going to leave in the morning and we would not be together again for another two months. It was hard for us to leave, as we would miss each other deeply and we still had no answers to my current medical condition.

CHAPTER NINETEEN

IT'S SHOWTIME

My life after being with Don in Anchorage was rather different. I felt reenergized and ready to make it through the remaining sixty days without him. My favorite past time was working as a DJ as the "Husky Club" after working hours. Something about the melodies of various music, made me feel better inside. When I wasn't working at the club, I kept myself busy participating in various small community service events. The biggest of all events started with an idea by a wild and crazy friend of mine. DL, as he was known, from the C.E. (Construction Electricians) shop, came to me with the idea of the century. His idea; bring the Christmas spirit back to Adak for everyone, including families that lived on the base. As for myself, I was game for anything that would put a smile on the faces of those around me, and would make time go by faster.

And so it was born, the first "Seabee Talent Show" on Adak. The date of the show was set for December 22, 1992. Just in time for the Holiday season. Our plan was to have eighteen acts with first prize being two donated round trip tickets on Reeves Aleutian Airlines to Anchorage. There was no charge for admission, to see the greatest show Adak has ever had, all you had to do was donate some nonperishable items for the food bank for our needy island families. *Yes, even Adak had its share of struggling families.*

As word got out, it seemed that everyone was getting into the spirit. Seabees from all shops and locations throughout the base did their part to donate their time, materials, and anything else they could do to pull this off. It became a phenomenal event and the talk of the base. Getting in on the act, our local Adak news and radio anchors, asked DL and I into the studio to do an on air interview. They wanted to add more to the already huge hype.

"Will you be there? Will you be able to say that you have seen the greatest show this side of the Aleutian Islands?" said the radio announcer with extreme enthusiasm. "In our studio today folks, we have DL Franklin and Fallon Bentley, both Seabees from Public Works. They're the creators of this very first Adak Seabee Talent show that everyone is buzzing about. Welcome both of you to our studio today."

DL was beaming and you could see the excitement as he stood in front of the microphone.

"Thank you for having us." We both replied simultaneously.

"So, please, tell the residents of Adak, what sparked such a wonderful idea?"

"We wanted to bring the Christmas spirit back to Adak. Many of us are far away from loved ones. It's not easy being so isolated and sometimes we find ourselves unhappy and all alone. Our hopes are that everyone joins us for an evening of fun and entertainment that will be enjoyed by the young, the old, and everyone in between." DL took a breath and smiled.

I watched the radio anchor as DL spoke. He was truly touched by what was said and appeared to be glassy eyed. This was DL's baby, he loved radio and he sincerely believed in our goals, so I let him do most of the talking. I stuck to things that I knew best, thanking those who did their part to make the show what it's going to be, GREAT! The interview lasted fifteen minutes, but seems like only seconds.

"Again thank you both for joining us in the studio today. It was indeed a pleasure speaking with you. There you have it, folks, the first ever Adak Seabee Talent Show. Don't miss out on the event of the year!"

When we left the news station, we were flying high on cloud nine. We danced and cheered through the halls with excitement.

Yes, I will be the first to admit it, I loved the attention. It was our fifteen minutes of fame and I'm not sorry to say that it was slowly going to our heads and we loved every minute of it.

*   *   *

I was happy to have Jack as my supervisor, he was great about allowing me time away from the shop to attending production meetings between

DL and I, and of course the numerous volunteers to get this show off the ground. Everyone had their assigned duty, and everyone was important.

Our command was very surprised about my sudden enthusiasm both with work and getting involved with the community more extensively. They saw a side of me that they had never thought existed before. Much to their disbelief, I really was a multi-talented and an outgoing person. *Ok, I feel like tooting my own horn a little.* I never gave my health a second thought as we planned, scheduled, and prepared for the wildest ride of our lives. DL and I had already decided in the preplanning stages that we were going to be the Masters of Ceremonies, but we wanted to do an act in the show as well. We wanted to create and be part of a very memorable finale, but we were stumped on what act we should do. We kept envisioning some type of song at the end of the show. It would prove that Seabees could carry a tune. There was one song that we both were drawn too, "You Don't Bring Me Flowers" by Neil Diamond and Barbara Streisand. Two things were against us, it was a slow song, really nothing to get up and dance to. The other problem, DL just couldn't get his voice to allow him to sing one word in the song. The word was, anymore. He hated how his voiced sounded. I have to say, he was a trooper and kept practicing, but with no luck, until his creative and outgoing crazy side hit him – hard.

"Fallon! I got it! I know how we can pull this off!" exclaimed DL, as he quickly entered the paint shop after morning muster. "I couldn't sleep all night! It's GENIUS! I couldn't wait to tell you!"

"Have you been practicing or something? Have you been drinking? Slow down. Tell me what's going on in that unique mind of yours." I didn't know what to expect, but with DL, I was ready for just about anything.

"Barbara is not going to sing with Neil!"

"She's not? Ok Smarty…who's she gonna sing with?"

"Bob!" He said with the biggest shit eating grin I have ever seen.

"Bob? Bob from your shop?" I feared the worst and hoped he wouldn't say yes that it was Bob.

Remember I still had sandwiches missing from my picnic basket, getting better, but still clueless at times.

"BOB DYLAN!" He yelled out.

I burst into a roar of rib tickling laughter, "That's GREAT! Nobody will ever expect that one. We'll have them all laughing their blues away."

"Yes we will!" He laughed just thinking about it.

DL could imitate Bob Dylan and many other performers with sheer perfection. Nobody, including our talent show crew knew what our intentions were and as hard as it was, we kept it highly confidential until our performance.

*   *   *

It was thirty minutes until curtain time. Nerves, pacing, butterflies, and endless questioning, about the outcome of the show, filtered through the minds of all the performers and production crews. DL and I kept each other calm, though to this day cannot recall how.

"DL, Fallon, I can't believe all the people waiting to get in and the theater is just about full!" exclaimed Roger from the projection booth. He was equipped with a two-way radio head set that connected to ours and several others backstage. He had a small window that looked into the Bering lobby just outside the theater. "Take a peek you are not going to believe it!"

We peered around curtains and were astonished.

"Fallon, did you expect any of this?" DL said in awe.

"Never in my wildest dreams," I muttered, with a sudden case of severe stage fright.

We couldn't believe our eyes as the auditorium quickly filled resulting in a packed house with standing room only. We had exceeded the safety limit of patrons, but even the fire and police departments were there to be a part of the hype. There was no way they were going to miss this. More reports came in over our headphones.

"Hey guys, we need someone to bring us more boxes A.S.A.P! Families are bringing bags and arms filled with food donations! Please, someone, bring more boxes up here fast!"

We were saved by the clerk working in the Mini Mart located just outside the theater. She quickly scrambled up a few boxes to help keep the donations organized, and business was booming in her store too.

This was not what we anticipated. As we both made our way to the back of the theater to start the show, there were people everywhere. Families and friends, strangers and familiar faces waiting in amazement and wanting to see for themselves if this was indeed going to be the show of the century. We had asked for assistance from the police department to help us get through the crowd and to keep the main aisles clear for our entrances. It was utter chaos and a pure adrenaline rush as people pushed and shoved to speak to us. *I loved every bit of it.*

Over the house speakers you could hear an officer asking patrons to please keep the main aisles clear as they would be used several times throughout the show.

"Ok, this is it DL. Take a deep breath and say a prayer, your dream is about to come true." Taking another deep breath I exclaimed, "Let's shake things up and rock the roof of this place!"

I then needed a quick moment to regroup. *I can do this, I can do this.*

"Are you ready Fallon? Take your place for our entrance, this show is about to begin." DL asked calmly.

"I'm as ready as I'll ever be," then I took another deep breath.

"ALL RIIIIGHT!" He yelled from deep within him for everyone in the audience to hear. He was pumped and ready.

Then suddenly it happened, the moment we had been planning for six long weeks was taking place at this very moment. The house lights went down and the music began.

"That's our cue!" we both said with a smile and in our own special spotlights we both jogged down the two side aisles and met together up onto center-stage.

The audience cheered, clapped and whistled as the show was now underway. To make our transitions move smoothly between acts that needed additional set up time, DL and I also created ways to keep the audience continually entertained. We had drawings for prizes donated by base shops and home business owners. We also arranged for a couple special guests – Santa Clause, who passed out candy canes during the intermission, and Elvis Presley. Yes, the King was alive and well on Adak thanks to DL's ability to impersonate Elvis and my ability to run a mean sewing machine and hot glue gun. The crowd went wild with every moment the show moved forward. People laughed until they cried, they cheered and sang with the music, and some even danced in the aisles. It was what we had envisioned from the very start plus fifty levels more. But never in our wildest of wild imaginations did DL and I ever expect the response we got when we did our version of Bob Dylan and Barbara Streisand singing, "You Don't Bring Me Flowers."

The crowd roared when DL took the performance to a whole other level by using his harmonica to add to the twist. Even I didn't know of his added intentions and had to do my best not to laugh during my singing. As we completed our act and took a bow, everyone in the audience rose to their feet and gave us a standing ovation that lasted over five minutes. We smiled at each other as we knew we had done what we set out to do.

After the prizes were awarded, DL and I said an extra special thanks by having those who helped on our crew, come out by name for all to see. They were honored that we had recognized them too. We also surprised them by arranging a celebration at one of the Longview-A barracks lounges to watch the video replay of the show, enjoy delicious snacks, drink strong alcoholic drinks and do what the Seabees do best, find a reason to party long and hard. This was the best reason ever.

* * *

My choice to participate with the show was the best decision I had ever made. Not only did my feelings of depression completely go away, it made the time pass at record speed. What also went quickly was the week after the show before going on leave to be with Don and then he would be returning back to Adak with me, to start our new lives together. I have to say, I didn't get much work done with all the calls, letters, and visits by people to express profound joy for making their Christmas on Adak one they'll remember forever. Yet of all the responses DL and I had gotten, it was an anonymous letter that touched our hearts. Written in the brilliant of red pens on beautiful stationary, it simply said,

"The Christmas spirit is alive and well on Adak – Love Santa."

Chapter Twenty
Distant Cries for Help

Since our arrival back from the three weeks of leave after Christmas, living in Adak, Alaska began to have its pros and cons. I think I can safely say, that those who had been stationed on Adak, during my tour, would agree. Many times, it gave its residents a feeling of entrapment with its limited services and its incredible distance from the mainland. The mainland was otherwise known as the lower 48. You couldn't just hop onto the next plane which was the only limited means of transportation to and from the island if the weather cooperated. Any time people wanted to depart or arrive on Adak, they had to give a minimum of a 24-hour notice. This also included government officials. Active duty members or specialized contractors wanting to depart from the island had to submit a request known as a chit.

The problem about being active duty was that was not the only requirement. A chit also had to be submitted and approved by all commanding officers connected to the department that you worked in. In most circumstances, a chit was returned within 72 hours, five signatures, and a comment of approval by the commanding officer of Public Works. Yes, in most circumstances you were approved, but disapproval could also result. All it took was one person to refuse to check yes next to their signature. This became a constant reoccurrence, for many personnel, after I returned from my treatments in Tacoma, Washington. Big changes were on the horizon, and I was thankful that health wise, all was fine in the Land of Oz.

Being so isolated from the lower 48, I felt I was working for a secluded underground private government within the military. Several of the upper ranking officers suffered from a serious God complex. I believe that they thought they held a special power. In their minds, nobody was going to get on or off the base unless they wanted them to. Because of this, many things happened up there that were brushed under the carpet. Most commands knew they had 24-hours before an inspector or higher dignitary would arrive, so they had time to create the illusion that everything was grand on our tiny island.

I was beginning to feel that I was falling victim to this secluded government escapade when in December of 1993, the unthinkable happened to me. I found out on December 6, I was approximately six weeks pregnant – the one thing I was told could not happen if I wanted to continue my duties on Adak. Upon my learning of my pregnancy, I immediately called my doctor in Tacoma, for some guidance. After several connections, I finally heard his voice.

"Good afternoon, Dr. Branzell speaking."

"Yes, good afternoon Dr. Branzell…this is Constructionmen Bentley… Fallon Bentley, the one with ITP, from Adak," I said, hoping he would remember me from his large list of patients.

"Yes, I do remember you, how could I forget anyone wanting to stay in Adak for duty. How are you feeling? How is life in Adak? It's been… what, since you were in Anchorage for some medical follow ups that I heard about you? I never heard anything bad, so I marked your chart that all was ok." He replied sounding a bit rushed. It was obvious he had patients waiting.

"Well, sir, things are not going all that well …you see … since the time you heard about me, Dr. Palmer got angry. He felt that I had gone over his head by asking the doctor in Anchorage to call you about what was going on with my health. Since then he has completely and utterly ignored my continued request for help, but that's not why I am calling." I said hesitantly, "Sir…I…um…just found out that I'm six weeks pregnant."

"Pregnant! I was under the impression that you were unable to have children. You did tell me that, correct?!"

"Yes, sir, my gynecologist told me that many years ago."

"Are you finished taking your steroids? That could have a serious effect on the baby," he said very concerned.

"Yes, sir, but I have been feeling very weak and thought it was due to the pregnancy."

"Your body has been through a lot in these past few months, and being pregnant could cause some serious medical conditions or could even cause your condition to spontaneously reoccur. My feelings are that you should be back in the states where your health can be monitored more efficiently. I will make some phone calls to your caregivers there as well as fax a letter of recommendations to them and your command."

"Thank you so much for your help." I felt that a giant weight had been lifted off my shoulders.

"I will be in touch with you *very* soon," were the last words I heard before he hung up the phone.

Dr. Branzell kept his word and made several attempts to contact my doctors in Adak, but to no avail. All of his return phone call requests, over a three week time frame, had received no responses. At one point he had tried calling my command to get in contact with me, but I was never informed of the call. He finally got a hold of me at my home in Adak, during a lunch break. He requested that I get a fax number for both my command and for the Adak Branch Medical Hospital. That was not going to be an easy feat with everyone knowing what I was up to.

With the help of an insider I worked with, located in Public Works and the Medical Center, I was able to secretly obtain many direct phone numbers and fax numbers. When I returned to work after my lunch, Jack came in and told me that I need to report immediately upstairs to the administration office. They wanted to see my ASAP!

"WHAT NOW?" I thought. But I knew perfectly well that it was because of the letter that the doctor, well on this letter it was signed Lt. Colonel Branzell, had faxed.

Now being that I was well versed in the strategic military tactics of C.Y.A. (Cover Your Ass), I also knew what I would say and do.

I would point the finger at the Adak Branch Medical Hospital. I'll play up my, feel bad for me kitten eyes look, along with my very best imitation of the dumb blonde. This is exactly what I did. *People forget my hair color comes from a nice little box. I was not born with it. There is nothing dumb about me.*

I was to do to them, what they had done to me, when I asked for a request chit I had submitted, but was told it was lost or they knew nothing about it. I was about to give them a taste of their own medicine. I denied any knowledge that Dr. Branzell was aware of my current health conditions. Truly an Oscar-winning moment.

As I arrived in the office, there was at least five command members stewing in a small circle, all interested in a piece of paper. When I requested permission to enter…all eyes were upon me, and ready to enter me into the largest butt kicking contest of the North.

"Constructionmen Bentley…would you care to explain," said my first class supervisor of our builder shop.

My thoughts were a raging flood consuming a small unsuspecting town. *"I'd love to explain that your ass should be brought up on sexual harassment charges. You are always trying to touch the woman in our shop. How you get behind us and motion as if you were doing it doggy style so the guys laugh."*

"FALLON! Care to answer the question?"

"About what?" I responded with my kitten eyes and innocent game face.

"This letter from a doctor in Tacoma, Washington," said a Senior Chief, looking really pissed off. "What's going on here?!" he bellowed.

"Sir, would it be ok if I could look at the letter so that maybe I could find some closure to this situation?" I spoke with my best Marilyn Monroe voice with a twist of my New England accent.

He was easy to sweet talk, as the rumor had it, he was easy.

"Here read it, but don't run off with it…I want a copy for my files."

"Thank you, Senior," I said with a smile and a small nibble to my lip, while trying concealing the little dancing devil on my shoulder. It was hard not to read without a grin coming across my face as my eyes took in every line.

December 7, 1993

Department of the Army
Madigan Army Medical Center
Tacoma, Washington 98431-5000

Reply to
Attention of
Hematology/Oncology Service

Re: Fallon Lake-Bentley, AD/USN
SSN: 20-000-000-0000

To whom it may concern:

Fallon Lake-Bentley was a patient at Madigan Army Medical Center in July of 1992. She had a disorder (autoimmune thrombocytopenia) characterized by a low platelet count, which can be associated with a high risk of hemorrhage. She was treated successfully and returned to duty. This disorder can recur spontaneously and particularly during pregnancy. When this disorder relapses during pregnancy there may be an increased risk of fetal hemorrhage.

Mrs. Lake-Bentley should be stationed near to or referred to a medical facility that can monitor her periodically for platelet counts and for the presence of antiplatelet antibodies, which is the best indicator of fetal hemorrhage risk. This care is available at Madigan Army Medical Center through the hematology Clinic and the Obstetrics Clinic.

If I can be of further assistance, please call me at (555) 555-2504/2505.

Alexander V. Branzell
LTC, MC
Fellow, Hematology/Oncology Services

Dr. Branzell, had done exactly what he had promised he would do to help me. After the command received his letter of recommendation, they contacted the Adak Branch Medical Hospital. What a shock it was to my command when they discovered that they had also received a copy of the same letter on their private fax machine number. They knew someone was lying. *To quote a song from Britney Spears, "Oops, I did it again…I'm not that innocent."*

CHAPTER TWENTY-ONE

HEAVENLY GUIDANCE

I was only a month pregnant with my first son Dallas, and I was home alone while Don was out plowing the roads of our little island. I was lying on our couch trying to ease my tension of dealing with my command. It was just after dark and the house was illuminated with only the lights from our television set and our little Christmas tree. I was covered up with a quilt that Don's mother had made him many years ago, and laid my head on a soft pillow as I watched a Christmas special on television. I started to worry about the baby and prayed it was going to make it to term. I worried that with all the stress I was dealing with, would my pregnancy go smoothly?

"There is no way I'm going to fall asleep, being this tense." I thought to myself. Yet being pregnant, it didn't matter, sleep always came easy and I drifted off.

"Come with me," said a comforting voice.

I felt refreshed and well rested, but something was very different. As I turned to stand up, there before me it stood.

"What a beautiful elevator," I said softly.

I entered and the doors closed behind me. It was crafted like no elevator that I had ever seen or been in. It was made of hand-etched glass and gold. All I could think was that I was on heaven's elevator. As it went up I could look out and gaze down upon the beautiful landscape of the island. The snow had stopped and the yellow of the streetlights made the new fallen snow glisten in the shade of sparkling gold.

"Breathtaking, simply breathtaking," I said in amazement.

Before long we reached high enough to meet the clouds and there was nothing more that could be seen. The elevator stopped and the doors opened to the sound of Nickelodeon music and the smell of flowers and burning chestnuts. It reminded me of a trip that my mother and I took to New York City at Christmas time during my high school years. I stepped out into a park like setting. To my left there was a stone wall and wrought iron fence cascaded with beautiful pink climbing rose bushes. In front of it sat a young couple on a wooden park bench. There was a man selling chestnuts from a vending cart with oversized bicycle wheels and an eye-catching rainbow colored umbrella. Many people were walking by me and would say hello, when my attention was drawn to a lady walking towards me. As she grew closer to where I stood, she began to reach out her hands. She seemed very excited to see me.

"Hello Fallon." She said with a smile.

"Nana?"

"Yes, it's me."

"Nana...you died." I said in disbelief that she stood before me. "Did I die too?"

"Oh no. I have something I must tell you. Your baby is a boy and he is going to be fine, but you will face a long hard road in order to be home with him."

I looked at her as she spoke; she was no longer pale and her long dark hair with auburn highlights was silky and colorful. There was not one sign of aging to be found. She moved without the restrictions of a stroke that she had suffered when I was very young. Her dress was red velvet that she had accented with a strand of pearls and a pillbox hat that matched so nicely. She removed her white gloves and touched my hands. They were her hands. They were Nana's hands that were soft and smooth just like I had remembered as a child.

"I am sorry that I had not come to see you more before you died, I was so confused about what I was doing and who I was. Living in Meredith was just not working out and I knew I just had to get away. Then the dream to find my mystery man, I just had to find him. That is why I joined the military as I knew he was in the military. I found him, Nana, his name is Don and I know you would have loved him."

Beside her stood a tall and slender man, yet he was turned away from me and I could not see his face. He was dressed in a dress blue military uniform and wearing his Dixie cup white hat.

"Nana," I said as I tried to keep from crying, "I am sorry."

"I have to go now, remember you have a long road ahead of you, but you will already know the answers."

"Answers to what?" I replied as the vision of her faded into a cloud of white.

"Fallon, Fallon."

"Don is that you?"

"Fallon, wake up I'm home."

I opened my eyes and there he stood, cold and covered in snow.

"Snowing? It's still snowing?" was all I could say to him.

"Yes, you must have fallen asleep. I got us McDonalds for dinner. Are you feeling any better? Are you able to hold anything down if you eat?" Don said in his sweet caring voice.

"Uh...ya...sure."

"That must have been some dream. You've been having a lot of those lately haven't you?"

"Yes, and they all feel so real. It kinda scares me sometimes."

It wasn't until I told my mother about my dream that I found out the man in the uniform was her father. He had died when she was a very small child. He had also been a Seabee in the Navy back during WWII. What was very haunting about this dream was when my mother had indicated that I described an outfit that my Nana had worn to my mother's wedding.

Little did I know that my life would soon be filled, with more of these tell-tale twilight sleep dreams. Some would offer answers to future events. While others were only just images for me to decipher their meanings. Taking the information my Nana had commented about in my heavenly encounter, I was ready to take on anything that was coming my way.

* * *

After several attempts to get someone to listen within my command, the walls I kept slamming into got larger and larger. I was the talk of the command, and nobody wanted to hear what I had to say. Many throughout my chain of command became the victims of a terrible and contagious illness called selective hearing. They were working diligently on getting my new command transfer orders changed from the projected date of June 21, 1994 to April 16, 1994, and they were making sure I was transferring alone. They were going to make Don stay in Adak. Their plan, if he was still here alone, the possibility of his being sent to another battalion was high. They would finally separate us. It was after I had exhausted all avenues and completely followed all military guidelines, including numerous requests to speak to the Captain of the base; I made the conscious choice to get our congressman involved. My letter read as follows:

Attention: Gov. Alan Tremont

My name is Fallon L. Bentley. I am an active duty member of the United States Naval Service. For the past two weeks my husband, Donald R. Bentley, also active duty Navy, and myself have been trying to get his orders changed to transfer from Adak, Alaska on June 21, 1994 to Annapolis, Maryland on April 16, 1994.

The reason we are asking for this change is due to the letter received from Lt. Col. Alexander V. Branzell. M.D. of the United States Army at Madigan Army Medical Center in Tacoma, Washington. Last year I was repeatedly seen by my Navy doctors here in Adak, Alaska for chronic fatigue and lower abdominal pains. I was told repeatedly that it was just a female thing and was given Motrin and sent on my way. I then suffered from a bad tooth infection and was given a high dose of a drug called Vibramycin for 10 days during the month of May in 1992.

On July 18, 1992, I was taken to the emergency room for repeated lower abdominal pains. When they did a routine CBC blood test, they discovered I had a very low platelet count (29 thousand to be exact). Low platelet, otherwise known as autoimmune thrombocytopenia, ITP, is when the blood becomes very thin, water like and is unable to clot. For example if I were to cut or bruise myself in any way, I could have bled to death.

The Army doctors believe that my condition was caused by the drug I was given in May. It was stated in my medical record prior to my entering the military that I was allergic to medications ending in CIN, such as Penicillin, Erythromycin, etc. I was still given this drug and ordered by the doctors here, to complete the entire prescription.

I was transferred to Madigan Army Medical Center on July 20, 1992, but instead was sent to Bremerton Naval Hospital. The doctors were very undereducated on my condition and placed me on a five-day liquid diet. I was only there six hours when they were notified by Madigan I was to be sent to them. I was admitted for seven days and my condition was stabilized with 80mgs of prednisone, another treatment for ITP is the removal of the spleen.

I was released from the hospital and placed into a medical holding company unit the twenty-eighth day of August of 1992. The only reason I was sent back to Adak, Alaska, was due to the fact I told my doctors I wanted to return and that I was told by past doctors that I was unable to have children. Otherwise Madigan would have not approved my return to Active duty in Adak, Alaska, due to the risks involved. On December 6, 1993, I was notified that I was into my sixth week of pregnancy. My doctor in Madigan has issued a letter confirming my risks. He has also made phone calls to the doctors here, but once again, the Navy doctors do not understand the risks involved and won't consider the risks until something happens to me again.

They did place me on a light duty chit that states no prolonged walking or standing and no lifting, thinking that my condition will not return. As stated in the letter from my doctor in Madigan, this condition can spontaneously happen.

All that we have been asking is that my husband be allowed to transfer with me in April of 1994 to Annapolis, Maryland. Because of my condition I would be unable to take on the responsibilities of getting our household goods, carrying my bags and pets onto the planes to Maryland, and to find permanent living quarters within the area. What would happen if my condition were to return during this transition period of getting settled in a new area?

My husband had done all the proper paper work that the Navy has required to have his orders changed. But because of a few Navy medical doctors here on Adak, we are at a standstill that could be life threatening to myself and our unborn child. I don't understand why we support these people 24-hours a day, but they refuse to support us during our time of need. I have wanted children for many years, and I don't want to lose this child because my real doctor is from the Army. I can't stand the thought that myself and our child could be placed in danger because some Navy doctors here are undereducated and don't understand my condition, which I have to live with the rest of my life because they gave me a drug I am allergic too. We ask that you please help us in our delicate situation. I personally thank you in taking the time to review our situation.

If you need any further information please contact me at (907) 555-5555 or (907) 555-0000. Again thank you.

Sincerely,
BUCN Fallon L. Bentley
U.S.N.

*   *   *

After Governor Tremont received my letter, a call was made to my command at Public Works. How do I know this? In the eyes of everyone, in my chain of command, was the incandescent flame of fire that also colored their faces in the same fashion, when they would see me. I honestly believed that if they could have gotten away with it, I would have come up missing. *Fish bait to put it bluntly.*

We were also instructed to follow our chain of command when dealing with *all* situations by filling out the proper request forms known in the Navy as chits. *No shit, been there, done that, have copies of them!*

I had already done everything that they were telling me, as if it were my first time. How quickly they forget they were the ones that taught me the C.Y.A.'s of the Navy. I knew how to, and did, always cover my ass. I kept copies of all the proper request chits I submitted to speak with various people that made up my command, including my request to speak with the Captain of the base. I was a pack rat, I kept everything. *Thank God for email now.*

Funny thing though, all of these request chits that I had submitted and had copies for, would be mysteriously circular-filed or otherwise thrown away. They also got clever, with every request date I was asking for to speak to the Captain of the base, they would schedule a spontaneous and mandatory uniform inspection. How pathetic!

Every day I pondered over and over if I had the right to contact my congressman about my situation. Did I do the right thing? *Your damn straight I did!*

After what seemed like months of endless confrontations and non-stop verbal harassment from numerous Public Works commanding officers and the commanding officers of the Adak Branch Medical Hospital, Don and I were finally granted orders and transferred on April 6, 1994, to begin a new life in Annapolis, Maryland and become a part of a new unit, Construction Battalion Unit 403, Naval Station Annapolis. It was just on the other side of the river from the United States Naval Academy.

Hope filled my heart when I found out that the Naval Academy was where my training for LDO (Officers Training School) was located. A light began to shine on the horizon.

CHAPTER TWENTY-TWO

THE CALM, BEFORE THE STORM

Everyone in their lives has experienced both hope and heartbreak. My family is no stranger to this concept; in fact, sometimes I think we invented this process. But seriously, I know that what it boils down to is that life happens. These next two chapters were by far the most challenging to put into words. The magnitude of emotion that my family and I had endured is a cold, disturbing reality, which I know that I should have heeded the guidance and advice of those concerned. Seek therapy.

Instead I adapted to a process of blocking bad things out in my mind. Slowly over the years I have been forced to come to terms with many sad and life threatening moments, that with each revelation, a new door, within my subconscious gives me the ability to smile, accept, and in even some cases, forgive.

One thing I never blocked - *spring of 1994*. Nobody told us or could have ever prepared for the permanent personality altering event that was going to turn our lives upside-down.

* * *

It was April 1994, and we had just signed the papers on the purchase of our new home located in Annapolis, Maryland. This was a big deal in our lives outside the anticipation of our first child. We were so excited to be living off the base. We had both agreed on the choice, to buy a home, months before transferring from Alaska. Thought again, many within the service did not agree. *They wouldn't be consistent if they did.*

Their opinions were that the only way to get the true military experience was base housing all the way baby. I am not saying I didn't fully agree, base housing did have a few fringe benefits; no maintenance work, no rent payments, no utility payments except for the must have, cable television. The biggest benefit was the freedom to move or transfer at the drop of a hat. There were no worries of having to give a landlord notice of vacancy, or having the hassles of selling a home.

These reasons for us, were understandable, but the drawback, so many families living in such close quarters offered very little space and privacy. Community roaches, was something that we were given a heads up about, that plagued some of the base housing in Annapolis, before it was renovated. The only downside to our owning a home off the base, having to leave the house earlier to get to work on time due to traffic.

Life was going as planned as we began our daily routine with our new command. We were now part of Construction Battalion Unit 403 aka, CBU 403. It was located on the Naval Station side of the Chesapeake Bay. Don enjoyed working with the Equipment Operators and Mechanics. I unfortunately, was place in the front office to work the desk, due to my pregnancy. They felt it was too risky to be working in the builder trade. *Ok, they expressed a little concern.*

I hated the idea of working up front with all the officers of the command. I swallowed my pride and accepted the jokes of the other Seabees working in their trades. I was now the newest, in what was known in the military as, an office Twinkie.

During the first part of May, I began to develop, as one would say, anxiety attacks that were in no relation to my job. The more I tried to shake it, the more intense it became. Every time I'd start thinking about the future, this form of stress and worry would come over me. I feared what would happen to Don and the baby if I were to die? *I know, just a tad bit morbid for someone about to become a new mommy.*

At the same time I was thinking like this, the news was reporting, on a daily basis, the health concerns of former First Lady Jacqueline Kennedy Onassis and her battle with Non-Hodgkin's disease. There had also been a story about a professional hockey player, who had been also battling, Hodgkin's disease. I was captivated by these two stories and followed their outcomes intently. I developed a strong interest in learning all about these two diseases and how they affected the body. It wasn't until I learned that these two diseases were forms of cancer, that I was paralyzed with fear as it cut through me like a dull steak knife.

"Why?" I wondered.

I was deeply saddened when I heard on a special news bulletin on May 19, 1994, Ms. Onassis, had lost her battle with Non-Hodgkin's, while the Hockey players Hodgkin's had appeared to have gone into remission. Along with the sadness of the loss of the First Lady, the yearning to have to know more about Hodgkin's disease filled my every waking thought. Who knows, maybe reading about these illnesses was not a good idea for someone dealing with ample hormonal emotions associated with pregnancy. Either way, these unexplained anxieties had found their way into my daily thoughts and dreams.

*   *   *

The day was a sunny Monday morning, late in the month of May. It was May 24, 1994, to be exact. I was looking forward to my first visit with my new OB-GYN, following our morning muster at the command. My last exam had been in Alaska, so it had been about a month since I had seen any doctors. My medical care was transferred to the National Naval Medical Center in Bethesda, Maryland.

I was excited to see how my unborn baby was doing. Hearing the sounds of my little boy's tiny baby heartbeat was always calming. It made me think of the melody of a slow song being performed on a violin, very angelic. It made every bad situation that I had experienced, simply fade away. A little person was growing inside of me, a life that was created by Don and I, a tiny miracle. This day, however with the excitement, a sense of worry and uncertainty was looming.

As we got into the truck to head to my appointment, I turned to Don. With all the strength one would have, I could not keep these words from falling from my lips, "Don't be surprised if they admit me today."

"What? What in the world would make you say a thing like that!" he remarked with extreme concern.

"I just have a bad feeling that something isn't right." I responded calmly.

"Do you think your I.T.P. is back? Do you have any of the symptoms? Is it the baby? Tell me Fallon!"

"No, it's none of those things."

"Then you're just over thinking things. You do that so well. I bet you're just nervous about delivering the baby and thinking how painful it may be. Don't worry sweetness; everything is going to be fine. Isn't that what you keep telling me?" He smiled. He loved to put my words back in my face.

"I guess so." Not accepting his words of encouragement eagerly.

"You're due date isn't until August, so relax." he said with a smile of assurance.

I didn't fully understand the reasoning behind my initial comment, yet I did know it was going to happen. None of my past appointments had indicated a reason to be worried or concerned. Nothing suggested that the baby or myself, was in any type of danger.

The only that was different, but seemed to be of no concern, was a small lump in the tissue over my right collar bone. It had been there since my pregnancy began. Each time I made mention of it in Alaska, no one, including my doctors, seemed alarmed. Well at least no one until this time. This appointment was going to be like none I had ever imagined, but I was not afraid. Somewhere inside myself I was preparing for a long journey that somehow I already knew about, and knew the answer to as well. I chose to refrain from continuing this conversation with Don, and went on to baby names.

CHAPTER TWENTY-THREE

THE DIAGNOSIS

"Good Morning Mr. and Mrs. Bentley," said Mrs. Robbins, my doctor's assistant.

"Good Morning Ma'am," Don and I replied in unison.

"So do we know what we're having? A boy or a girl?" she grinned as if she had the magic answer.

"I feel it is a boy," I said confident in my response.

"The moms are usually right, we'll see." she replied as she began to exit the room.

"Wait!"

"Yes?"

"Is my doctor a man or a woman? Then shyly tipping my head down asked, "What size hands do they have?"

"Excuse me?" Don responded in disbelief that I would even ask such a question.

Now I don't know the feelings of every woman in the world, but to me there is just something about going to the gynecologist just has my undies in an uproar. Then to be told, put your legs up in the stirrups and scoot my ass to the edge of the table; that just sounds so wrong or kinky depending on who's undergoing the exam. Since being pregnant, these appointments now have added the displeasure of extreme tenderness, especially when the doctor starts feeling around inside my personal cervical cave. *The word vagina just sounds so complicated. Don't you agree?*

I found that with my previous exams, doctors with longer fingers were able to perform an exam with minimal pain. As for the doctors with the short stubby fingers…well, you do the math.

Without a second thought, she quickly calmed Don down with her reasonable reply. "Don't worry hon; this is not a question that has not been asked before. Many mothers have pain associated with these exams and prefer someone with slender hands. I'll be right back if you have any more questions, ok dear?" Then she went into the adjoining room to inform the doctor that I was ready for my exam.

I was so relieved to see that my new doctor had slender hands. I am also pleased to report that the procedure was successful, no pain was felt. The baby seemed to be growing nicely and that the heartbeat sounded very active. Things were going as planned and that by his calculations, I would be delivering somewhere in the first part of August. As the doctor prepared to leave, Don quickly mentioned the lump over my collar bone.

"A lump?" He questioned, "What lump?"

"You can feel it, and it is the size of a navy bean." I said, rather blasé.

The doctor stood in front of me and with his hands began to feel behind my ears, down my neck and across my shoulders. He repeated this several times, never once making any kind of comment.

"Give me a few minutes. Wait right here, don't go anywhere." He said with a rushed sound to his voice.

What was going to be a few minutes was quickly becoming a half an hour. Don and I had no clue what was going on and began to envision all types of bad scenarios. When the clock had indicated that nearly forty-five minutes had passed, my doctor and three other people came into my examination room. All wearing name tags and patches on the white lab coats that said, Hematology.

"Hematology? Hematology? Why does that sound familiar?" I thought as I struggled to remember where I had seen that name. *"MADIGAN! TACOMA! My I.T.P.! Was back! NO! Please NO!"*

Don stood in a daze and remained silent. He couldn't speak, and looked to be in total disbelief. There was absolutely no doubt, he immediately knew what that clinic name stood for.

"Fallon, this is Dr. Mulligan, and her assistants from the hematology clinic. They want to run some tests on you today and tomorrow.

"Tests?" I said, waiting for my words I spoke earlier in the day to Don, to be put back in my face.

"We are going to admit you. This way you won't have to drive back and forth in the beltway traffic and if we have additional tests that we may need, you'll be here at the ready. Most of the tests cannot be performed until tomorrow morning."

"Yes, I know."

When I looked over at Don, he was astonished at what he had just heard and tears were affecting his strength to hide his fears. I stood up forcing the doctor to refrain from pawing over me. I needed to hug Don, I needed to touch him, and I needed him to know that whatever lay ahead of us, we were going to face head on, together.

*   *   *

The next 24-hours were filled with very little sleep and lots of needles. Something I despised more than anything, needles! Doctors were performing blood work, x-rays, ultra sounds, blood pressure readings, you name it. If they hadn't done it, I am sure they were thinking about it. But the worse for this time frame, a needle aspiration of the lump to see what fluid or tissue, if any, it contained. I will admit that I was doing my best to keep up a great front of no fear. When they had to put a needle into my collar bone tissue, I couldn't understand why they needed to go in so deep. *Little did I know.* I found it harder and harder to keep from getting upset. Don held my hand through the entire procedure and talked about what type of decorations were we going to put in the baby's room.

His conversation stopped when the fluid from the lump was placed on a slide and put under a microscope. There was an immediate hush that froze the movement in the entire room. The last thing I remember hearing, one serious statement… it's malignant. It was a form of cancer.

What was to be an overnight stay was quickly changed. I was rushed over to hematology to do additional blood work and to have a patient record generated. They decided they wanted additional tests that included a C.A.T. scan and a bone marrow biopsy that could not be scheduled right away. Having been through a bone marrow biopsy, I was glad to know that it was not going to be done right away and was something that mentally I had to get ready for. If I had my way though, it would not be done at all. But it was important that they knew all they could before making any decisions and these tests were vital.

The day light hours slowly faded into a dusky evening shade of blue grey. I got back to my room just before a dinner plate arrived. Don had decided that he was going to go home to get a clean change of clothes and let the command know what was going on.

"I'll be back, first thing tomorrow, ok?" he was spent.

"We'll be waiting for you." I said with a smile as I put his hand on my belly so he could feel the baby. "Don't worry, were going to be just fine. You go home, take a nice hot shower and get some sleep."

He then pulled me to him and wrapped his arms around me. I always felt so safe in his arms, that I wished that his arms would also be able to pull this cancer out of me.

"I love you Fallon. We can get through this, right?"

"Yes, together we can. Whatever they find, it is not going to hurt me. I won't let it."

You could see the depth of his pain as he gathered his things and slowly walked out of the room. He didn't want to go, but we both knew it was best. He was so tired from the night before. The hospital was nice enough to give him a lounger to sleep in since I didn't have another person in my room, but he was too worried to rest.

I think my ability to remain calm during the past 24-hours, was so that I could keep Don from reliving the experience we faced with my blood problem in 1992. I knew that this time things were going to have a direct impact on how I would live the rest of my life. But I wondered why it was that I took it upon myself to learn about Hodgkin's disease. It was at the moment, I knew what the doctors were going to tell me. Never in my wildest imagination did I ever think I would be told I had cancer.

"Cancer? Life or Death?" Were the words filling my runaway train of thoughts, as I walked over and turned the lights off in my hospital room.

"I don't want to die, please God, I don't want to die. I want to see my baby grow up. I can't leave Don all alone to raise a baby. I don't want another woman raising my son! I don't want to leave them! I need them! They need me! What did I do to deserve this! I am sorry for the bad things I have ever done!" I repeated over and over again, while sitting on the corner of my hospital bed in the darkened room staring into the night from my window. I tried many times to stop the tears. Tears of hate, anger, revenge, fear, guilt, worry, hate, and anger. My tears of self-pity were the worst.

"I WANT IT OUT OF ME!" I screamed out loud.

Yes, at one point I honestly believed that if I ran far away, it would go away.

"No Fallon, you've got to be strong, you have to be strong for the baby, for Don, for yourself!" I thought as I tried to smile through the heartbreak.

"Running away won't make your illness disappear," said a voice from behind me.

With only the accent of the hallway light entering the room I could only see her silhouette. Worried that she would turn the light on, I turned and peered out my window again to hide my sorrow.

"Do I know you?" I asked trying to place the familiar voice.

There was a long pause in her response.

"Yes, I think you do." Her voice was pleasant as it carried through the darkness.

"Who are you?" I asked again.

"You will have a long journey and will follow a very hard road, so that you will be able to stay home with your son. Always remember you know the answer. Best is yet to come."

"You will follow a very hard road, where have I heard that?"

"Nana!" I cried out as I turned so that I could see her face.

No one was there. I ran into the hallway looking to see who the person was that stood in my doorway. The hallway was empty.

Nobody could move that fast, I'm at the end of the hall. Who are you really? Where did you go? How do you know about my dream?

My mind was racing and I could not catch my breath. I walked up to the nurse's station and asked if he had seen a woman come by there. His response was that the ward was closed to all visitors and that there would not be any female nurses or doctors on duty until 11:00pm. Still dazed and confused, I walked back to towards my room, I didn't believe it, but yet, I knew what I had seen. I was not crazy.

As I lay in my bed I knew that my illness was, Hodgkin's disease. Nobody had told me this. My doctors were still trying to determine what the cancer was. I already knew. I had known long before I even mentioned the lump on my neck. What makes this whole situation even more of a mystery, not only did I know what my illness was; I also knew what the cure was too.

"But would anyone listen to my new revelation?" I wondered.

The next morning Don had gotten back to the hospital just in time to hear the news about the test results of the cancer cells from the aspiration of the lump.

"How are my babies doing?" he said with his always perfect smile.

"We're just fine. Did you get any sleep?" I said worried at how red and bloodshot his eyes looked. I am sure it was a combination of crying and a lack of sleep that was the cause.

"I couldn't sleep at all last night, Fallon." He said while yawning. "We have been through some serious shit. I am afraid to go through it again and this time something will happen to you."

I was worried what he might be trying to say. I know there are men out there in the world that could have never handled the medical crap that we had already been through. I knew a few personally that couldn't take it and left their wives, life, marriage, and even their kids. It was just too hard on them.

How Don was able to deal with all this, I'll never know. But one thing I did know, no matter what, not this or anything else was going to pull Don and I apart.

"Don, I had this strange thing happen to me. I have got to tell you, you're not going to believe it. I know this is going to sound like I am crazy, but I am going to be fine and I know what my illness and my cure is. The road will be tough, but we will get through it together, trust me." I said, feeling extremely confident with what I was saying. I knew this to be true.

As I began to tell him the story of the lady in my room last night, Dr. Mulligan, and another three other fellows, as they are known in the department, came into my room to break the news to me. Before she had a chance to speak, I told her I knew I had Hodgkin's disease. Much to their surprise of how I knew this information, they confirmed that I was indeed correct and even more amazed how well I was accepting the news. What they didn't anticipate was when I told them what my cure was. Radiation therapy followed by the removal of my spleen.

That part they didn't want to discuss, but they could see that I was ready for any treatments that had in mind for me. With that, a game plan was underway.

* * *

Knowing that my mother had just lost someone to cancer, calling to tell her my diagnosis was heartbreaking. I kept a positive tone of voice when I broke the news to her. She could not believe what I was saying. I went on to tell her what the plans were at this point, that I would be starting a regiment of chemotherapy, that they felt would not endanger the baby. My treatment was called, A.B.V.D. Which are the first letters of each chemical in my treatment cocktail. Adrianmicin, Vancristine, Bleomicin and Doxarubicin. *Yes, three of the four ended with CIN and I was concerned.*

The Doxarubicin was not going to be administered until after the baby was born as that could have caused him complications.

Also on the list of to do's was to undergo a neck biopsy, have a Hickman Catheter placed into a central vein in my chest, and the worst thing of all, a double bone marrow biopsy. This time they were going to take a sample from the left and the right side of my hips. All of these procedures were going to be done with no anesthesia, only regular Tylenol for the pain. The biggest thing about the operating room procedure, this twisted form of torture was all going to be attempted while I was pregnant. There was no waiting for baby. They would induce me closer to my due date.

I was determined, in spite of the pain, I was going to get through this, somehow, someway, my goal – *I would beat this disease for my baby and Don.*

CHAPTER TWENTY-FOUR

A PERFECT EXAMPLE: TREATMENT OR TORTURE?

Going through the bone marrow biopsy this time, other than being pregnant, was not much different than the procedure done at Madigan. The pressure of a needle the size of a number two pencil, actually felt good in a warped way, it was when the marrow was aspirated into the syringe, I felt that same intense pain. There are just not enough words in the English language to explain this kind of pain. If you have ever broken a bone, well take that broken bone and have someone step on it right after it's been broken. Even that is still not enough to describe it, but rather close. One good thing about a bone marrow transplant, if you are a donor, they put you under anesthesia. Thank the Lord.

I got the bone marrow test completed, so to me the rest was going to be a walk in the park. *So So Wrong!* To prepare for my surgical procedures for my catheter and lymph-node biopsy, I pondered the thought that if given the choice, I would have opted for the bone marrow test again.

Now be it known, that even though I was determined to get through this, I was and still am, a very jumpy and unpredictable patient. But what I was about to be put through was total terror.

"I can't do this! Please let me up! Please!" I screamed with horror. I feared the procedures that my body was about to undergo. "Please Stop!"

Brilliant flashes of light blinded me as I tried helplessly to fixate on the turmoil that filled the room. Endless touches of unknown hands, position me to sit onto the hardness of a cold steel table. As if I were part of a sick sadistic form of bondage, my arms were bound with a sheet. Slowly I was helped to lean back onto the sheet and table to become my own restraint.

My breathing-labored as the utterances and commotion intensified as the silhouettes in the glow of the lights grew closer to me. I was also informed, before we entered the operating room, I was not going to be given any pain medication, just locals in the areas where they were doing the necessary procedures. This intensified my anxiety to the fullest.

"Are we ready to begin?" A distinguished voice, questioned. "You should feel extremely privileged Petty Officer...this surgical unit is the one we use for the President of the Unites States."

Maybe another day and place, this would have made me happy, but this comment did not comfort me at all.

"Please! Put me to sleep! Give me something!"

Though muffled by a cloth surgical mask, I somehow understood the deep voice that answered my cries. "Relax ma'am, I am going to give you a local, just a little something to take the edge off. As far as we know, this medication won't hurt the baby. I'm sorry that we can't put you under, it's too dangerous."

Finally someone was listening, they knew I was frightened with what was about to take place. Following an increased coolness into my left arm, I could feel the tenseness, throughout my body, slowly subsiding. Whatever the drug was, it worked quickly. Images became rather blurry, but I never revealed its effect. I knew I needed more.

"It isn't working! Please stop!" Knowing perfectly well that it was working, just not enough to put me to sleep and relieve my fears and concerns.

Again, another short burst of coolness danced into my wanting veins. Still never revealing its effect, I pleaded for more.

"We must begin the procedure" ordered the surgeon.

I lay there unable to avoid the prick of the needle as it entered the tissue framed by my right collar bone. As the needle was pushed deeper, warm bursts followed by sharp stings radiated across my shoulders and up into my neck. The constant pain was nothing I had ever felt before, until the event that shortly followed during the procedure.

"Nurse, how is the monitor on the Petty Officer's baby looking? Any distress or change in the heart rhythm?"

"All is reading normal at this time Sir."

As the deep voice spoke into my left ear to keep my attention off the procedure, A startling intense and overwhelming pain ripped through my body. I shrieked in intense horror. "WHAT ARE YOU DOING TO ME? STOP...STOP...STOP! Get it off my arm! Get it off my arm! IT'S HOT! IT'S BURNING ME!

"Get what off...OH MY GOD! LT! The cauterizer! It's on her arm!"

The entire surgical unit quickly scrambled to assist. They couldn't believe what they saw, and the smell of burning flesh was stomach-turning.

It was a new fellow, who was trying to build up OR time, that was being instructed on how to remove the lump from my neck. He was using the cauterizer to keep larger veins from bleeding heavily. Even though he was new I tolerated the idea of him doing the procedure, it was when he dropped the intensely hot iron onto my arm, and not realizing this, that pissed me off.

It was so hot that it felt ice piercingly cold. The smell, oh how that smell of burning flesh would not seem to fade away. I knew that if it was making me sick to my stomach, the others in the room must have been feeling the same way. I was extremely stressed out and I wanted out. I had enough. Because of the added stress, there was a rapid spike in my blood pressure. The doctors feared it would endanger the baby and had no choice but to make me comfortable.

"We're not anywhere near done. We'll have to give her something for the pain," said the head surgeon. "Nurse, please tend to this burn before we resume our procedures."

"Yes sir."

This time they gave me pain medication a little bit at a time, to which I would tell them that I still couldn't feel it, but I could. They had no idea what I was up to until I started singing "Winnie-the-Pooh" and the baby was also moving around as if it was on the highest of highs. The doctors knew I had been given a little too much, I love me, medication. They kept all the monitors on, watching the baby and I very closely, while they continued taking numerous samples of lymph-nodes out of my neck to test for additional cancer.

I knew this wasn't going to be the last of my many trips to the operating room. It was going to be a long, ongoing process of treatments, surgeries, and more needles that I could have ever feared. Yet, I never felt like I was going to die from this cancer and all I had to do was convince my doctors to believe me and what I knew my treatments were to cure me.

I also knew they'd never believe I got this information from a heavenly dream, and worse, if I told them it was my Nana, who died in 1990, that helped me see this, I would be deemed crazy for sure. I had to somehow get them to see the future as I did, but decided to keep the information, some of the information, to myself. Crazy was not a label I wanted added to my medical record.

CHAPTER TWENTY-FIVE

THEN AND NOW

Such a long journey, so many moments, so many memories. So fast, the years have passed me by. How I ache for the new days of my military career... How will I...

"Excuse me...Petty Officer Bentley...Ms. Bentley, are you ok?

I jumped when I realized that the true reality of it all was that I was not in the world in which I reminisced.

"Wow, where was I?" I said somewhat dazed and a bit confused. "Did you call for me Lieutenant?"

"Yes, Ma'am, I did...are you ok? Do you need anything? You look a bit pale."

"No thank you...I am ok. I'm lost in thought is all," I replied in disbelief. I just couldn't fathom I was still in the waiting room anticipating my hearing.

"Excuse me, Lieutenant, what time is it?" I asked, then smiled and chuckled when I realized the phrase I had just said.

"It's after nine o'clock; the board members should be calling you and your representative in any time now."

"Thanks," I said while still pondering the phrase that brought Don and I together.

What time is it? Oh Don...God if you could just be with me right now. I need you to hold me and reassure me that all is going to turn out just fine. I'm so afraid. Will they understand? Will they listen to me in this hearing? GOD HELP ME!

I had been so lost in my memories I never realized that the lights and a small television had been turned on in the room. Another military member, a woman, had come in and was watching the news while she awaited her hearing that was scheduled for ten o'clock.

"Guess they're running late today," I said, trying to make conversation.

"Yes, I guess so. No surprise. The desk clerk told me your case was to be heard at nine. Have you been in yet?

"Nope…nothing new though…after more than ten years of the Navy life there is one thing I have learned…"

"What's that?"

"Hurry up and wait." I responded, rolling my eyes back in my head.

She laughed, there was no doubt she totally agreed with both my statement and the added facial expressions.

"So why are you here today?" I asked, without making it sound like I was writing a book. Little did she know, I thought, holding my sarcastic giggle in.

"I had some medical problems and I am here to re-appeal a decision the board made some months back. How about yourself?" she replied in a quiet tone of voice.

"I'm here fighting for, what I believe in and what's right. This has been an ongoing issue since July of 1995, and this unnecessary process has taken me eight years. But I will tell you that today I am leaving here the winner of the battle." I remarked semi-calmly, trying to hold back the adrenaline rush I felt coming over me.

"Petty Officer Douglas, can you step into my office for a few minutes?" said a voice that I assumed was her counselor.

Once again I was alone with the endless sounds of office phones ringing just down the hallway. It must have been my attorney's office, I mused. He never answered his phone when I called him. I decided to sit down and relax for a moment to review my answers to tentative questions that may be asked during my hearing. The one big question that kept coming into my mind - why in the world was I there in the first place?

Why am I here? Do I have enough evidence to prove my case? Will I win? I have to win…I didn't do anything wrong; the military did! They didn't help me when I needed them the most…thank God I got stationed in Annapolis. The Alaskan command sent me to Annapolis to be spiteful and never realized, when then did, they saved my life!

As I sat thinking about my questions and answers, I found myself quickly returning to a special place in my memories and my mind, our home in Annapolis, Maryland, after all my cancer treatments were complete. I honestly believe that going through the treatments was easier, than coping with life and the constant unknowns that follow.

I never realized that, it was harder on the people who were bystanders, than being the one, undergoing the cancer treatments. It's also hard on the patient, to talk about what they have been through, if you live to tell about it.

CHAPTER TWENTY-SIX

LIFE GOES ON

It was early November of 1994, when the Navy Hematology team told me there wasn't anything more they could do to cure me. I had relapsed during my chemotherapy and they decided that I would be better off to try a protocol at the National Institute of Health, which just happened to be right across the street from the naval hospital.

The Navy wanted no part of what I believed would be my cure – Radiation therapy and a spleenectomy. It was at N.I.H. that I felt like the doctors and nurses were the ones who saved my life, because they finally listened to me about what I believed my cure was. N.I.H. tried me on a protocol that was another form of chemotherapy. I understood they wanted to avoid any unnecessary surgery if at all possible, but noted my treatment suggestion in the back of their minds. The new chemo cocktail was called E.P.O.C.H. It was a form of chemotherapy that you wore for an entire week that was in a fanny pack and connected to a new catheter that they had placed into my chest.

It would continuously pump the chemicals into my body for a full seven days. I had to undergo this treatment once a month. Following the treatment I had to take special medications and the nurses trained Don, to provide me with GCSF shots to aid in my immune system recovery and control any possible forms of neutropenia. The last thing I need was to catch a cold or flu bug.

Still to this day, I do not know what E.P.O.C.H. stood for, but I do know that its name was also created from the first letters of each drug they used. As for the GCSF shots, because it came in the form of a needle into my skin, I didn't care to know. Now because I still had a current hazmat license that I had obtained from ample training in Adak,

I would disconnect myself from my treatments. Don and I would store everything into control containers and we wouldn't have to return them to the hospital until the following month for treatment. Because of this, it saved us from driving almost a hundred miles, round trip, to Bethesda almost every day.

But in spite of all our training and hard work, it still did not result in any change to the growth of my cancer. In January of 1995, I relapsed once again and the chemo regiment that I was on was stopped. The fellows pondered a bone marrow transplant, but that too, would not be in the cards for me. Finally they heeded my suggestion and sent me to the radiation clinic in February of 1995. It was there, I knew that it was going to reduce the tumor and I would soon enjoy a new life with my cancer in remission.

I would lie on the radiation table, and would envision, mini angels with big garage brooms, sweeping the cancer out of me and onto the floor. The technicians told me that like clockwork every day, during my treatment, I would fall into a twilight sleep and sing very angelically. I wished someone had recorded that, because I can't carry a note in a paper bag, much less sing. Ten weeks of radiation treatments, that also included a spleenectomy, caused the tumor to begin to shrink and then fade away. My treatment worked. I was finally graced with a day that all cancer patients dream of, a road that leads to full remission.

My road to remission began one sunny morning, on the 21st day of June at 11:05am. The fast paced life of being a cancer patient, the center of attention, to most, came to an abrupt halt. No more daily visits to all the clinics that I had come to know, that rendered me the ability to walk their halls while blind folded if I had to. No more sincere, yet sympathetic smiles from the numerous doctors and nurses that I had gotten to know by their first name. What was once daily visits, were now only going to be once a month and if all went well, could someday be once a year, then once every two years and so on and so forth.

It was on this day that I was going to be sent out into the world to try to get back to a normal life. *A normal life, YEAH RIGHT! This was going to be anything but, a normal life and nobody on the outside could see my uncontrolled mental destruction taking shape in my mind.*

Outside I was bubbly and cheerful for all to see, but on the inside, a loaded fast moving, out of control train, with a granite mountain side as my breaks. At any point in time, I was going to slam head on into it, and shatter like shards of glass from a broken Corelle dish. The National Institute of Health became my security blanket and I was being told I had to part with it.

I made my rounds and said my good-byes, and gathered all the support I could. I was going to walk out of the radiation clinic for the last time. I was dazed, yet I felt my legs take one small step at a time towards the basement elevator to day light. This was my last day as a patient...the LAST DAY. Many thoughts filtered thought my mind.

Who in the world would I talk with when everyone is back to work? Will I know how to be a good mother to my son? What if my illness comes back before my next appointment? Will I see my baby grow up? Would my husband remarry if my illness came back and I died? GOD! HELP! ME! I know with all my heart that my illness is going to stay in remission, but how? How do I know this? Why? Please show me the answer...SHOW ME THE WAY!

With those feelings, I filled with a strong push that came over me with quickness, an overwhelming sense to just run away, take my family and never look back. I honestly wanted to believe that running away from Maryland would confirm that my illness would go away forever.

As I waited for the elevator, I head a familiar voice yelling from down the hall.

"FALLON! Fallon please wait!"

Looking around I saw my radiation nurse, Alice, who had listened to many stories of how sick I felt some days, to how I ended up here in the first place. She was never judgmental and she always had an ear or shoulder to lean on while she listened to my fears and dreams. These were usually my main topics of open discussion.

Alice took me aside to express her feelings about what lay ahead of me. She seemed very concerned as she was the only one that knew of my fears of trying to get on with my life. She had suggested that it would be in my best interest to join some type of support group, for patients who have finished all possible treatments and only see their physician's once a month. Her reasons were that many people develop a high-dependency during their days as a patient, whether it was for their doctors, clinics, drugs, and yes even immediate family members. For some, an anxiety sets over them when their newly added daily routine begins and their clinic appointments become spaced further apart.

Being as stubborn as I was, I insisted that I was going to be just fine and I didn't need to sit in any support group and feel bad for myself. My life was going to be normal again. In my mind it was going too happened overnight and life would be as it once was. *I don't and probably will never have a full picnic basket. Still clueless.*

For the first time in all our many days of endless conversations that we had, she looked me straight in the eyes and said to me with most sincere tone of voice, "Please, for GOD SAKES, Please, FALLON, FOR ME! Please think about what I am trying to say. I see it in you already, constant extreme personalities, some good, some bad, but I can tell you, your family will not understand! You are going to need support more than you know. Life outside these doors is not going to be a walk in the park. Great, you have conquered the illness, it's fantastic, but Fallon can you face the bigger challenge – can you conquer yourself? The waiting and the endless wonder of the unknown will consume you. I have seen this in so many patients. One day when you least expect it, you will have to deal with all that you have blocked, repressed, locked in the back of your mind, or where ever you put the pain of what you have been through. You will one day be triggered by something and you will be forced to face it...you had and could have again...CANCER! This is indeed something that you should not be dealt with while you are home alone all day. I fear depression, for you."

"Okay I will think about it, but cannot promise you anything, but if I think that I am in need of some help, I will call you." *Said like a true alcoholic, which I can honestly say I am not. I was in pure denial of a problem.*

"You can call me anytime, here are all my numbers including my home number," she said with a breath of relief and a smile. "I'll be waiting for your call." *A call that would never come.*

"Thanks for everything," I said with a cheerful response as the elevator signaled its arrival. I boarded the elevator, turned around and leaned against the back wall just in time to see and hear Alice saying good-bye and wave as the doors closed. This would be the last time I physically saw Alice. Two months later she moved to the West Coast.

* * *

All was anything but normal in the months following the daily grind of doctors, exams, blood work, and treatments. Over the next ten months, the mental game of wait, wonder, and see, was like watching an ice-cream sundae melt in the summer sun. Just as Alice, had predicted, my life just went from bad to worse. Dealing with the lack of energy, the adjustment of a day filled with a new baby to tend to, housework, bills and budgets with no money to compensate either, and trying to be the best wife I could be, slowly consumed me like quicksand. I felt I was losing the fun and outgoing person I used to be. Due to my mother's work schedules and funding, she could no longer fly down from NH, as she had once done while I was going through treatments just after Dallas was born in July of 1994. Don's supervisor's at the CBU, were less willing to give him any time off to help me, and my neighbor down the street, that I talked with every day, was now facing her own battle with colon cancer. All of this was no-doubt, the topping on my fast melting sundae. I had not come to terms with the emotional stress that my mind had been put through. I had done just what Alice had said I had, during my days to remission I blocked the emotional pain, and like a bad job, just went with the motions to hurry up and get it done. The endless wonder, would I stay in remission, would my cancer return? This was something that took over and haunted me daily as it twisted me into a world that felt lonely, cold and dark.

As the months slowly slipped away, more secondary problems reared their ugly heads. The biggest and most devastating issue was my extreme dental decay. The radiation had done its share of damage on my teeth, and soon a mountain of bills began to add up. The dentist was a person, that in my world or worlds I feared, as much as a life without love, the thought of ever losing my husband and son, and the worst, death. I hated needles and could never find a way to just calm down as the work would be done. But during this time of a filling here, a root canal there, there was a point that I found a happy place that could be described in three words – powerful pain medication. It was then I began my dance with the Devil himself. I would always ask for the tablets so that I could cut them into quarters, nothing to drug me to the point of numb, just enough to help me bypass the sounds of silence, that turn to the loud darkness just before my twilight dreams. Was it an addiction? I'd like to think it wasn't. Did it help me in anyway? No. It would be hard to get up in the mornings, but family just thought that it was my body still recovering from what it had been through. Could it have been fatigue or the pain medications? I believe it was a bit of both.

I began to figure out ways to get prescriptions, all they had to believe was that my pain was worse than it really was. I achieved many Oscar-winning performances, if I do say so myself. If one dentist would stop providing, then I would find another and another. Honestly, I did have a lot of dental issues that did require extreme treatments and pain medication was a must. But with all the stresses, old and new, that plagued me, I found that if the dentist gave me a strong local, I rather enjoyed the vibration of the tool that etched the root from my gums. The pain following my procedure, well let's just say, it was nothing compared to the five total bone marrow biopsies that I had in the years past. It was just an extreme feeling that gave me something different to worry about until my new pain prescription was filled.

Yes, I say this now, I became dependent and began many months of self-medicating to sleep at night to rid myself from the dark thoughts that told me that I was going to end up alone in the world, nobody was going to stay with someone who had cancer, that I was ugly, fat, undesirable and always would be. But the most consuming feeling I faced, feeling ashamed that I took away my Don's dreams of moving.

I watched his inner grief grow like a tumor, with no signs of a cure. Every day I tried to reach out and comfort him, the more I felt that I had lost a part of the man, I loved more than life itself. Watching him slowly develop a hatred for people, the world, and even going out to public events was hard for me. Sometimes I'd take a half a pill, just so I wouldn't cry myself to sleep with him near. I found that sometimes when he would call home and I didn't know he was on the phone, I'd hear his conversations while I was on the other line. I would always hear, people saying, how much he needed to move back home, that life would be better once he was back. I understood that his family and some friends wished for his immediate return, but I could never understand, that for the time being, why they couldn't just be supportive that he had a good paying job, a home, his health, and a wife and son, that soon became two sons, who loved him. Just a change of a few simple words would have helped him tremendously. Maybe it was that they never realized that they too, were adding to his altered personality and depression.

Over the years, I slowly felt that I was always going to be known as the other woman, in the eyes of his family and some of his friends out west. *Could I be over thinking things? Don, say's I am an expert at doing that. Okay, yes, I will say, I do agree with this statement 30% of the time. But the actions of others is how many a times, this thinking is created.*

During a few of our trips out West, I always felt intentionally excluded from some things that included Don and his family. I recall a time during a family vacation with my mother, when we stayed at his family farm. A family member arrived in her sports car and whisked him away, like on old boyfriend, leaving me, my mother, and our boys alone. It hurt me deeply that I was never invited to join them. Yet what hurt even more was when Dillan remarked that Aunt Carol was taking daddy on a date, as that is the way it appeared to him and you know kids, they have a way of putting things. But sadly, this was not the first time this remark had been made to me, by others, about this odd behavior.

Although several other negative moments come to mind, that made us feel left out and unwanted, I'd rather block the thought with the hopes they never surface again. I tell myself that maybe it is just because they have not seen Don, for so long they forget that he is more than just a son or brother, he a father and a husband, or maybe Don told them how unhappy he was in Maryland and they misunderstood, that it was the location not the marriage that he was unhappy with. I also wondered did they blame me, as much as I blame myself for not having the financial means to move back to Nebraska. Either way, I would love to do things with them as a family, if only given the chance. For the most part, I always enjoyed being with them and the great stories they told of a famer's life and the places they have seen in the world. I'd love to operate a tractor and even fool around with Don, in a golden wheat field under a warm summer sun, while listening to "Fields of Gold" sung by Sting. This city girl has a lot more country in her than I'm given credit for. I guess only time will tell.

This feeling of being excluded whether intentionally or unintentionally, I found myself on numerous occasions pondering the idea if my cancer did come back, would I do the treatments, or would I just give up the fight, so my husband could have my insurance money to move home so his friends and family could have him all to themselves.

These thoughts would come and go, but I wouldn't let the idea settle too long in my thinking. I'm his wife! I am the mother of two miracles! Nobody was going to take my place! My boys needed me and I wasn't going anywhere – I was here to stay! When God is ready to see our big move to a new state, I'll be there with my bags in hand and bells on. *Sometimes, when you try to control destiny and mold it to what pleases you, it turns out to be nothing like you planned. But we should never regret anything we do in our life, in the end it makes us who we are.*

With all this endless thinking, there was one worry that had its very own permanent place, just behind my left ear, inside my brain – my death. I feared leaving my husband and Sons, alone to live on in this world. I wanted this madness in my mind to just go away. I could sit at our dinner table with my family and smile, as my mind was screaming silently for someone, anyone, to hear me. Now taking pain medication, even a quarter of a tablet, would make me very groggy, but one thing puzzled me, no matter how it made me feel, when my baby boy cried or reached out for me, my mind was instantly free from any affects.

I never told my family or my husband, until recently, what I had done to myself, instead they all thought I was just moody, a royal bitch, or who knows, maybe even bi-polar. I lost many friends along the way. *It will all make sense to them now. It's strange what people do to themselves when they are hurting. And Lord knows when someone starts to think they are not loved or they feel unwanted, one can start going downhill fast.*

CHAPTER TWENTY-SEVEN

BABIES SONG

Now for some of you, I can hear it now, "FALLON! WHAT ABOUT YOUR NEWBORN SON! Where is he in all of your turmoil?"

Dallas was always by my side, day and night. He was now my new security blanket and I feared that having chemo while I was pregnant with him, something beyond my control, would happen to him. With my new mentality, I wouldn't let him out of sight. Sometimes he would sleep in his crib, other times, I would sit on the floor gently cradling him in my arms. His sweet baby smell, the feel of his little feet against my arms, he was so small and innocent, pure. How peaceful it was listening to his every breath, while at the same time, I was ready to be there at a moments' notice if he stopped breathing. I would sit and listen to my music softly as I rocked him to sleep and myself, calm. This was my daily routine every day during nap time. The only sounds that would enter my mind were the melodies of the music and the angelic sound of small breaths. You could have dropped a bomb beside me, and I would not have heard it. I was in a world where nothing else mattered; nothing else could enter, until my Don, walked through the door.

There were still appointments that I needed to go to, but now my sweet baby boy was no longer allowed to be brought into any of the exam rooms. The clinics really frowned on it, but I understand they didn't want to expose him to any harmful illnesses. I knew if I had an appointment, I would purposely keep this information to myself until the last minute, I would then ask Don, to take off work, so that Dallas could go with us. Don was quick to figure out this little stunt, and it didn't last long. I had no other choice but to find childcare, it was as simple as that. I couldn't deal with the anxiety of being away from Dallas, or leaving him with a babysitter or childcare provider. He was the strength that got me through the long and lonely days both at home and all my appointments. Here was this tiny baby boy that was in my life, so innocent and pure, he needs me to see him through life and I need him for the very same reason.

As time continued to move forward, when he would take his naps after playtime, the house was so quiet and lonely. I would stand over his crib and cry as his little body was changing as he grew through the months. My baby could not be a baby forever and this hurt. I knew that he was going to need more and more as he developed his skills.

Could I really be the mother he needs? How can I help him if I can't even help myself? Alice warned me.

On a day while my son was napping, I decided to take a hot bath in the middle of the day, something I had never done before and was totally out of character for me, but had turned a corner in my soul. I opened the window that was directly over the tub and inhaled deeply. The new summer air was so refreshing even though it was very humid. Tranquility and peace made their appearance as the smell of the air danced within my senses.

I lay submerged in the warmth of the hot water as it wrapped around my body like a cocoon and framed my face. It was very calming feeling as I lay staring up at the window. Suddenly I was aware of something that I had not felt in a very long time. My hair was long enough to sway around my head in the water. My hair was growing! Now for some this moment many not be that big of a deal, but to me it was the spark that ignited me to regain control of my emotions and my life. Life was going on, and no matter how I wanted control, I could not stop the future from coming into our lives.

Don and my baby boy were the only reasons I needed, and I had them both. Day by day, life began to change for me deep within my soul. One night at a time, I slowly stopped using pain medications, and would fall asleep knowing that I was loved and was learning to love myself again. Yes, there were still the occasional days of pity me parties and the what if's. I found ways to restructure my thinking and I began to do what I loved best, to help me heal my broken soul. I listened to the melody of music all day long. *Maybe that is why Dallas has had such a strong love for music growing up.*

While coloring with Dallas, when he got older, I started to dream an old dream of being a published writer one day. I also had accomplished another mile stone when I finally found the ability to move myself from beside my sweet boy's crib to another room near-by. Now when my son would lay down for his afternoon naps, I would sit on the floor of our spare bedroom and take myself anywhere the music would let me. If I felt like crying, I would put in a song that would make me sad yet I would only allow myself the length of the song to cry. One cool spring morning in April 1996, I decided to play a specific song that I remembering hearing when I was in Adak. The song embraced me with its beautiful melody, it was by Dolly Parton and the name of it was "She's An Eagle When She Flies." It's hard to explain what happened to me as I listened to the words that she sang. It was as if I had been an old flashlight, always dim and dark and had been given a second chance on life, with a new pair of rechargeable batteries to become the brightest light I could be. I knew who I was. I knew what I wanted in my life and I knew this change was not going to be easy. It was this moment that had me reaching for pen and paper and set me on a course to write my memoir. As the music played, my pen danced gracefully across the paper giving birth to words that had been entombed in my mind of looked doors, for so very long.

Who am I, a survivor! I will fight this illness and continue with my life with my husband, my son, my family. I CAN! I WILL! I SHALL! I WILL SURVIVE!

From this point on, I was at peace with myself and ready for anything life had planned for me in the future. I knew that I would have moments when I would need the medication again, and yes I did, but with the bad, good came out of it and I learned to cope on my own.

* * *

Each month my appointments would reveal that I was still in remission and would be scheduled later and later in the years to follow. In addition to marrying my love of a life time, and the birth of my baby boy Dallas, another wonderful miracle happened to us. After being told that having another child may or may not be impossible after all my treatments and radiation therapy, we were blessed with another beautiful healthy baby boy. Dillan joined our family in June and was born on Friday the 13, 1997. God was indeed watching over us, not only did I have another sweet baby boy; he took a day that I once thought was full of crazy superstitions and made it a perfectly innocent day. Our family was now complete.

CHAPTER TWENTY-EIGHT

BIRTH OF A ROSE

For the past several years, I had been searching for Don's birthmother. I was determined to keep my promise to him that I would, since the evening of his 22nd birthday. Born on February 24, 1970 at 8:29pm in Denver, Colorado was all I had to go on, which made the task at hand, daunting. Over the years I had let this promise take over me, and at times made me very angry for wanting information that would not offer any answers. I continued with this search throughout all my medical treatments and the overwhelming anticipation when both my boys were due into this world. I think I became more focused on finding his mother, when I found the strength I needed to stay healthy for my sons and Don. I took my anger and fears and used my promise as a positive tool to my own inner healing to continue winning the battle against cancer, as well as finding closure for my husband.

We learned on his birthday in 1997, through contact with the children's home, that he was adopted from, and his birth-grandmother, that his birthmother Anne, had passed away, in August 1996, after a long battle with breast cancer. With the loss of her daughter, we then waited for more than a year before asking about family medical history or information on the birthfather. *Information that we didn't realize, she had no intentions on reviling.* The only information that we were ever given was about his birth mother, and even this information was very vague, was her first name, a couple pictures and her date of birth and death. The only information we were ever given about the birth father, was that he was in the Navy and had seven siblings.

Then it seem as though we had been written off, never to hear anything more about his mother again. *That was the way her mother wanted it.* We had repeatedly asked the Children's Home numerous times, about family history to have for our son's medical records and for Don's as well. They would only give the basic information from the previous contact with Anne's mother. This was not good enough for me. Trying to obtain the information we needed was impossible without legal assistance, something we could not afford, and so decided to leave well enough alone.

*   *   *

In the past I was known for being the type of person that had a hard time believing in things that I couldn't see. At times my heart and mind would not open to the thought of a high power to help me.

I know there were two moments in my life as a child that kept me in a closed state of heart and mind. The first being a time while I was playing with friends outside of my childhood home. They were insistent on teasing me for believing in Santa Claus. So I decided to go and ask my mom, I knew that she wouldn't lie to me, and she didn't, she told me the truth. The other moment I remember, as if it just happened an hour ago, that affected me for many years to follow. This was the day that I asked our minister of the Weirs Beach United Methodist Church, a question about God. As a young child, the lessons of the Bible were often sad and I never fully grasped the difference between God and Jesus.

As we were making our way up the stairs from Sunday school to the morning services, I wanted to know where God lived if he created the earth, and made the mistake of asking the Minister this question in front of the other kids. Now, you have to understand, I always thought our minister was God. He was as appalled with my question. Without skipping a beat he said to me that I was not welcome in his church and escorted me out the door. He didn't want anyone around him that was questioning the belief of God.

Alone I sat on the front steps of the Church as the doxology filled the room with its glorious melody played by the pianist. I was only nine years old and had been kicked out of God's home. I felt like such a bad person and it was then I immediately became fearful of anything that had to do with Church and religion. For many years following as a child, I'd go to the church, but it wouldn't be without kicking and crying the whole way.

"If only my mom knew." I thought as I was growing up. But being nine, I believed she would never take me seriously and would think I was lying to get out of going to Church every Sunday.

I kept this secret to myself until Don, took me to his family's place of worship at the Hull United Methodist Church in Harrisburg, Nebraska, in January of 1993 to introduce his new wife to everyone he knew. When you hear about victims who repress things in their lives and later on in life they happen to surface, or in a better expression, something triggers them to remember, let's just say, that was the day that I was forced to deal with the pain and hurt from my childhood that I had blocked over the years.

As I sat with a smile to hide my anxiety of being inside a Methodist Church, I melted into soulful cry when the doxology began to play. Don's friends were baffled as to why his, new wife was crying. Don, my savoir, helped me understand this bad act and to find solace. Over time, I eventually shared with the congregation members why it was that I was so sad that day that I graced their church for the very first time. I was humbled by the amount of support and understanding that they gave to me.

These days, I am able to enter any Methodist Church. I no longer allow the pain of that day, so many years ago, to rent a place in my mind. I have evicted it. Though I have been away from the Church for so long, I still do not grasp all the stories of the Bible, and to this very day, when the doxology plays, I smile and know, I survived and I am not a bad person.

* * *

At the young age of nine, other things began to surface spiritually, that I was not aware of their significant meanings, but harboring the anxiety about Church, at the time, I did my best to cope. My first encounter of what my doctors tell me is the gift of second sight, was when I was woken by sounds coming from my desk at the end of my bed. A ghostly image stood before me that actually looked like my mother.

"Mom, what are you doing in my desk?"
But she never answered.
"Mom, is that you?" my young voice quivered.
Now in some of the reading I had done in the library, some books remarked that sometimes spirits would take the image of someone who we were not afraid

of, to help those still on this earth, get used to the idea that we could see spirits and not be afraid of them.

At the age of nine, I wouldn't have cared if I knew them or not, it scared the shit out of me, when the ghostly figure rose up; turned to look at me, and then started moving towards me. At that point I became a shaking mess and dove, my head, under the pillow and covers, waiting for the image to touch me. *It never did.* No way did I want to see anymore. Clearly the guidance of a minster or some church affiliate could have helped me see my gift and I could have understood it a lot sooner than I eventually did.

For many years to follow, I experienced numerous dreams of people that had since passed from our world and onto the next. Some would talk to me and tell of things in the future. Others would help me find answers to questions that I longed to know. I never took any of the dreams seriously until I found Don, my diagnosis and the birth of my sons. Then what opened my mind completely to the possibilities of having this gift, was a soon to be special visitor.

*   *   *

My husband has exchanged birthday cards, for years, with a friend that shares the same month and birthday and it was that time again to start looking for a card. For some reason he felt that rather than mail out a card this year he was going to call her. He picked up the telephone at 8:15pm on their birthday and wished her a happy day. Wanting to surprise Don, I sat in the living room preparing to wish him the same when the clock said 8:29pm. As I got up from the chair and rounded the corner to go into the kitchen where he was, I felt a sense that something was very wrong.

"Fallon, you need to talk to Marietta," Don said in a shocked and saddened voice. "She was diagnosed with breast cancer."

"It's ok Don, she is going to be fine. Give me the phone, I'll talk to her." I said to him in a whisper as I took the phone from his tightened grip. "She'll be fine, I know she will."

After talking with her and assuring her that everything was going to be just fine, I felt a sense of being wrapped in a hidden blanket of warmth. That night I could not sleep and I kept seeing a light appearing on the hall walls just across from our bedroom. Telling myself it was just the streetlight, I would try to close my eyes and sleep. Still I had a feeling and

I would again find myself staring at the walls as though I was supposed to see something, and before long I did.

"I am seeing things. I am just tired, that's all." I said to myself trying to keep from fears tight grip. "It…IT… IT CAN'T BE!"

But it was. It was a shape of a cross with the glow of a soft yellow light that appeared to look warm to the touch. I couldn't speak or move as I became transfixed on the glow of the light. I slowly found myself falling into a comforting twilight sleep that lasted only fifteen minutes, but felt like it had been hours. When I awoke, I could only remember a shape or color with no further details. This happened for the next few days in the exact same way. I found myself after each sleep going through a multitude of every emotion that my body could experience, all at once. Worried, I made an appointment with a doctor here in Annapolis. I wanted some guidance as to what I was going through and why. I explained to her, the complexity of my dreams and that I kept seeing something during this sleep, yet I could not remember what it was exactly when I got up in the morning. She told me that what I did remember to write it down as soon as I woke, that maybe that would help me make sense of it all. So as directed, I did just as prescribed.

On the seventh day after his birthday while cleaning through some of my old papers and letters, I stumbled on to the first letter from the Nebraska Children's Home. When I picked the letter up, I turned to the picture of Don's birth mother he had on his dresser. *Little did I know my mouth was about to change my life as I knew it.*

Once again I felt the anger build within. I was so mad at her for not letting us know who she was, that I took the framed photo from off his dresser and began screaming and yelling at it.

"WHO ARE YOU! WHAT RIGHT DO YOU HAVE TO KEEP US FROM KNOWING YOU! ALL HE WANTS TO DO IS LOVE YOU!" I screamed this over and over until I was hoarse and weeping.

As stated in the letters from the agency that his birth mother was very active in her religion and with her church. I found myself saying these words to her.

"IF YOU ARE SO INTO THE LORD THAN SHOW ME A SIGN, ALL HE WANTS IS CLOSURE! ALL HE WANTS IS TO LOVE YOU! SHOW ME SOMETHING AND I WILL LEAVE YOU ALONE DAMMIT! I was frustrated and consumed with pure exhaustion.

That evening, I was shown a sign. It was more than I had ever expected in my life. I slipped into a relaxed sleep like the nights before, but one thing was very different from nights passed. This time I could see, hear, feel, and smell. All my senses were at work. I felt my body moving as I walked through a house with yellow walls. A woman sitting in the front of a fireplace asked me to come and sit by her. She had asked what I was looking for, to which I replied nothing and looked away.

She again asked me what I was looking for, so I showed her this picture I had of his birth mother, in my jacket pocket. I explained that all I had was her first name, date of birth and death.

"I know Anne," this woman replied.

When I heard her say this, I turned around in my chair and found myself walking backwards in a cemetery with voices saying that I didn't believe that she had passed on. *The voices were right.* In a split second, I was covered by a white sheet.

I heard a voice then say, "Is this who I think it is?"

I lifted the sheet off and found myself in a room looking out this big picture window watching Don and an older man by the name of Dean, walking towards the house in a wheat field. I turned around and there before me, stood his birth mother. Her voice was soft and she looked so young and beautiful. I told her about my promise I had made to her son so many years ago. Both men walked in the door and I said to Don, this is your birth mother. His eyes filled with now tears of happiness as she took him in her arms and they both walked away.

As they walked away, I heard soft music playing that sounded like the song from Cinderella. A dream is a wish your heart makes when the day is through and if you believe in your dreams, they too will come true. I turned to look back out the window and suddenly all the stars in the sky were circled around me. Through the splendor of the star lights I saw this beautiful vision of an angel appear. She spoke to me and said she wanted me to create an image of her to share with others, as our world needed peace.

"How could I create something as beautiful as you?" I asked.

"With love," she replied in a flawless voice that woke me back into the reality in which I lived. I laid there the rest of the evening staring into the darkness as tears of joy rolled down my cheeks onto my pillow. I had been touched by the love of an angel.

The next day I began putting together the angel that I had seen. My husband and I named her "Rose" but her birth name would be Rosemary. I felt the urge to want to show her to all my friends and family members as she was so important to me. They wanted to know how, did I come up with the idea to create "Rose". They also wanted to know, if was she a pattern from the local craft store, or what. So many times it was hard to explain how she came to be, I feared that people would not believe me, if I told them the real story. So my explanation was that she stands for beauty and will comfort all that touch her, like a dozen red roses. I never really knew the answer behind the angel and sometimes I even questioned it all myself. *Did I really see something or was it all my imagination?*

One night as I was watching the Learning Channel, the host was talking about the Virgin Mary as they began to display drawings of her.

"OH MY GOD! DON! THAT'S ROSE!" were the only words I could say.

I was overcome with emotions. I was breathless. Tears began to roll down my face as I again felt rushed with every emotion like the nights of my dreams. This was the angel that I had seen, but what confirmed this and answered my question, if this was all just a figment of my imagination, was what the host went on to say about Virgin Mary. I realized then, I would never question the unknown again.

"The best way to describe the Virgin Mary was like the symbol of a rose and was often known as "Rose," said the host "To all that have felt her and have seen her, would find peace and believe in the strength of a higher power."

I finally was able to put the pieces together. Don had always told me his favorite number was seven. It took me seven days to see Angel Rose before I could create her.

Is the angel that I saw in my dream, the Virgin Mary? Were the stars that surrounded me that night, spirit lights of friends and family that have passed on and have earned their wings by helping me?

So many thoughts filtered through my mind. I knew the answers after seeing these pictures and the words about Virgin Mary, I felt as though my heart and soul had been given wings. A way to help, with a gentle healing, that all of mankind seeks. So many who have Guardian Angel Rose with them speak of how they just want to have her in their presence. There is a comfort about Angel Rose that makes one relish in the glow that she is part of a higher power. This assures me that God is forever in our presence and watching over each and every one of us.

I thank you God and all your glory, for giving me so many miracles of life, love, family, friends, health and the new miracles that are awaiting me and my family.

* * *

I am so happy to say that Marietta, is in remission and doing well to this very day. Marietta, may God bless you and continue to bestow all his strength, love and guidance to see you through to each new day that is born. May you also have your guardian Angel always by your side.

CHAPTER TWENTY-NINE

FROM BAD TO WORSE

Being a woman in a man's military offered many trials and tribulations along my journey. Being accepted as a team player to work alongside the men in the Seabees, was even more challenging than fighting a battle against my cancer. This was a task not easy to overcome, but was something I wanted more and more if I was going to make this a career.

"Were the woman in the Seabees, using their shovels to lean on or work with?" This was an endless comment often expressed by all the men. If you wanted respect, women needed to learn a shovel was not for leaning on and you needed to be able to bust your ass and hold your own just like the rest of the men in this man's military.

As I endured my own blood, sweat, and hidden tears, their respect was slowly, and I emphasize slowly, earned. There were days when duty went from dusk to dawn, but I kept my strength and carried on with the task at hand. A mission some will never see, especially through my eyes. With each day I was faced with, I put forth 200%. At the time they understood that I would never be on the front lines of a war, but rules change and that day could come. Day by day they took me under their wings to allow me to be within their ranks and be part of their growing team. A team that I felt was taken from me, suddenly, like an unexpected death, when I was told, that I could not continue to remain on active duty. I wanted the choice, but this time there wasn't any. I was supposed to be the active duty spouse, and my husband wanted to be, the stay at home dad, but life would have its way again, and our plans were thrown to the winds of change. The command he was presently stationed at did their part to make Don's life miserable, and again it was because of me. At one point they had even threatened to transfer him to a Battalion in Mississippi, just so he and I would be separated. It had been three years since we had transferred from Adak to Annapolis, but still our old command had done enough damage to sabotage Don's military position, no matter how hard he tried, he was never promoted to second class.

In June of 1997, just after the birth of our second son, Don ended his military service to work for a construction company that was eventually closed for its shady practices. But all things happen for a reason, so people say, and low and behold, two years later he was hired to do something he knew very well, working the grounds at the Pleasant Plains Turf farm in Annapolis, Maryland. It was right up his alley, as he grew up, a wheat farmer's son. He was accustomed to tractors and farming. It didn't matter if he was planting seeds for wheat or various types of grass; it was the best of both worlds. He got great city pay with the freedom of planting and harvesting just like his days on the farm when he was a kid. Don seemed content.

*   *   *

I took on the roll as the stay at home mom even though I was still in the military. I had not been discharged and I had been placed on a TDRL, which stands for Temporarily Disabled Retired list. Technically, I was home awaiting orders. In my mind, they wanted me out so that I would no longer be a problem they would have to deal with. There was no way I was going to let them discharge me from the service without my full benefits.

With cancer, you never know when or where it will reveal its ugly self in the future. I couldn't take the chance of it returning. This was something that happened to me because of a prescription overdose, written by a military doctor. I felt I was right to fight this battle so that I could receive my VA benefits. At the same time I was filled with anger and some hostility to fight, I was having mixed feeling about getting out of the service too. Maybe I could overcome this too, and my family could be like all the other military families in the world, and travel. I had made third class while I was undergoing my treatments, how hard would it be?

My life before my cancer was filled with non-stop energy. I was involved in everything and yes, I'll admit it, I loved to be the center of attention. To me it was to have my evaluation sheets filled with endless jobs I had done, volunteer time, plaques, written recognition, and a multitude of jobs recognized by others and followed by ample, well done, letters of thanks. I knew what to say, and what they wanted to hear and if anyone could get those perfect evaluations through bullshit, kissing someone's ass with words, and not having to sleep around – then Fallon was your girl. I lived for this, I felt validation that I was needed and important, with an ego that was fueled by the thought that the job couldn't go on without me. My ego died in a fiery crash of rage when I found out, not only could the jobs go on without me, they did. Once I was home, I felt as though the military looked at me as if I were a used paint brush, why bother cleaning up so it can be used again. No, instead they got everything they needed out of me and threw me away because it appeared old and so over worked.

With the stress of fighting the military, keeping my promise to Don to find his birth mother, and the pressures of my family and his, my personality once again took a serious hit. I would speak my mind without realizing the emotional repercussions of others. And Lord help the person who worked on a day that I had an appointment. Front desk clerks feared me and my unexpected tempers. If it wasn't my way, then it wouldn't happen and that was it. I became a royal "Cast Iron" bitch. I had absolutely no tolerance for family drama, which had plagued me for years, or any drama for that matter. I never felt truly accepted by many family members on my side and on Don's. No matter what, I felt that I was the bad guy, because I loved to walk to the beat of my own drum. With the bullshit that I had been handed since my entering the service, I had to be this way to protect the real me. The shy, quiet, non-confrontational person that lived with in that I had locked away.

One reason, they claimed they got so mad at me, and I'll always remember, I am told that I blame others for my problems. But it wouldn't be until much later in my life, that I realized that the only person I chronically blamed, was myself for not speaking my mind. Rather than addressing problems when they arose, I would just take on their problems, which usually didn't have anything to do with me. Clearly something was happening to me inside the depths of my soul. I became very untrusting of others and began to fear the outside world. I began to believe this was all planned, that the Navy could have cured me earlier, but they didn't want me. They got me for a cheap price, and now it was time to upgrade. *I should have listened to Alice.*

I still never called Alice like I had promised. I never called anyone else to help me though this, I was going to do this on my own. My ego and my fear, at this point, needed a bucket to be carried around in, as my brain was not big enough to hold it all. I felt I knew what was best for me and I refused to join any type of support group. My mind was set; if I stayed home then nothing bad could happen to me or my babies. I took myself from the outside world. I would not go out with friends when they called, I wouldn't drive to the store, and I would wait for Don to come home to take me where I needed to go. Oddly enough, I would drive my boys to elementary and pre-school without any problems. What a crazy brainy mind I had. If something was going to happen, I'd be there to help them, not a bus driver or some stranger. This was the way my mind processed much of my thinking.

When my kids were in school, my days were filled with endless calls to Congressman, lawyers, doctors and financial advisors. This was not a good thing. Nobody wanted to fight the military, everyone said, that I couldn't win this and I should take whatever they were willing to give me. I had to get them to hear me, I just had to, but every road I took, every call I made, always ended with the same, "I'm sorry Fallon, and we can't help you."

I had it drilled in my mind that the military could not just let me out of the service and expect me to fend for myself. I was already worth over a million dollars with all the medical services and treatments I had gone through. *If only all those services paid me in cash.* How could anyone like me, in such debt, pay a medical bill like that in the real world? Things were crazy, the more I thought I had control, the more I was losing it. In my life, things never went as planned, and I was thrown surprises when I thought all had failed. I found myself watching one door close in my face and then another one would open. I couldn't help but stand back, scratch my head and say, "What the hell?"

In all of the endless fighting with the military, my promise to Don, for some reason was always at the front most of my mind. It didn't matter what time of day it was, the thought would come and go day and night. Even as I pursued my quest to fight the government, Don's promise was always on my mind.

CHAPTER THIRTY

DON

On February 17, 1998, I was filled with a deep worry, never really comprehending why. The good Lord had decided that this would be the day that I would be given my test of tests. I had no idea that my self-pity, the military and my family drama, all this would no longer matter to me, when Don came home from work.

The day was slowly turning into the shadows of night, and the kids were anxiously waiting for their dad to walk through the front door. How they couldn't wait to wrestle and play with him. Don has always been a great dad to our kids and to the other kids we'd meet along the way in our life. He was the father that I wish my dad could have been to me. He has always been a loving, caring, and kind soul with not one mean bone in his body. The kind of person that you knew, people wanted in their life, and even at times, idolized his simple ways. And yes, I can say I get jealous when I take notice of the ladies trying to sweet talk him and try to lure him to the mirage of greener pastures. He says I'm crazy, but deep down, he likes that I get jealous. To him it's another way, other than saying I love you, to show him how much I really do love him. He truly means the world to me and my soul would die without him.

When he finally got home, his skin was pasty in color and he moved slowly. He could barely stand up.

"Don! What's wrong?" I feared the deathly look he was wearing.

"I don't know Fallon, something isn't right."

"We need to get you to a hospital, now!"

I got the kids dressed and into the car, then ran back into the house to help Don back to his feet. By this time he was unable to walk on his own. I couldn't help but think that the man of my dreams could be dying beside me and there was nothing I could do. I got him to the emergency room at the Fort Meade Army Base in Odenton, Maryland. They got him on a stretcher and quickly wheeled him away, leaving me and our babies alone in the waiting room. Usually I was the one that was being rushed here and there, with Don left behind. This was all new to me. I was unsure what I should do. We sat there for about two hours when a doctor came into the room.

"Mrs. Bentley?"

"Yes, that's me," I said trying to keep Dallas entertained so he wouldn't wake up his baby brother.

"Ma'am, I just don't know what to say. We did all we could…"

Before he finished his sentence, I froze. I was engulfed in a stir of emotions and my voice was paralyzed. I could feel the hot tears streaming down my face, but I could not wipe them. I couldn't move. The room was spinning around me as the lights grew dark, I had fainted. When I came to, I began to scream uncontrollably "NO! NO! Tell me this isn't so. I can't live without him. DON PLEASE! PLEASE DON'T LEAVE ME! Oh my God, I can't breathe. HELP ME! I CAN'T BREATHE!

I could feel the sharpness of the stabbing knife of fear as it pieced every part of my body. I was completely out of control. Dallas looked up at me, not understanding why mommy had fallen to the floor and then woke up yelling. He was crying because I was crying, which also woke up Dillan, who also began to cry.

"WHAT THE HELL IS GOING ON OUT HERE!" yelled another man, wearing a white doctor's lab coat. "Landford! Answer me! What is going on?"

"Sir. She thinks her husband is dead."

"Where the hell did she get that idea like that? Never mind!" and he turned to help me.

"Mrs. Bentley…MRS. BENTLEY!!!" shouted the doctor as he grabbed a hold of my arms. "Your husband is alive! He's alive! Please ma'am, sit down and gather yourself. I am so sorry for this misunderstanding, please let me explain to you what is going on with Don's health."

After we all stopped crying and the doctor got me some ginger ale, and a couple nurses catered to the boys, the doctor updated me on the situation. He was stumped. He and his staff had done numerous lab and urine tests, but nothing registered to make a diagnosis. They were only a small hospital and felt it would be better if Don went out into town and got a second opinion. They gave him medication, to help him with the pain, and place him on IV antibiotics just to rule out a possible infection that could have been missed.

They told me that usually kids are not allowed in the emergency room, but they would make an exception this time, when they found out what had happened in the waiting room. A nurse took me aside and apologized for the way Technician Landford, took it upon himself to speak to me, without knowing what was going on. That he was not the doctor and had no right to share any patient information of any kind. That only the doctors speak with families.

The nurse helped me by watching Dallas and pushing Dillan around in the stroller as I went into where Don was. He lay there, motionless and his eyes closed. I waited and watched to see if his chest would rise as he took in a breath, still fearing that the doctors were wrong again. He was calm, but still very pale in color. He seemed to be pain free, but that was only the pain medication doing its part to take the edge off. Something I knew firsthand about. I just stood there and stared at him, then smiled with relief when I saw him take a breath.

You see on movies when something traumatic happens, people lives flash before their eyes. Well that is an excellent way to describe what I was going through as I stood there. I could see all the moments we had shared together. I could hear his laugh, I could see his hypnotic smile, I could feel his arms around me, and I could even smell his cologne. The thought of being told he died, ripped me apart. That somewhere in the waiting room, my heart and fallen out of my chest and possibly rolled under a table for a stranger to find and take apart piece by piece. It was a hurt that was going to stay with me for a long, long, time. How would I ever tell him what just happened? Nobody wants to hear something like this. I never was strong enough to get into great detail with Don, about this, as the pain is far too great, still to this very day. *Now he will know the whole story as he continues to read my words.* Don will know what really happened that night and why I treasure every second we have together and never take life for granted.

"Thank you God. Thank you Angel Rose." I thought *"Please make him better. I love him with all that I am."*

It wasn't until Dallas, had giggled over something the nurse had done, that Don opened his eyes and looked at me. I just stood grasping hold of the privacy curtain staring back at him, telling myself he was alive, he was alive.

"Come over here sweetness." He said in a whisper.

"I love you so much." I said, trying to keep my composure, but broke into tears.

"Fallon, why are you shaking?"

"I was missing you." And I gently kissed his forehead and took hold of his hand. My prayer had been heard. My love of a life time was still with me. That was all that mattered.

CHAPTER THIRTY-ONE

THE MEDICAL MYSTERY

Don was released from the Military hospital, with several prescriptions and doctor's orders to go to a near-by civilian facility, if he didn't feel he was getting any better. We got back to the house just after six in the morning, and without missing a beat, I got him and the boys settled down and into their beds. What a night it was. I was hoping that, the only thing my sweetie needed, was lots of sleep, so he could get back to being the healthy Don I knew. While the house was peaceful, I took the time to take a long hot shower and try to get myself in a better frame of mind. This whole ordeal scared me more than being told I had cancer. I could not envision my life without him, and I didn't want to either.

As I stood in the warmth of the water, without fail the phone rang. My mom was an early bird and would call the house every other morning by seven. *I think she was trying to get me on her schedule.*

"Hello?"

"You home?" said my mother, always greeting me this way.

"Yeah," I said with a long sigh.

"You sound tired Fallon, are you ok? What's going on?"

"Don is sick. He came home last night in bad shape. I ended taking him up to the military hospital in Fort Meade. Doctors don't have a clue what is going on with him."

"What about the kids? What did you do with them?"

"I bundled them up, and took them with us. I had to wait in the waiting room. Later on a nurse stayed with them when I went in to see Don. *I never told her what happened to me in the waiting room. I was not going to relive those feeling again.*

"So they don't know what is going on?" shocked they didn't find something on his test.

"No"

Suddenly there was a loud commotion coming from the bedroom. Don had gotten up to rush to the bathroom and had fallen down. I told my mother I'd call her back and quickly dropped the phone to help him.

"Don!"

"Fallon, something is wrong. I think I passed out. I don't know."

I got Don, to the bathroom and stayed with him to make sure he didn't pass out again. I knew that this medical problem of his was in no way over. Whether he liked it or not, I was taking him to the Anne Arundel Medical Center. This hospital had always been great to me when I had illnesses and pain. They were quick to get answers, but a bit slow in the emergency room. I'm told this happens because some patients don't have health care, so they utilized the ER as a doctor for their medical needs.

I got him and the boys dressed and loaded into the car again. This hospital was a little more accepting, of the kids and I, staying in the room with Don while he waited. However, these rooms were very cramped. Honestly there was not enough room for family or visitors. I gave the nurses the paper work from the night before and all the names of the medications he had been taking for the past 24-hours. He moaned in pain, and his color was lighter than ever. As I was speaking to a nurse, Allison, about the foods he had eaten, fluids, and how he was feeling when he came home, another nurse come into his room.

"Mrs. Bentley, I am going to have to ask you and your children to leave the room." said this unknown person, with a bedside manor resembling razor sharp porcupine quills dipped in acid.

She clearly didn't want me there. Taking her attitude personally, I quickly responded in a rather nasty tone. "I'm sorry, I know kids are not allowed in the emergency room, but I don't have any family or child care for them and my husband..."

Before I could finish my sentence, she quickly interjected a sneer followed by another round of nastiness.

"Ma'am, I don't care that you brought your kids. Your husband, as you may know, is very sick and he needs his rest. He's not going to get it, with you and Allison, the wanna be nurse assistant, chatting up a storm. Let the real nurses, make him better. You and your kids need to go in the other room. Thank you!"

"Really, wow, I had no clue, I just thought since we didn't have anything to do today and we are just so loaded with cash, we'd come into the emergency room to hang out and see just how many real nurses there are here. I know I'm not looking at one right now." *Ok, not the smartest move, but what the hell? She was a joke. Her ego needed a good ass kicking.*

"Fallon, it's ok. I'll make sure they keep you posted. Please hon, they are just trying to make Don, as comfortable as possible." said Allison, "I won't keep anything from you. I promise."

Allison just had a way with her tone that you knew she was not going to let anything happen to him. She gave me a sense of relief, but still deep down, I was bitterly angry with the way nurse bitch addressed me. She knew I would not forget her and my complaint to management. *I am happy to say, and not because of me, she no longer works for this hospital.*

I took the kids for stroll to find a soda and chip machine to help pass the time. Dallas insisted that I let him put the coins in the machine. Dillan just slept and snuggled with his blanket in the stroller as if nothing was wrong in the world today. As we walked back to the ER, Nurse Allison came up to me.

"Mrs. Bentley, the doctors are in with your husband. They want to do a spinal tap on him."

"Now?"

"Yes, so if you want, I'll sit outside the room with your boys and you can be with your husband."

"Thank you so much. I really do appreciate it."

Allison, was a real trooper, she had gotten a coloring page for Dallas, and rocked the stroller with her foot to keep Dillan a sleep.

As the procedure began, Nurse Bitch and doctor so-and-so, explained what they were going to be doing each step of the way. Don yelled in pain as they started to push the needle deep into his back.

"It's ok honey, count, that's what I do, just count. It will take your mind off..."

"DAMMIT! WHAT THE FUCK!" he yelled out with all his strength. "What you're doing hurts!"

"Clearly Mrs. Bentley, you're a distraction. Please leave the room, now!" said Nurse Bitch. *The best nurse on staff. NOT!*

The doctor also looked up at me, and I knew, that he also wanted me to leave. Don, was hurting too much to care if I was in the room or not. It was so hard to be just outside his room, listening to him yelling out in so much pain. Don, was not a big one for doctors and hospitals, so for me, that was hard to hear and not being able to be there for him, even harder. Without fail, Don had been by my side each and every day. All the months I spent in and out of the hospitals and treatments that I had to undergo, never once did he complain, he was always there.

Our time at AAMC, was another day, of blood tests, urine samples and now a spinal tap, only to find nothing. There were never any answers, just a growing pile of discharge papers, as Don, had been in and out of the emergency room four times in the course of seven days. With each day, he got weaker and weaker as though each day was his last. With his birthday only a couple days away, I was hoping this would be what would make him feel better. But his birthdays were not ones he looked forward to, as they would always remind him of biological parents. Who were they? Where were they? Why would Anne's mother tell us she wished for no further contact? What was she hiding?

I had always known he was born in Denver, Colorado as that was on his birth certificate that his adoptive parents received when they adopted him. I finally found the hospital that he was born in, as the Children's Home and indicated in a second letter back to us. I think this may had been an error on their part, but for me it was a clue.

I believe that after all my hard work, this time something would result. The only result I did get, just when I thought I had the answers, was a dead end. I had been informed that where he was born, was torn down due to a huge fire and that the records of the babies born there, had all been lost. I don't know why, but I still sent my information about my search and what I was seeking. I knew it would be a long shot, with only just a birth mother's name, date of birth and death, no real personal information or consent, there would be no way to get or find anything I was asking for. His records had been permanently sealed in a Denver court house and we didn't have the money for a lawyer. But who needs a lawyer when you have a mouth like mine. I was about to open it once again and wide enough to insert my size 11 foot.

CHAPTER THIRTY-TWO

A PROMISE BY MAIL

On the night before his birthday, I feared that this would be the day before Don's passing. I couldn't stomach the idea that my honey may be dying, and nobody had an answer. I needed to do something – anything. Now, since my dream about Angel Rose, I always felt she was just over my shoulder guiding me to do the right things. No more pain pills, no more hate or hostility about what I had been through, just good thoughts and was thankful to be alive. On this night, good thoughts were thrown to the wind.

Remembering a time in the past, when I yelled at his birth mother's picture demanding answers, Angel Rose came into my life and brought her to me. So, would I repeat this process again? *You bet your bottom dollar I would, I did, and then some!*

The boys were all cleaned up, fed and all snuggled down for the night with their blankets that Grandma Bentley had made them. If anything could put them to sleep, it was a bottle or a warm cup of milk, a back rub and Grandma's blankets. I checked on them, and when I knew all was well, I quietly went back into the bedroom, took the photo of Don's birth mother off his nightstand and went into the upstairs living room.

Looking at the picture while shaking it in my hands, I could feel myself filling with rage and anger. I found the words spilling out of me like hot lava, no control and would hurt if you were in its path. I demanded answers and I wasn't willing to wait.

"HE'S YOUR SON, BUT YOU CAN'T HAVE HIM NOW! If you love him, you will help him! Help him stay with us, and get better for our boys! You

have no right to take him now, when you were never there for him to begin with! They need a father in their lives! There is nobody that could fill Don's shoes! NOBODY! CAN YOU HEAR ME!? IF YOU CAN THEN SHOW ME ANOTHER SIGN! BUT IF YOU'RE GOING TO TAKE ANYONE, THEN TAKE ME! I WILL DIE FOR HIM! I WILL DIE FOR HIM! I WILL DIE FOR HIM!"

I don't recall what happened after that. All I knew is that I woke up the next morning on the couch, listening to the sounds of Dallas, playing with his trucks on the kitchen floor and Dillan was starting to fuss for a bottle.

"Wow, what happened? Dang my head hurts." I said, out loud to myself. "What time is it?"

I felt I was hung over but I knew I had not had anything to drink, not even water. I said good morning to Dallas, and got Dillan his bottle and a desperately needed diaper change. He was sporting a diaper that I swear was at least five pounds. *Poor baby.*

Once I knew the kids were settled, I went into the bedroom to check on Don. He was breathing very shallow and his skin was a pale purple with an odd clammy feeling.

"Oh honey, what can I do to help you? What?" I whispered close to his exposed ear. "I need a magic wand to take your pain away. I love you so much, please get better for me. Better yet, get better for your sweet baby boys. They miss you."

But he didn't respond. He was breathing, but was not talking at all.

"Please Angel Rose, give me something, anything. I need a miracle." I thought and then began to cry.

Don slept, with an occasional moan, but nothing more. I felt like I was at a loss and in many ways, I was trying to get myself ready. What was God going to choose to do? I tried to walk out of the room to let him rest, but feared going too far from him at the same time. So I leaned against the doorjamb to our bedroom. I watched his every breath as I reminisced about the good times, and how I missed looking into his beautiful blue eyes. I couldn't help but keep staring at him, wanting so much to hear him say something, anything. He could yell at me about my endless clutter, it wouldn't have mattered; it would have totally thrilled me, just to hear his voice again. But he was lifeless.

I put Dallas in Dillan's room with the gate up so they could play together while I went outside to get the mail. As I opened the door and stepped out onto the front porch, I was embraced with a familiar and yet powerful feeling. One of comfort, such soothing warmth surrounded me, like many arms holding me ever so gently. My vision became transfixed on the mailbox. I saw a mail truck parked in front of it, but in the blink of an eye, it was gone. I knew this feeling, I'd felt it before, I'd even seen this before, but how? When? George. Angel Rose. Yes.

My body moved to the mailbox. It was like I was walking on air. I don't remember the ground beneath my feet. I don't remember anything to either side of me. What I could see had a soft golden color that twinkled. It was heavenly. When I reached out and touched the mailbox, my breathing became restrained and my soul slowly filled with all the emotions I had once felt when I discovered the identity of the Angel in my dream. When I opened the door, the box smelled like mildew, very musty and smoky. There was an envelope inside. No return address was on it, and it was only addressed to me. *What could this be? It smells terrible and feels like it's wet. But how could that be? It's as dry as a bone.*

I was not prepared for what I was about to discover. I turned the envelope over and opened it. When I looked inside, all I saw were the words on a folder that said, "Baby boy Brown."

"No, this can't be real." I fell to my knees and began to weep, "It was my promise to Don."

I grabbed the mailbox and pulled myself back onto my feet and then quickly ran to the house, yelling Don's name. I didn't care who heard me. But just as fast as I was moving, I then suddenly stopped. My attention was drawn to the sounds of the mailbox door shutting.

"Hi Fallon, have a great day."

It was my mailman. *"But how could that be?"* I thought, puzzled and confused by what had just happened. "I just got the mail and saw the mail truck already. No way, it couldn't be."

"DON! DON!" I yelled his name, as I ran into the house, "DON!"

"What?" he said in a shallow voice.

"Look what I found in the mailbox!" I said with sheer excitement. "It's all about you. It's filled with all your answers. It's your entire birth record, names, places, people, everything!"

When I handed him the folder, he sat right up as if he had never been sick. The color was slowly returning to his face and body. He voice got deeper and stronger and his eyes grew brighter and brighter. I just stood there in disbelief that I was really seeing him recover, in a matter of minutes, before my very own eyes. I was standing and witnessing a true miracle.

"Happy Birthday Honey. I told you I keep my promises. But I had a higher power help me on this one."

All afternoon, he sat on the bed, reading the story of his infant life, and about the time he did spend with his birth mother. It was not her choice to give him up, but it was the best thing for her to do at the time. But Anne had done something that I don't think her only family knew about. In the faintest of pencil on the last page of Don's birth record, a name appeared. We would later learn that this name was his birth father and we would soon meet him.

Still to this very day, I have not seen Don filled with such an overflow of emotions, as I did that day. I knew what he was feeling, as I felt it too. To watch him as he read about the days before his birth to the days he spent in Anne's arms, before he was placed for adoption. He was finally at peace and he knew who he was and that she loved him. And I, I too was finally at peace. I kept my promise.

Thank you Rose. Thank you George.

CHAPTER THIRTY-THREE

THE CHRISTMAS SPIRIT ON THE ROAD

With all the madness and our fair share of troubles and hardships, we always found ways to bring life back into our emotionally beaten souls. Sometimes I would take the boys on a week vacation to one of Maine's great ocean beaches. Other times it was just a ten minute trip across town to the Sandy Point State Park to go swimming. I always found that every year from January to August, I was always had the urge to travel somewhere. Why wouldn't I, during this time frame, since my joining in the military, I would either be transferring locations or going on trips using the leave I had earned.

It's just something that is going to stick with me. Here it is, February, and I am already planning a trip to Lancaster, Pennsylvania to celebrate our wedding anniversary in May, and to Yale, Michigan to see Frank and Sally over the Fourth of July. I love the excitement of counting down the days until we were on the road to another one of our wild and wacky adventures. It was one winter trip that I recall that truly warmed our hearts and became our family newsletter to our families and friends. It is this letter that I would like to share with you.

*   *   *

Dear friends and family members,

We are safe and sound in the year 2000. Welcome to the New Millennium. In my story of event, for those of you who know us and to the newest family members we have just met, our newsletter takes us back to the holiday season of 1999. As most of you know, the rule of thumb in our home is that the holidays are kept here in Annapolis. But last year was the exception, when we found Don's birth father in North Platte, Nebraska.

So we made a family decision and the Bentleys of Annapolis, packed up the family truckster and began our journey to enjoy Christmas out west with family in Harrisburg, Nebraska and meet new family members along the way.

Now I don't know if any of you have ever seen the National Lampoons: Vacation or Christmas Vacation movies, but our family is the spitting image of the Griswold's when it comes to traveling. To know the movies, is to know that with our traveling, come great stories that will make even the shyest person laugh out loud. Part of our travel troubles usually begin days before the actual trip. The normal person would begin packing two days to a week before their scheduled departure. Not us, we wait until crunch time – the night before.

This trip wasn't any different. The night before our departure, we were changing the breaks on the car and packing it. Don and I had beautiful black circles under our eyes that we wore, along with big smiles and crazy Christmas sweaters, for all the family photographs. We were so impressed with ourselves, as we put the last suitcase into the Mercury Sable wagon, we had fit everything in without using the space between the kids in the back seat or using my solution, "Strap it to the roof" – until we went upstairs to find all the gifts that were to go with us.

After hours of putting together our adult size rubic's cube, the puzzle was finally solved, without having to weld the doors closed, or use any straps that would have made our car look like a rolling pot roast. Now in all the years I have been traveling, I do have a special tip for all the ladies out there that have small boys, or even big boys if they are willing, never forget to take two bottles with wide re-sealing lids and handi-wipes, this makes that side of the road pee break in the wind, much easier than risking pressure loss within the cargo hold. If it could only be that simple for women, trips would be ever so much easier.

On the first leg of the trip our troubles were minimum, the kids were just perfect angels, just heavenly, a dream come true. Don and I were enjoying lengthy adult conversations and laughing through most of Maryland, when suddenly it happened…they woke up. The cooler was raided to the point of empty, and the pee break games began. As the miles grew longer and the weather grew cooler, we realized during a stop somewhere between where we came from and where we were going, that we had forgotten something very important, we were not dressed for winter temperatures past the Blue Ridge Mountains. People stared as we entered a small restaurant section of a truck stop, to use the bathrooms. We always believed in wearing the most attractive travel wear that we could. *Not!*

Don was sporting a pair of red Nebraska sweatpants that had blotches of white paint on them and a short sleeve shirt that was covered in red juice stains, from the juice boxes the kids had wanted opened early in our drive. The boys were still in their footy pajamas and wrapped in their blankets that were covered in permanent mystery stains. Myself, I had on a pair over oversized pink, just your size, sweatpants with a grey Seabee t-shirt and sneakers with no socks. We were looking hot to trot. I meant that most sarcastically.

As we were getting ready to exit the building, a man from out of nowhere gave Dallas a dollar to get something from the McDonalds booth, said Merry Christmas and then walked off with a smile. It felt strange to think that our traveling clothes that made us feel comfortable, looked like a needy family to another, yet at that very moment the spirit of the season started to grow in all of us. Now Don tells me that I am a back seat driver that sits in the front seat to drive him crazy. Ok, yes, I do like to nag him, but only on one topic when it comes to our driving trips, and this one was not any different. As we began the drive again, I mentioned to Don to watch his speeding since the next state, Ohio, was hard on drivers who didn't follow the rules of the road.

Don always enjoyed our driving trips to the fullest – when the kids and I were asleep. Being in a station wagon filled to the brim and Don's sad country music, the only thing to do, other than pick our noses or poke our eyes out with our fingers, was to nap.

Suddenly this squelch of fear from Don's voice filled the car.

"GET UP IT'S THE POLICE!"

Sitting up from a dead sleep, I yelled out, "What's Happening?"

Don indicated that he was being pulled over by the police, yet made it sound like it was because he was not wearing a seatbelt. *Yes, my Don is a rebel. He won't wear a seatbelt.*

But as I looked around the car everyone including Don had their belts on.

Something was wrong here. Maybe there was smoke coming from some source on the car, or maybe we had hit someone or something, I just couldn't figure it out. Why were we being pulled over?

As I sat wondering what could be the problem, a large round-bellied officer came up to the window, pulled up his duty belt and then bent forward to make eye contact with Don and I and said, "License and registration" and then paused. He didn't look to terribly happy.

"Son, do you know why I have pulled you over today?"

Don looked at me with this cheesy; I'm so innocent, grin and then looked at the officer and replied with a question, "I was speeding?"

"Yes, Son you were. Do you happen to know how fast you were going?"

Knowing the speed limit was 65, he responded, "81 Sir?"

"I clocked you several times just to be absolutely sure you had your foot almost to the floor. I got you at 80, 83, and 85, which one would you like your ticket to say?"

In keeping tradition with every road trip, Don was about to receive a welcome to Ohio speeding ticket just in time for the holidays. We chose door number one, the 80 mph and a $197.00 fine, 'tis the season to give and the Ohio State police were actively doing their part.

The kids had gotten into a small box during dad's traffic stop. They had found the little gifts that I had gotten them to make our different stops easier. I decided to give them each one present and the rule was, with each stop we made they could open another one.

While Don was getting his gift from the police the kids were opening theirs. Beep, beep, beep, were the constant sounds that filled the air, from a pocket sized Simon game that Dallas got from the gift box and Dillan was making sounds for his new mini sized toy Tonka dump truck. Also in the box were sheets of window clings that I had gotten at the dollar store. The kids were having a lot of fun with the mini gifts and putting the Christmas clings onto the windows of the car. Once again the spirit of the holidays filtered back into our Santa land on wheels, and we continued onward.

As the purple of a dusk sky faded into darkness of the evening, we arrived into the city of Indianapolis, Indiana where we were spending the night. Don and I had been here back in the summer of 1996 and it was because of the indoor pool and family size hot tub, we chose to stay here. The lights of the Christmas decorations around the city sparkled with a magical twinkle. I imagined that we were the modern version of the wise men and an angel, following the Christmas star to Bethlehem. You could feel the excitement and wonder as the kid's ooh and awed with each Christmas tree they saw.

We got our room and brought some of our things into the hotel. We were finally going to eat real food since our trip began, but found out that the restaurant in the hotel did not serve dinner, only breakfast and brunch. Getting back into the car we found an Arby's just down the road from where we were staying. There we sat enjoying, ham sandwiches with curly fries and hot cocoa. We watched the sky as it teased us with spitting snowflakes that lightly dusted the ground. People were filling their cars with their special holiday finds and we chuckled at the funny Christmas songs that were playing over the speakers.

After dinner, Don took us over to a CVS so we could pick up some candy canes and the new Rudolph Ornament from the holiday classic television show "Rudolph the Red-Nosed Reindeer."

After a long day of traveling, followed by food and fun in the pool, Don and the kids snuggled under the covers watching a Christmas show, but soon feel asleep. I sat up listening to the company Christmas party that was going on in the pavilion next to the pool and worked on painting some snowman ornaments. Trying to savor every moment of the evening, I tried to imagine what each one of my three little boys must have been dreaming. Yes, even at Christmas time Don is a little boy as well. At about 11:30pm, I too put my head on a pillow and followed Mr. Sandman off to dreamland.

Morning came quickly and we got our things together and had breakfast before heading out. The restaurant was all a buzz with the talk of the serious snowstorm forecasted and was following the path of our travels from the west. The kids were anxious to see their first Christmas snow, but as for Don and I, we knew we had a long trip ahead of us and could spell trouble. The skies began to turn from a beautiful sunny morning into a serious steely blue-grey. As our trip got us onto Route 80 the weather began to show its harsh side. The traffic began to slow down and the roads were changing quite rapidly as the snow fell faster and faster. At times it was hard to keep the collection of snow off the windshield so that we could see what lay ahead of us. Motorists were everywhere but on the road. Many of which had fallen victim to the large ditches at the bottom of steep embankments along the highway due to the slick conditions and poor visibility.

The decision was to keep going at a slow and steady pace, easy on the gas, light on the break and keep a good distance from the person in front of us. As we entered the state of Iowa, we stopped at a Flying "J" truck stop for fuel and food. Breakfast just didn't hold anyone over, so we were going to get quick simple food, donuts and milk, but not before a restroom stop as well. As I came out of the restroom with both kids, I happen to see a horrified look on Don's face.

"What's wrong now, speeding ticket flash back?" I asked sarcastically.

"Worse!" he exclaimed.

Now I have to tell you, Don always has had the special ability to find mystery gifts in his food, whether it's bad mayonnaise or big winged six legged things in a sandwich, but this number one mystery prize was something he would remember forever.

"Look at this Fallon, this is not right!"

I walked over to where he was standing and looked into a display case of donuts. Thinking it was some crazy new flavor or something, I stared into the case as Don reached in and pulled a four foot thick black hair from the display case. The best part was when two donuts in the case also began to move because each end of the hair had been cooked into the donuts. I was relieved to see that they were something that was cooked in the store and wasn't a favorite brand like Krispy Kreme or something.

Trying to find humor in the situation and make Don laugh, I couldn't help but comment, "You know Don if the hair was a bit shorter you could throw them over your head and wear them as donut ear muffs."

"Yummy, I'm hungry now." Don said in an unsteady and about to be sick voice.

"Mommy can we get donuts?" Dallas asked unaware of the event that had just taken place.

"No, they're having a two for one special and we can afford it. I think it would be a better idea if we look for ones already packaged." I said trying to keep a straight face. Don glared at me.

The kids and I found the goodies we wanted to snack on and Don finally got the composure to go on with looking for some kind of goodie for himself, when I just had to do it, and it took all I had not to laugh.

"Uh, Hey, Hon, would you come here and pay for this, I forgot my change in the car." *Not really but you'll love this.*

As he approached the counter a deep voice said to us, "That all?"

He looked up and was stunned; there in front of us was the owner of the four-foot thick black mystery hair she had cooked in her donuts.

"I'm out of here. Fallon I'll be in the car with the kids." shaking his head in total disgust.

He handed me the money for the kids and I, put his packaged food back on a near-by shelf and walked out the door sputtering while I laughed myself hysterically to the car as I followed behind him.

I was always taught what goes around comes around so because of my insincerity for the situation at the Flying "J", his gratification and my personal payback was on the horizon.

Getting back up onto the snow-covered road, I ate my goodies and sang songs with the kids and would tip my head to one side and shine a big cheesy grin when I would make eye contact with Don. Yes, I thought I was a funny girl.

"Oh Fallon, you'll get yours. Payback is a bitch, just you wait and see." laughing in his most sinister voice as he smirked when he looked at me.

"Ya, ya, ya, you're all talk." feeling on top of the world for the moment.

As our drive continued, a small pain began to roam and grow in the pit of my stomach. Thinking that I must be either hungry or nervous about meeting Don's birth father, I brushed it off. At about noon time we stopped at a Pizza Hut that was in an outlet plaza still in Iowa. We had a little lunch, but due to the stomach pain that I was dealing with, and would not go away, I didn't eat much. Maybe it was the elastic in my sweatpants or maybe, oh this wouldn't be good, maybe it was gas; this was going to be a fun.

Don asked if I would do some driving so that he could take a nap. Now going on long road trips with us is a process like a puzzle. Everyone and everything had a place so that all the doors could and would stay closed. Don, wanting to nap in the front seat where my position as a passenger was, would mean the removal of three blankets, one pillow, a crushed bag of chips, and the apple juice bottles that were being used as portable urinary stations for the boys. We must also not forget the ever dreaded and always full of shit that took up 90% of all my foot room, my overstuffed purse.

All of these things would need to be taken out. I would then have to get Don settled, organize the chaos, and try to put this puzzle back together around him so he could nap. Wanting to do my part, I decided I should take my turn behind the wheel. While dealing with my gas pain, I was able to get everyone and everything piled back into the car and off we went. The kids took their naps along with daddy and so it was just me, my gas, and I.

I had only driven about 100 miles when I just couldn't sit this way anymore. I desperately wanted to lie down, as the pain was so intense. I had tried to sit in every safe position I possibly would while driving, which included pulling my sweatpants down to mid-thigh to take the pressure off my stomach. *Yes mom, I had clean underwear on.*

I was going to have to give the wheel back to Don until this stomach pain went away. I can't tell you how many times I wished for the fart of farts to be released. My stomach was so bloated it looked like I had swallowed a huge beach ball. It was terrible. All I needed was a huge wicker basket, lots of rope and a match, and I could have doubled as a hot air balloon.

We stopped at this little blip on the map and Don and Dallas, went into this makeshift store that used to be a Dairy Queen just about 50 miles from Council Bluffs. Don had this craving for Gummi Bears and so he and Dallas got everyone a drink and of course packages of

Gummi Bears. It was a quick stop, because not everyone had to get out of the car, so there was less organization time required to get back onto the road.

Don kept making fun of me because I had my pants down around my knees, a pillow against the door for my head and my jacket to cover up with. I was a mess. I was dealing with a full blown stomach virus and all I wanted to do was try to sleep it off. I finally dozed off to dreamland and was able to rest a little, when again I was woken by the sounds of Don's voice screaming out a solid twenty dollar word.

"FUCK!"

"Don? What's the matter? Are you speeding again?"

"No. I just broke a tooth on one of these Jurassic Gummi Bears. Son of a bitch!"

"Little ears babe, little ears."

Thank goodness it was a tooth that had a root canal and was not painful just very sharp. He got on his portable phone and called his mother in Scottsbluff, Nebraska and asked her if they could get him a dental appointment when he arrived or the day after he got there.

"What next?" I said, "This just isn't our day."

Usually it is always something with the boys; whether it was potty breaks or car sickness, being bored or fighting. For me, it was pee breaks when there was no place to stop, and for Don, it was driving balls to the wall to get as far away from Maryland as he could. But we'd never trade the experience for the world. What's the fun of having a Griswold Family trip, if you don't have the ups and downs along the way?

It was a wonderful Christmas spent with family and old friends at the farm in Harrisburg, Nebraska. We split the time between his family and the newest members of his family that lived in North Platte, Nebraska. We rang in the New Millennium with Don's birth father and all the friends and family on that side of his additional family tree. We are glad that time and finances allowed us, this first time Holiday travel, out west were Don grew up. It was a time that we will never forget.

* * *

We have enjoyed many trips as a family since that memorable drive to the west. We have traveled to the top of the Rocky Mountains, where my mother actually touched a cloud. Several places immediately flood my mind as I think of all the places we have been as a family; Mt. Rushmore, Devils Tower, Fort Laramie, Yale Michigan, Orlando Florida, Estes Park, and so many more wonderful and exciting places. My kids have seen so much of the United States, so much more than I could have ever dreamed of seeing when I was their age. Don on the other hand, did quite a bit of traveling when he was young and doesn't mind going on trips, as long as they don't include busy cities and take him to or through his great state of Nebraska.

Of all the trips, the best one was the trip that took us to North Platte so Don, could finally meet the man, who gave him life, Michael Dean Way (this is his real name). Mike never knew he had fathered a child with Anne. I'll never forget that moment when they first looked at each other, an instant connection formed. I always said they were twins because they both wore blue jeans, fruit of the loom pocket t-shirts to put their smoky treats in, and they both had a little belly. The only difference was Mike was about two feet shorter. Don had gotten his height from his mother.

How they laughed and talked about their wild times during their Navy careers. Yes, Mike was a military career man, but the most haunting thing about this, was when Mike told Don that his last duty station was at the Denver Military Enlisted Processing Station in November of 1988. This just happened to had been the exact location and time frame when Don had entered the military. The shock and awe moment of the year was when Don, looked through his military paper work, after we got back from our trip, to see who signed him into the service. *I can still hear him now and the hairs on my arms and legs are standing straight up as I share this.*

"Fallon?" he spoke in a monotone voice and was accompanied by a facial look of utter disbelief.

"Yes," I answered trying to understand his tone and look.

"Remember when you told me years back when I asked you to help me find my birth mother and you said I had already met my dad face to face."

"Yes"

"How did you know that?"

"One of my weird dreams, why?"

"You'll never guess who swore me into active duty and signed my enlistment papers."

"No way, Mike?"

"Fallon, how could you have known that we met before? You didn't even know anything about me."

"A soulful connection." I smiled, "As I have told you before, all in a dream. I love you honey."

Another one of my sixth sense mysteries had been solved all in the name of love.

*　　*　　*

It is with a very heavy heart that I must tell you, that on October 29, 2010, at 5:53pm in a VA hospital in Cheyenne, Wyoming, Michael Dean Way, had passed on to his new Navy base in the sky. Rest in Peace Senior Chief, you will be missed.

CHAPTER THIRTY-FOUR

CHAOS

Schedules, phone calls, appointments – it was one thing after another! I found that I was become more extremely tense and completely overwhelmed. The kids had started school and things were not off to a good start. The Bethesda Naval hospital doctors had not done their part to complete my medical addendum, a requirement for my final medical board. *Whenever that would be.* Also, it had to be turned in by the ninth of September 2001. If it wasn't, I could possible lose what little pay I was receiving from the military. Losing any income from out family budget was something we would not recover from, unless we filed bankruptcy.

As each day slowly passed, sorrow filled my days, as though wet rice had been placed in the hour glass of time. I had this irrational anxiety that convinced me my mother was sick, that she was going to die. I found myself crying uncontrollably for seemingly no reason at all.

"Maybe my worrying about my mother was due to a serious illness she had a few years back?" I questioned myself each time I got upset.

In her right leg she had developed streptococcal, a flesh-eating bacteria, and had to be rushed to the hospital. The doctors reported that if she hadn't arrived when she did, she would have died within two days. I knew I had been experiencing uncontrollable crying, but I had no reason to believe that this was why. She has been in great heath since her recovery. I was overwhelmed with a tremendous amount of unknown loss.

Maybe I just need to stop thinking about everything so much. Maybe…just maybe…I have too much free time on my hands, or maybe I am not making enough time.

School had been in session for approximately a week and a half. I thought that with both boys being full time students, it would free up some of my time. Now I could get myself together and focus my thoughts on getting my book writing caught up. Unfortunately, this did not go as planned. Instead I would spend long hours in front of my computer writing mini paragraphs of what I fantasized would become the memoir of the century. *Yes, I am the dreamer of all dreamers.*

The only problem was, each word that appeared before my eyes took me back to places of anger and disappointment that I wasn't ready to deal with. So I put it off and just kept telling my family the book was almost done. I just never thought with each day I put it off, the pressures of those wanting to read my words began to weigh heavily on my subconscious. Quickly I became consumed with, an all too familiar feeling, the desire to sit alone quietly as the world went on outside my door. I did better about letting the boys go to school without me having to drive them every day. I would put the kids on the bus in the morning and retreat to the computer downstairs in the family room telling myself again, this would be the day I would finish my book. But as the days grew closer to the first part of September, I could not take the words from my mind and put them into print, and I couldn't understand why. Each of my attempts always resulted, in the same old, pity me song and dance.

'What is wrong with me? Why can't I get myself together, make the calls to the hospital, get these people in gear! Get your papers done! Stop volunteering so much! Focus more on home and family! Mom is fine! Stop worrying! BUT WHAT IS WRONG WITH ME! HELP ME SOMEONE! HELP ME! HELP ME STOP MY FEARS AND THESE TEARS FROM TAKING CONTROL OF ME! UGGGHHH!

It was the morning of August 31, 2001. I was getting into my usual "pity me" routine, when I was startled by the sound of a knocking at the front door. I ran upstairs, quickly wiping away tears of frustration. When I opened the door, I was relieved to find it was my friend, Edward that I had gotten to know while volunteering with the PTA at our sons' school. He was an officer with the Annapolis Police Department and a reservist in the Air Force branch of the military. These were two careers that always held my interest, but now unable to do either.

He was dropping off more uniforms to have the rating badges changed. Again I had come up with a way to make a little extra money, sewing patches on uniforms. The extra money was nice, but just to have someone stop by once in a great while, got me through many lonely days. I don't even think he knew this. If he did, he was respectful and kept it to himself very well. I am sure he could see that I had been crying when I opened the door. Felling self-conscious, I didn't want to explain why I was so red eyed and emotional. I just laughed it off and became my cheery, nothing is bugging me, self again. *A classic Cybil moment.*

I would on occasion look forward to his stopping by, as this was my only adult interaction I had until Don would come home from work. Now somewhere in this eclectic head of mine, I had this perception that if you wore a uniform you were somebody special. In my mind I felt that I was no longer important because I didn't wear mine anymore. My once perfectly shined inspection boots and pressed uniform had fallen victim to a dust covered cruise box stowed in our garage. To be in the presence of someone who wore both the military and policemen uniform, and actually spoke to me, made me feel special. *Dumb hua?* Our talks would only last ten to fifteen minutes tops, when he did stop in, due to his limited personal time. He was indeed a work-a-holic. When we did get a chance to talk, our conversations always revolved around our experiences in the military and how we both agreed on how political the military had become.

On occasion I would get a sense of comfort to discuss my latest saga of fighting the military with him, as the topic was often hard on Don. One way or another, I was going to get compensated for my medical issues. Overall, I enjoyed and preferred listening to his adventures as a military member, a police officer and the gal in his life that he married one beautiful day in June. As he spoke I never once showed how much I though what life must be like if I could be in his shoes, as a police officer, even for just a day.

Having the additional military duties in his life really made finding personal time very difficult. Now knowing his new wife, Patricia, very well, I think I can safely say that his military days were very stressful for both of them, but love would prevail. Being newly married, he couldn't express it enough that he was looking forward to having more time with his new bride and to do the job he loved, police work.

During his visit this time, he was unbelievably cheerful. I could see that he had something he was just itching to tell someone. He smiled as he told me his time was just about up in the Air Force and he would be a permanent civilian soon. I don't think the he ever expected the twist that life was planning for him and his family.

He gave me all the information as to where all the new badges were to be sewn. We agreed that he could pick them up on the following Monday morning. Needless to say, my sewing machine had other ideas.

Now I have to tell you about my love hate relationship with my sewing machine. It is over thirteen years old and just as moody as I am when I'm in the middle of a week of menstrual cramps. Because it decided to give me bobbin and tension troubles, I was forced to take it in to be fixed and would not get in back for about ten days. Worried I called Edward and told him about my situation. He completely understood, as this was not the first time my sewing machine had given me trouble. I was relieved to know, he was not in any rush to have them back. I explained that I would be getting my machine back on September 10th, and he could pick his uniforms up on the morning of 11th.

Exactly ten days later, I got my sewing machine back just as the technician had promised. I had every intention of getting his uniforms ready so that he could pick them up on Tuesday morning. I had gotten all but one shirt completed, when a severe case of "pity me'" had overcome my thinking again. Now, having a Masters in professional procrastination, I should have taken five more minutes to finish the job, but instead decided to get up early in the morning to finish it, which is a joke, as I am the worst person to rise any earlier that eight in the morning.

Oddly enough something serious had my thoughts wrapped up as tight as a size twelve girdle being forced on by a size twenty body. Nothing was going to give in or give me an answer. As the day went on, I began pacing from room to room. My hands were cold and clammy, and I couldn't speak without the urge to cry. When my kids returned home and found me so upset, they just chalked it up as another bad day for mommy.

Shortly after dinner, around 6:30 that evening, I had this tremendous sense of loss and was terrified that something had happened to my mother. I made several phone calls to her home, but there was no answer.

"Mom, where are you!? Please God let her be ok! Mom, please pick up the phone!" I said over and over that began to scare both Don and the kids.

With every attempt to reach her, there was still no answer. I paced around the house feeling helpless and still was unsure why I was so worried.

Don kept telling me, "Sit down and relax. She is probably at the store or a school meeting."

When the phone finally rang, I leaped to my feel and quickly rushed to the phone, knocking down a half-filled laundry basket that needed to be folded. I was slightly relieved when I saw her name appear on our caller ID panel.

"Mom!" I said frantically and short of breath before the receiver got to my ear.

"Fallon, what is the matter?!" She said in a frightened voice.

Taking another deep breath I asked her, "Are you ok!?"

"Yes why? What's wrong? Fallon, you need to calm down!"

"I just had this terrible feeling that something had happened to you."

"I was at the grocery store to get a few things," she replied, still concerned about the tone of my voice.

Hearing her voice helped me put my fears at ease, but I still had felt that at any moment I would start crying again. She told me that she felt I was just stressed out and that I needed to establish a good routine. Mom was always right about this topic; I was never the one for sticking to a daily routine. I always waited until the last minute or simply put it off until the job became so overwhelming, I would want to quit. We talked for a good two hours, and by the end of our conversation I felt that she was fine and I had nothing more to fear.

"You were right, Don. She was at the store," I said. I hated the fact that once again, he was right.

"What did my ears hear? You said I was right?" He said as he proudly lifted his chest.

"Yes, you were right. There, you finally heard me say it," I quickly responded, trying not to boost the adrenaline of ego that was consuming his mind like volcanic lava on a near-by Hawaiian village.

"I told you so. Do you feel better?" he said.

"I guess."

"What do you mean, you guess?"

"Something just isn't right, I feel something bad is about to happen… but what? I have not a clue."

He knew that something was eating at me and knew that I needed a different train of thought.

"I put the kids to bed so you could talk to your mom. They are asleep, but I told them you'd give em' hugs and kisses, aren't I just wonderful?"

"But of course," I said with a smile. "Thank you honey."

"I am going to take a shower, and I am going to bed. I'm beat."

"That sounds like a good idea." I replied as I went to give the boys their good night kisses.

I quietly tried to maneuver through the minefield of plastic army toys, matchbox cars and micro-machines that lined the floors of both kids' bedrooms. Not an easy task, but I did make my way to their beds without requiring a Band-Aid or a 911 call afterwards.

I took an extra-long look at their innocent little faces, kissed them good-night and whispered to them, "I love you." For some unexplained reason I just didn't want to leave their rooms. I stood there in the hallways between their rooms. Worried, wondering, waiting – waiting for an unknown event.

I got into bed and waited for Don to finish his shower, so he could then dry off and then crawl into bed beside me. I wasn't until I felt him against me that I finally drifted off to sleep.

*   *   *

Don had already left for work when I awoke to feel a cool and gentle autumn breeze tickle my undressed shoulders from the open window over our bed. To add some amusement to my day, I enjoyed watching pieces of dust like particles dancing in the rays of sunlight that filtered through the partially opened louver window blind. A perfect fall like morning filled with the sounds of Dallas and Dillan watching cartoons and my alarm clock, that kept reviving itself after having its snooze bar assaulted by me every ten minutes. *Come on, be honest, you do it too.*

I would have loved to have slept in, but it was already 7:15, and the kids had to get ready for school. I got up, got them dressed, fed them breakfast, and then took my shower and got myself ready. I decided that I would make the day special and take them to school rather than ride the bus. To them, this was a very big deal and quite a treat. We left for the school at about 8:35am and the announcer on the radio was reporting that a plane had either crashed or was going to crash in the Pennsylvania. Before I could get the rest of the report, Dallas decided to put a tape in to listen to. To us, the morning of September 11th, was like any other day. We were unaware of what was taking place in America. I dropped them off and went back to the house so that I could finish the shirt for Edward. As I completed what was left of my sewing, the doorbell rang.

"*Wow, he's early.*" I thought to myself.

I opened the door expecting Edward. To my surprise, there stood two older ladies. They were trying to do their best to solicit their views of religion. They believed religion would stop the hatred in the world. Now I don't want to disrespect their beliefs and religion, but my honest opinion is that everyone has different religions that they practice. I find it very intrusive for those who choose to go door to door to push the issue and practices of their religion. Before you know it, we'll have to put on our mailbox what faith we are just to keep some from knocking down our doors thinking they know it all. My family and I are Methodist and I find it rather troublesome to have someone knocking on my door to preach the word of God that is not of my faith. Now this has gone on for several months, and I have asked politely, each time, not to return to my home. This latest visit only place me in a position to finally be rude. Even after I became uncouth, they still insisted on coming into my home. My philosophy – No means no, get the hell out!

In the middle of one woman's persuasion, I finally said goodbye and closed the door. I looked up at the clock that read 8:59am, and realized that Regis and Kelly would be on in few minutes. Watching them helped me to de-stress, big time. This was good, as I was in dire need of a pick-me-up after being preached at by two people that I don't even know, on a topic that I was rather uncomfortable with.

As I walked towards the television, I was overcome with terror as a wind shear of fear ripped right through me.

"They are going to die!" I screamed but didn't know why. I went into the kitchen for drink of water; I couldn't believe what had just happened.

"Is this what our Vietnam veterans suffer from when the have flashbacks." I pondered, *"But why would I have a flash about something I've never seen before?"*

As my jitters began to subside, I went back into the living room. I turned the television on, only to become transfixed on what was being broadcasted before my eyes. So unimaginable. The words, so haunting.

"We are just currently getting a look at the World Trade Center. Something has happened here, flames, and an awful lot of smoke from one of the towers. We are trying to determine, what that is. Whatever has occurred has just occurred within minutes." It was clear that the reporter was in total disbelief as to what she was seeing. "Flames are shooting out, smoke is shooting out."

"This isn't happening. It's a dream; I'm dreaming...I have to be!"

Hoping that my concerns and sorrow were triggered by clips to a movie, like the movie "Independence Day." I proceeded to jump from channel to channel. Numerous reporters, all sharing the same words of concern for those possibly trapped or hurt inside the building. Their reports began to hit hard as a realization set in, these events were actually taking place and I was watching it live at that very moment.

CHAPTER THIRTY-FIVE

A NATION MOURNS

During this horrendous moment, I felt the same irritability and the sense of loss that had come over me daily during the past few weeks. This was a place that had a special meaning in my heart from a past point in my life. Now it was at the mercy of nature's feared fury, fire.

In 1984, my mother and I embarked on a Christmas show and shop bus tour of New York City. One of the highlights of our trip, going to the Windows of the World indoor observation area to view the City from high a top of the World Trade Center. I got many pictures so that I could relive the amazement of standing at the top of one of the largest buildings in the world. It was then my mother and I bonded into friendship, from what was a mother daughter relationship. It was a time that has always kept a special place in my heart. I had hoped to have enjoyed a moment like this with my own children one day.

I watched, in disbelief, the black smoke billow from the outside of the buildings.

"Put the fire out! Put the fire out!" I yelled at the television over and over.

Then a view from the Pentagon appeared. Slowly it was being reported that these crashes were intentional and were acts of terrorists. I changed the channel. Something kept my focus on wanting to see more of what was happening in New York. Before my eyes, I saw the explosion of the second tower and the endless replay of a second plane crashing into it.

"Both towers of the World Trade Center have been hit by aircraft, both are in flames. There is black smoke coming from both of the towers." paused a female reporter, trying to find the words, "Ah...ah...it's a horrific scene here, debris is flying through the air. Clearly this is not an accident. Officially this is an act of a terrorist. We now have reports of a fire at the pentagon, clearly not an accident. The F.B.I. is now investigating a report of a plane high-jacking before the crashes at the World Trade Center this morning. We will keep you posted as more information is provided."

Not only the events of what was taking place were being televised, nothing had a chance to be edited. It was all being broadcasted live. Before the Nations eyes, people were seen jumping to their death. As I stood there, tears, streamed from my eyes. Then suddenly, I was breathless. Again I could see the floor joints, people standing in the stairwell. Screams of terror engulfed my thoughts as razor sharp chills raced throughout my body. I knew it then, these towers – they're going to fall.

What madness! A form of torture for those inside! A LIVING HELL! WHY! How long will these buildings remain standing? God! Please make these thoughts go away. PLEASE! HELP THESE PEOPLE TO SAFETY! How long would God make them wait, before he would come to take so many innocent lives home with him? Would the people get out? People in the elevators, GET THEM OUT!

I was lost in the surrealism of what had been about an hour since I had first turned on the television.

"It wasn't happening, it was a sick joke!" I thought as I remembered the special report on the death of Princess Diana. We were watching Saturday Night Live when a special report aired. It was just ironic timing that it fell during one of their mock news skits. Don and I could not believe that SNL would air such a sick joke. Much to our surprise, the joke was on us as the footage went on for more than then minutes and other stations were also airing the auto accident she was involved in. Sadly, we realized that what we were seeing had actually happened.

The screams of the news anchors snapped me back to focus on the events taking place. The south tower was buckling at the point of impact. At a great rate of speed it crumbled to the ground, taking the lives that may still be inside.

"OH MY GOD! NO, NO!" I screamed at the top of my lungs.

"A situation that started bad just gets worse and worse." Were the words spoken by another reporter just after the south tower had fallen.

"The World Trade Center south tower, which was hit by a plane, followed by an explosion approximately an hour ago, has collapsed. If you are just joining us this morning, you are in for a horrific surprise…"

On my radio, a similar report, "Just minutes ago the South Tower of the World Trade Center collapsed to the ground. One tower is standing at this point. Although there's no report on casualties, the loss of life is presumably profound."

It was not long after, the second tower soon followed suit and it too, took with it mothers, fathers, policemen, firemen, brothers and sisters and so many more. The news reported that the plane crash in Pennsylvania was also part of a terrorist act to crash into what they believed to be the White House or the Capital building. All air traffic was being grounded until further notice. When they began to mention the safety of children located in the near-by childcare center close to the World Trade Center, I yelled out. "MY BOYS! I NEED TO GET MY BOYS!"

I rushed to the phone to call Don at work to inform him of the events that were taking place.

"That explains the big boom that I heard earlier." He said, still trying to make sense of what was taking place.

"I thought it odd that everyone I passed on the highway, as I made my delivery, was on a cell phone."

"Don, I have to get the kids, come home…PLEASE come home! I love you."

"I love you to, I'll get home as fast as I can, don't worry. You just worry about keeping yourself and the kids safe."

Since my cancer diagnosis, I had mastered a new skill. When faced with a major crisis, I can be as strong as steel, as well as, calm, cool, collected and stress free. The little things, it's best to drug me up, put me in a straight jacket in a rubber room and throw away the key.

Without a second thought I had turned everything off in the house, and was out the door. I immediately rushed down the porch steps, got in my car and made my way to the school. If something catastrophic was going to happen, I was going to have my babies with me, no matter what!

The school lobby and office was filled with terrified people experiencing mass confusion. Parents and guardians had the same maternal instinct, wanting to get the children home. I have to give credit to the faculty and staff of Germantown Elementary School. They to, handled the situation with ease. Calmly and effectively, you would have thought they had been training for this day, for years.

Still being some-what connected with the military, we had always been told that in the event of an emergency on a grand scale, we were to report to the base.

My thoughts on that idea, *"A military installation was the last place to be."*

My children could sense that there was something terribly wrong as we made our way out of the school.

"Mommy, why are there so many people at my school today?" Dillan said. You could see that he was feeling a bit nervous.

"Mommy just wants you both to come home early today."

"I heard something was on fire." said Dallas trying to repeat a conversation he had overheard between some parents in the hall near his locker.

On the way home, I tried to explain without scaring either of them, "Something had happened that hurt a lot of people." They were accepting of this explanation for the time being.

We got back to the house and I had the kids put a movie into the VCR so that they didn't have to see first-hand what was happening. It seems that every television channel was reporting on the events that were taking place. Don called to establish a plan, that in the event of an evacuation I would meet him at a specific location. His preference was to head west. Our rendezvous point would be just a location we know well in West Virginia.

As I hung up the phone, I flashed back to a night that I was awoken from or horrific dream. In my dream I am walking through the hallway of our home here in Maryland. I find my way to my bedroom to where my husband is sleeping very peacefully. I slowly sit down on the edge of my side of the bed. I look up to see a bright white flash. "I love you" I say out loud to my kids and husband as things are being blown away. I felt no pain and the only one sound, my voice saying good-bye. To this day, I refuse to change my furniture around in my room, in the same way that it was in my dream. I guess this is my way of thinking that I can harness any future events of mass destruction.

I quickly shrugged the images of the dream.

"No! This can't happen!" I said quietly to myself.

My thoughts were filled with so many fears and questions, but nothing spoke out-loud to scare my boys.

I am so angry, just kick ass and take names later. They had no right to do this to America! What have we done to deserve this! Life will no longer be as it once was. Don please, come home to us. My Children, what does the future hold for them? I should call my mother. Should I pack a bag if we have to evacuate? Where is a safe place? Is my grandmother ok? Is my mother ok?

I was entirely numb with no sense of what my next move should be. It was the voice of my younger son, Dillan, asking for a cookie, which helped me refocus. Throughout the day, I listened to reports that came over a low volume radio in the kitchen. All the information, still the same, it was indeed terrorism and the death totals would be in the thousands. Don finally walked through the back door at about 4:30pm. It was only then I let part of my guard down. The boys did not hear him come through the door. That was probably a good thing as I desperately needed to just hold him. His reason for being later than he'd hoped was that the traffic was backed up. Everyone, I'm sure, was trying to get home to their loved ones. I went towards him and fell into his arms as the strength within me fell apart. I finally felt safe as he held me close. Hearing him say that everything is going to be fine, comforting. Yet all the strength that I had built up during my cancer treatments and life experiences in the military could have never prepared me for this day. I feared that it was inevitable that our country would go to war. Life, as we knew it, was going to change forever.

"But did this mean that Don could be reactivated?" I shuttered to think of the possibility.

While changing their movie, the kids had seen on the television the collapse of the World Trade Center, but were unaware that this was live. To them it was just another movie with special effects. When they were finally aware that Don was home from work, they quickly told us of what they had seen.

"Daddy, you know what, we saw a big building fall down in the smoke." said four year old Dillan.

"It was just a movie." replied our older son Dallas, nonchalantly.

Don sat down and tried to explain that what they had seen on the television was not a movie. Some bad people were the ones who had done this to these buildings. We made it very clear, to both of them, that they never speak to strangers and if something goes on at school they are to listen to the teacher's instructions. That we would get to them as soon as we could if something were to go wrong. They were happy with this explanation and as if nothing ever happened, asked their dad to come and wrestle with them. They showed no signs of worry, but then again, being as young as they were, I think that is what protected their minds from harm.

Life for my friend Edward and his family drastically changed on September 11, 2001 and the days to follow. What were once Police badges that were being sewn onto uniforms of blue were now military badges being sewn on khaki colored shirts, pants and jackets. What he thought were just a few more years in the reserves, were immediately changed to full active duty. He was called on 9/11 at 11:30pm and told to report to his unit at 5:00am the next morning. He worked at Andrews Air Force Base as a Security Controller (Dispatcher) on the midnight shift until October 22, 2001. He was then sent over to Bolling Air Force Base in Washington, D.C., his new assignment, Assistant Flight Chief.

During these new and additional duties, that disrupted his family life and duties with local law enforcement, was a constant worry on the minds of all. Would his unit be sent overseas to enforce our homeland security? On August 19, 2002, fears became reality as he and his unit embarked on their Journey to Saudi Arabia. I feared that if he was going to be sent, then the Seabees could recall Don and Frank to do another tour in Saudi Arabia, even if they had already go out. That was something I had feared for a very long time, and was relieved as the years passed one by one and the call never came.

While Edward was overseas, Patricia and I got to know each other very well and became great friends. My prayers were always said for Edward and Patricia, as they walked the journey of his military duty to fight and defend our great nation and to rid the world of terrorism. My prayer also went out nightly to our military men and woman of our armed forces.

May God bless you and keep you safe from harm. We will prevail.

***

I am happy to report that Edward came home and he eventually got to enjoy his retirement day from the armed forces. Today he is still employed with the Annapolis Police Department, and lives with his beautiful wife, Patricia, here in Annapolis.

CHAPTER THIRTY-SIX

WIN OR LOSE

What a series of emotional journeys that had been bestowed upon me. To best describe my journey as I look back on the events that I encountered would be as this, walking through the Sahara Desert with occasional food, water, and shelter. That each day would bring up hills and down, that bad would do its best to contain me, but good would always prevail when the innocence of my boys and the loving soul of my husband, would walk in the door after a long day. So many days I wanted to just give up, to close the door to the endless drama and just fade away. It was when I thought that there was truly no hope to find an ending or some form of closure, a spiritual feeling would come over me as if God's hands would extend before me. With his love and the love of my family they helped me continue on the right path and believe in the strength within me and to remember that there is always hope and what was important, my family.

With all that had gone wrong over the last several years and I believed that all hope was lost, I got the call that I had been waiting for on April 17, 2002. I would learn that Wednesday June 5, would be a day that would be become extremely important to both myself and my family. Yes, the final saga of my journey in the military would possible come to an end. This was the morning that my final hearing had been scheduled for. The day I had been longing and fearing since May 26, 1994, it was my chance to finally be heard.

* * *

The morning started out uneventful as I prepared for my hearing that was being held at the National Naval Medical Center in Bethesda,

Maryland. I followed my basic morning routine as I have always done for days that I had to travel to Bethesda. It was a humid morning with the hint of rain in the air. Traffic on the beltway was its typical regiment, miles of cars slowly moving in and out of each other over all five lanes. Everyone trying to get somewhere and each doing their best trying to find the fastest route. My thoughts didn't dwell on the topic of the pending hearing before me. It was the worry that I may not get back to attend the award ceremony being held at the school that my boys attended. Both of my boys were being awarded for perfect attendance and I had promised that mommy and daddy would be there. *Me and my promises are going to seriously get me into trouble one day.*

I arrived at the base at 8:10 am and was greeted with a smile from the on duty security guard checking military identification cards.

"Thank you, and have a nice day Petty Officer." said the guard with another full smile.

"You do the same." I said sharing a smile of my own.

Finding parking was probably the easiest task that I had to undergo and what made my day was that I found a space close to the air-conditioned overpass that connected the parking garage and the Medical center together. I only endured the humidity for about thirty seconds, which was fine with me. I made my way to a location of the Medical Center that was near building one.

Building one is a twenty-story tower that is filled with many departmental office spaces. I was to report to the ninth floor, which was, where all hearings and meetings with legal counsel members took place.

I stopped by the bank and withdrew ten dollars from my savings account and then went over to the Dunkin Donuts/Subway food court to grab a little something before heading upstairs. I didn't have to report to my legal counselor until 8:30 am. I got two glazed donuts and a pint of 2% milk, paid the cashier and was on my way. Elevator service was extremely quick and in a matter of seconds the doors opened to the ninth floor hall. As I was making my way toward the reception area I ran into Lt. Parker, that was also a legal counselor, just not mine. She had the personality of a professional lawyer, she was perfect for the case I had. She escorted me to the waiting area and reassured me that all was to be just fine today.

"Just sit and relax and don't worry." She said in a pleasant voice.

I was worried, worried that my legal counselor was not the right man for the job. I had about two months to meet with him, but his choice, the day before the hearing. His inability to look me straight in the face during the first visit, the day before, and his speaking ability with me on the phone would make anyone in this situation feel like a long tail cat in a room full of rocking chairs.

I had even commented that I wished that Lt. Parker could sit in on the hearing. My counselor came from around the corner, before I could explain why I wanted her with me. I am sure he heard everything I said, but I could have cared less. I just smiled and then changed the topic. He explained to me that my 9:00 am hearing was now being changed to 10:00 am. *Why am I not surprised, the Navy way – hurry up and wait.*

I was also very concerned about keeping my promise to my children that I would be home as I was unsure how long this would take. I didn't show my concern or worry to anyone and I don't think they knew, or at least they never suspected I had other things on my mind. Both counselors then left me to sit alone in the waiting room. The silence was often tickled by the sound of a bell that signified the arrival of an available elevator.

While I sat quietly upon one of five couches, I couldn't help but chuckle as I looked around the room. There was no doubt in my mind, that the military had a hand in the decorating. *Martha Stewart would not have commented that it was a good thing.* Along with the couches, two love seats and one chair all upholstered in that have to have color of the military, *and I mean this as sarcastically as I can be,* battleship grey. They were arranged so it appeared in this one room space, to look as if it had two back to back living rooms. Each area had a coffee table that had a limited display of outdated magazines of Golf Digest, All Hands, and the Naval Reservist News. I think someone was trying to make a point, retire, which was what I think the Navy had planned for me to accomplish on this very day. All I can say, "Not without my benefits!"

The room was painted in the every-popular military regulation color, eggshell white, accented with plastic roll out grey molding glued to the base of the wall. The room was finished with large potted green leafy plastic plants, a must for any home, if you didn't own water to keep real plants alive. As observant as I am when it comes to decorating, this was indeed something I would have never recommended, with the exception of the art work on the walls. The artwork was all inspiration posters of brilliant photos of natures' beauty accompanied by soul-filling quotes. They had been placed in black plastic frames and mounted around the room. This was the most attention getting part of the makeshift military waiting room.

As I read each one I felt as though it was speaking about each part of my journey since the day I entered the Navy. As I took a long look at each photo and then read each quote below, I took some time to reflect on what it was saying. I would like to share with you these quotes in the order in which I read them.

ACHIEVEMENT

"Unless you try to do something beyond what you have already mastered, you will never grow.

THE ESSENCE OF DESTINY
"Watch your thoughts, for they become words.
Choose your words, for they become actions.
Understand your actions, for they become habit.
Study your habit, for they will become your character.
Develop your character, for it becomes your destiny."

ATTITUDE
"The people who get on in this world are the people who get up and look for the circumstances they want, and, if they can't find them, make them."
~ George Benard Shaw ~

THE POWER OF BELIEF
"Believe in yourself. You gain strength, courage, and confidence by every experience in which you stop to look fear in the face...you must do that which you think you cannot do."
~ Eleanor Roosevelt ~

THE LIGHT OF INTERGRITY
"The soul is dyed the color of its thoughts. Think only on those things that are in the line with your principals and can bear the full light of day. The content of your character is your choice.
Day by day, what you chose, what you think, and what you do is who you become. Your integrity is your destiny...it is the light that guides your way.
Heraclitus
Greek Poet, Philosopher

"What a way it has been." I said to myself, "What a way indeed."

After reading and then writing these quotes into my journal, I took in a deep cleansing breath and then stood looking out the window pondering my journey and all the challenges I have faced.

At about 9:58 am another person arrived for their 10:00 am hearing. We talked about our medical history for a bit and the struggles that we have faced trying to get to this day. She seemed rather disappointed to learn that my 9:00 am hearing had been changed to 10:00 am, which only meant one thing, she too was going to get into her meeting later than she had planned. I have to admit that I was glad that I was going to be first. My hopes were that I would get people that already had their coffee, breakfast, and were in a fairly good mood. I was informed that when the board members were ready to have each case heard, there would be a signal. All they had to do was press a button in the hearing room that would make a large buzzing sound in the hallway. One signal was for just the legal counselors to discuss the case and their findings. Two signals meant the lawyer and the client were to appear together.

One long buzz finally signaled from a small metal box from just outside the door to the hearing room. My counselor immediately came from around the corner. Knocked on the door and waited to be told to enter. At about 10:38 he came out of the hearing room alone with an unconvincing look of disappointment. Again, something just didn't sit right, but I knew what it was, I didn't trust him.

"Well what did they say?"

"They, meaning the board, do not want to increase your benefits to 30%."

"On what grounds?"

"Excuse me?" he said in a pissy voice.

"I SAID! ON...WHAT...GROUNDS?! Did you hear that?" I said not willing to play his bullshit game.

"If you choose not to appear before the board it will stay at 20%, which is good as they wanted to drop you to 10% and even that is pushing it. So here is the deal at 20% or even at 10% you still get eight months of pay as a third class petty officer, but that means that your VA pay will stop paying you until it equals the separation check amount received by the Navy. You can also sign the check over to VA and continue receiving some monthly benefits from the VA. The last option is to still go into the hearing, keeping in mind that you will still receive a separation check amount that I explained to you."

"What do you think?" I asked him while the shock of what I was hearing faded.

"It's not up to me."

"I understand that, but what is your honest impression of the board members?" What were they feeling?" I asked in a stern voice trying to control myself and to maintain my composure.

"As I said, they would rather give you just 10%. So you will still get some money."

After his last response, I went silent. I pondered numerous scenarios, but not about what would happen behind the doors, my thoughts were, *"How much trouble would I get in if I punched my counselor out cold? What would I do next? I have got to get control of myself. I didn't come all this way just to walk away with a check that will only be received for eight months out of forever. It's not about money; it is about health care. Go for it! Go for it! Fight for your rights; be strong as he is not going to be the strength to see this matter through for you. You CAN DO IT SEABEE! It's up to you, your time to say what have been waiting to say all of these years.*

"It's not about the money! It is about what is right! I want to appear before the board!" I yell at him.

He looked at me almost shocked with what I was about to do. His response was very unsettling as he quickly left the waiting room and went back to his office to get what papers he had prepared. I was not going to let the negativity of his attitude stop me; I was going to take my time in the court room. I was going to be heard!

"Ok, let's go in." he said as he knocked on the door and waited for approval to enter.

I immediately hit the record button on my pocket recorder and walked into the hearing room.

Epilogue

The table was in the shape of the letter T. There were three board members seated across the top of the T shape and a single chair for myself was at the bottom and to the left side was a single seat for my lawyer. I was instructed, before entering, that I when I was in the hearing room I was to stand on the right side of my chair and report as ordered.

"I am Petty Officer Bentley reporting as ordered."

"Please be seated." replied the President of the Physical Evaluation Board, "This formal board will come to order, it is convened by the director of the Naval Counselor Personnel Boards appointing order date 27, March 2001 as attended. The case of Petty Officer Fallon Bentley has been properly referred for determination of physical fitness for continued naval service. Determination of entitlement to benefits authorized by title 10 of procedures governed in the operation of this formal board are contained in the disability evaluation. My name is Captain London, presiding officer. Good morning."

Sitting straight and tall with my hands placed on the table, one over the other, I looked directly into each of the members eyes as they were introduced and I responded with my greeting.

"Good Morning Captain London."

"The medical member for this board is Dr. Jackson."

"Good Morning Dr. Jackson."

"And the second line officer member is Commander Collins."

"Good Morning Commander Collins."

Usually it is customary to reply with a greeting followed by sir or ma'am, but I wanted to make the most professional impression I could make and chose to use their rank and rate. I believed we were off to a good start.

"All persons required to be sworn have been sworn. Petty Officer Bentley, please state you full name, rank, social security number and home of residence to which you reside." said Captain London in a strong military demeanor.

I responded with all the information that had been asked of me. In spite of a minor nervous sounding voice, I did very well and was very respectful.

"Very well, I have here an Eledgment of Right's form that has properly been filled out. Do you recognize your signature?"

"Yes I do, Ma'am."

"Do you fully understand your rights as outline on this form?"

"Yes I do, Ma'am."

"By whom will you be represented?"

"I will be represented by Counsel Lt. Charles Dawson."

It wasn't until I got a chance to review the audiotape, I had made, that I realized that I had given the wrong first name for my counselor. *Oh well.*

"Counsel please state your qualifications for the record." asked Captain London.

"None, none at all ma'am." That is what I was thinking.

"Ma'am I am qualified and certified in accordance with article 27 Bravo of the Uniform Code of Military Justice and sworn in accordance with article 42 Alfa UCMJ.

"Very well, is there any member of the board aware of any reason that would render or be unable to accord Petty Officer Bentley a fair and impartial hearing?

"No" replied all the board members.

"Let the record reflect a negative response from all board members."

It was at that moment that a hurricane of questioning began. The problem was, it seemed that it was the same questions over and over, but structured differently, as if to catch me in a lie. I also took notice that they didn't have any of the materials that I had provided my counselor for them to review. They were only given materials that were only pertaining to my current health and services provided by the military. I had provided my counselor with a slew of documentation provided by civilian doctors, hospitals, dentists, and new secondary illnesses in conjunction with my cancer treatments. I had all of this during our meeting the day before. He simply said it was irrelevant to the case and that it would not help me.

I could see that the board members questioned my information about having to be rushed to the hospital for an asthma attack that was a condition related to my radiation therapy, and two days later, following that ER visit, I was diagnosed with restricted airway disease.

Why did they think this way? My counselor failed to provide them any documentation to support what I was saying. My frustration fueled resentment and anger in me that I have never had in my life. I wanted blood!

That bastard! He didn't give them anything I had, NOTHING! So it looks like I am the liar here!

Such bad thoughts, so many bad thoughts, that if I had acted upon, I would have been taken to jail and be facing a military court martial. This counselor had screwed me, big time and there was no way he was going to get away with it. He had no idea what I was capable of, but he was going to find out the hard way.

"Petty Officer Bentley, I am hearing about all these doctor appointments and new illnesses, yet I see no documentation to support your claims." She commented, wanting an immediate answer.

Here it was, she had given me a moment that I could make history, but was I strong enough?

Pausing to ponder the repercussion of what I was about to do, the words came out of my mouth with grace and ease. "Ma'am I was told that these documents were irrelevant to my case."

Holy shit, I said it. I said it. Stay calm Fallon, stay calm.

I became a full powered overloaded freight train that had just derailed and was heading towards an unexpected town. I wasn't holding anything back any longer. My counselor just sat there, nothing he could say or do to stop me from being heard. Years of frustration! Years of anguish! The moments that I have been unable to remember with my baby boy because of depression. The pain, oh my god THE PAIN! Four years following my treatments, I was without anyone willing to help me with my dental disease caused by the radiation. I had to be active duty for any dental benefits. If it hadn't been for Dr. Caesar Romeo whose touch was as gentle as his heart, I would have lost all my teeth. Understanding both my pain and financial cost of this situation, he did everything under the sun to bring my dental care to a full manageable level, while at the same time, ensuring that my out of pocket expenses stayed within reason. I am blessed that he is still in the practice and my dentist.

I am sure that the board members were wondering what was happening, anything and everything was coming out and was being strewn across the table. Everything that my counselor said was irrelevant was now out for the board members to sift through and decipher the real facts that supported my fight to keep my benefits. I was here and I wasn't leaving unless I won!

I sneered at my counselor as he fumbled over his words of explanation trying to regain the confidence and trust from the board members.

When the president of the board turned and looked at me, I pulled out my one final dagger to prove that my counselor had made a bad choice with my case. I pick up the entire original medical record that was noted as lost in Adak, in the paperwork that they had, and put it on the table. Even my counselor didn't realize it was the original medical record. It was a five inch thick binder of all original documentation from the very first moment I stepped into an active duty role and when my medical fiasco began. I told my counselor I had documentation, but again, he told me it was irrelevant.

"Ma'am, this is what I have faced since I started this adventure. People who claim they will help me and never follow through" then I looked over at the only man on the board panel and addressed him personally. "Sir, what I am about to say is in no disrespect towards you. I am also not saying that every man is this way. Ok?"

"That's fine, continue," he said puzzled.

"Everyone I had to go to for help was a man! Don't get me wrong, some were more than helpful. Most were not. They would turn away as their views are women should not be in their Navy. They felt that if they made my life hell, I would just get out. My dreams were to be the officer of the family. My dream was taken away as soon as word got out that I was sick. I was sick, not dead!"

Then without warning, my emotions set in, but I kept my strength that was fueled with adrenaline, and went on.

"I don't know how many times I have to repeat myself. I have said it over and over again, my reason for coming all this way, the benefits. It has never been about the money! It's about my health care now and for the future!"

The room was silent as I wiped the tears from my eyes. I was mortified that I actually let myself cry. What a chick move. Yet, I think it wasn't that I was seeking the sympathy of the board, it was the weight that I had thrown off my shoulders. I had said my peace. I had finally spoke my mind. I didn't back down, something I should have done the when I was given the prescription I was ordered to take. Had it gone to court then, I would have had proof and it would have been over. Either way, that's here nor there, I had finally done what I need to do, I let it out. It was now up to them.

"Thank you Petty Office Bentley. Counselor, you and your client are dismissed. Would you please have a seat in the waiting room?"

"Yes Ma'am" was all he could say.

As we walked out of the room, I started to feel myself shake. I wanted to lash out at my counselor, get in his face, and give him a piece of my mind. My guardian angel must have been on my shoulder watching out for me as she graced me with two miracles that day. The first, seeing how angry my counselor was for the way I had made him look in front of the board members. He no longer wore his mask of ego, disgust was now the mask he wore, and I was proud that I had put it there.

"You don't know what you've just done." he tried to say calmly, as we entered his office.

You could feel all the eyes and ears of others wanting to know what the sputtering was all about.

"REALLY?!" All the documentation I had with me that covered the last eleven years. It wasn't your choice to decide what they should and shouldn't see! Oh yeah, that's right, it's irrelevant, which I guess means, no big deal to you! But obviously it was to them. You never once even looked it over or you would have seen it was the original record that you could have shown them to review! How else were they going to know the hell I have been through?"

"Well, we'll just have to wait and see what the board decides, which could take more than an hour" he said never once making eye contact with me.

I wanted no more to do with him and I left him pouting in his fancy leather chair.

"How pathetic! So childish!" I thought to myself *"He wasn't a lawyer, he was a billet filler!"*

Not once did my counselor come out to see if I was ok, and probably a good thing. Lt Parker and several others were very concerned with my emotional outbreak.

"Guess this was not a good day to get a spine," I said jokingly through my tears of anger.

"Hey, you've been holding this in for many years, by the sounds of it. Just relax." said an unknown lady who was just an innocent by-stander.

Now I don't know if the board members heard any of the commotion that had been taking place, and I don't know if they heard my next comment either. Everything that I was saying, I meant with all that makes up me.

"I'll tell you right now, if I don't get my 30%, I will keep coming back. It will get to a point that they will be so sick of me they will wish I fell off the face of the earth. I will keep fighting and get my own lawyers if that is what it takes! I won't stop until I get what I came for!"

Those around me knew that I was serious, but helped me stay focused on what was going on now. We were all startled when we heard the signal of the board members indicating they were ready to announce their decision. It had only been fifteen minutes, not an hour like I was informed. This couldn't be good.

Time moved in slow motion as I walked towards the door, I felt the familiar warmth that I had felt so many time before, when something great was about to happen. I felt at peace and assurance filled my heart. The door appeared bright and it gleamed with a golden glow. The same glow as the cross on my wall when I saw my guardian angel in my dream. I was unaware of the presence of people in the room. The space around me was clouded. When I walked into the room and sat down, something caught my attention. A single snow white colored dove perched on the sill outside the window.

"Petty Officer Bentley, the board would like to share with you the findings of your hearing." said the president of the board in a monotone voice.

Honestly I don't recall what was said over the next five minutes and unfortunately I had run out of tape to record it as well. But I did hear the most important information what was going to either end my saga or force me to begin a new one.

"We are granting you your 30% and are placing you on the full retirement list."

I was silent and lowered my head to cry. It was over…it was over.

I went out in the waiting room, in a daze.

What had just happened? What did they say? Did I get what I wanted? Yes and No. I got my benefits, but in my heart, I wanted to be told that I could resume the life as a Seabee.

My counselor was awe struck, that I won and had been given full benefits and 30% disability.

"I've never won a case with that board." He said.

Under my breath, but was heard by the secretary, I replied as I signed the remaining documents for my new military title of retiree, "We all know why you lose. Everything you do is half-assed."

"He didn't win! I did! I was the one, with the balls to win this case." I smiled as I thought of what I had just done.

I collected my papers and anything more that I needed to obtain my new ID card. Then I said my good-byes to Lt. Parker.

"Hey Fallon,"

"Yes Lieutenant?"

"That original medical record, how did you happen across that?"

"Let's just say, that a mystery man acquired it for me, any further information, I plea the fifth."

"Word of advice, many copies, stamped certified to be turn, over many locations. As for the original, safe deposit box baby. You did a great job!"

"Consider it already done, and thanks Lieutenant. You'll be hearing from me again in the future. This is so going to be in my book."

"One last thing before you go Fallon. Always remember, you don't have to wear a uniform to be important. You're a very talent and gifted soul, use those tools to the fullest."

With her final words, I smiled and headed on my way to get back to my boys and their award ceremony at the school. I was going to make it after all.

I took the elevator to the main floor. As I walked with a forced kick in my step back to the parking garage, the director of medical that was on my board, addressed me as we walked passed in the hallway.

"Good luck on your retirement Petty Officer," he said with a smile and thumbs up. You earned it."

"Thank you sir," I replied with a painted smile.

* * *

As I made my way back to Annapolis, I was faced with a level-headedness that I was now fully retired and scared as to what the tomorrows of my future would bring. I knew that as long as I had the support of my family and friends, if I could get through a cancer illness, find the love of my life time in the middle of the Bering Sea on the small island of Adak, give birth to two beautiful baby boys, and only lose my sanity now and then there was only one thing left to say.

"Well then my dear Fallon, I guess your game for just about anything."

One idea immediately popped into my head. A sequel to this book titled, "Life after the Military" – A Retiree's Memoir, yeah that just might work. Hoo-Rah!

A native of Laconia, New Hampshire, Stacey Bolin lived in Adak, Alaska and now resides with her husband and boys, in Annapolis, Maryland. She is a member of the Maryland Writers Association, has had her poetry, artwork, crime prevention programs, and photography published. She writes in several genres. She is presently polishing three non-fictional stories. The Crayon Box, Two small boys unite a community with their artwork to rid the neighborhood of crime. Window Prints, enduring life at the hands of an abusive father. In Her Words - The Sorrow behind Grandma's Smile, Grandma had always told Katie since she was a very young girl, that she was writing a book. Since Katie believed her to be the best cook in the world, she assumed it was a cookbook. But when Grandma's house was remodeled, after she passed, hundreds of written pages were found hidden in the walls. Grandma had been writing - about the abuse she suffered at the hands of her husband.

Through the Barracks Window has been her 22 year labor of love. What happened to her in this story is all truth, only the names have been changed to protect the innocent, and because the law says she has to protect the guilty too. Her hopes are to inspire people, with her words and her passion for music, to help them find their inner voice and strength that every soul possesses.